Unequal Opportunities

Women's Employment in England
1800–1918

Unequal Opportunities

Women's Employment in England 1800–1918

Edited by Angela V. John

Basil Blackwell

Basil Blackwell Ltd, 1986

First published 1986
Reprinted 1988

Basil Blackwell Ltd
108 Cowley Road, Oxford OX4 1JF, UK

Basil Blackwell Inc.
432 Park Avenue South, Suite 1505
New York, NY 10016, USA

British Library Cataloguing in Publication Data
Unequal opportunites: women's employment
   in England 1800–1918
   1. Women — Employment — Great Britain — History
   I. John, Angela V.
   331.4'0941   HD6135

   ISBN 0–631–13955–9
   ISBN 0–631–13956–7 Pbk

Library of Congress Cataloging Data
Unequal opportunities.
Bibliography: p.
Includes index.
1. Women — Employment — England — History — 19th century —
Addresses, essays, lectures. 2. Sex discrimination against women —
England — History — 19th century — Addresses, essays, lectures.
3. Women in trade-unions — England — History — 19th century —
Addresses, essays, lectures. I. John, Angela V.
HD6136.U54   1985   331.4'0942
ISBN 0–631–13955–9
ISBN 0–631–13956–7 (pbk)

Typeset by Dentset, Oxford
Printed in Great Britain by Page Bros, Norwich.

For Leonore Davidoff, whose constant encouragement and support of women historians and historians of women in recent years has provided a major stimulus to history.

Contents

Part III Women and Organization

List of Tables

Acknowledgements

The editor would like to express her gratitude to the following for permission to reproduce illustrations on: p.44 reproduced by permission of Leicestershire Museums, Art Galleries and Records Service; photograph taken by Ray Brown: p.70 from George Dodd's *Days at the Factories* (1843); photograph taken by Thames Polytechnic C.S.U.: p.94 reproduced by permission of the Manchester Studies Archive of Family Photographs; photograph taken by R.L. Bell: p.124 reproduced by permission of the Suffolk Photographic Collection: Inset: from the Arthur Munby MS; reproduced by permission of the Master and Fellows of Trinity College, Cambridge (Wren Library): p.152 photograph taken by Thames Polytechnic C.S.U.: p.178 illustration from *Mines and Miners* or *Underground Life* by L. Simonin (translated by W.H. Bristow), 1868 edition; photograph taken by Thames Polytechnic C.S.U.: p.206 taken from *A Short History of the General Union of Textile Workers* by Ben Turner (1920, p.129); photograph taken by Thames Polytechnic C.S.U.: p.234 left: illustration from *The Book of the Labour Party* volume 3 by Herbert Tracey; reproduced by permission of the T.U.C. Library; photograph taken by Ernie Greenwood: right: reproduced by permission of the Fawcett Society Library; photograph taken by John R. Freeman: p.260 reproduced by permission of the Varley Collection, University of Hull; photograph taken by Thames Polytechnic C.S.U.

List of Contributors

Joanna Bornat graduated from the Universities of Leeds and Essex in 1965 and 1980; she is an editor of the journal *Oral History* and Educational Director of a large national charity working for older people. She is co-author, with Chris Phillipson and Sue Ward of *A Manifesto For Old Age* (Pluto, 1985).

Gill Burke is a senior lecturer in Social Administration at the Polytechnic of Central London. Her interest in the Cornish mining industry has led her to investigate the wider links that Cornish mine labour and capital had with the development of the world mineral economy and the way the past illuminates current problems of scarce mineral resources.

Edward Higgs was born in Lancashire. At university he studied Modern History and wrote a thesis on domestic service. He is an Assistant Keeper at the Public Record Office and is currently working on the history of the nineteenth-century censuses. His mother was in service.

Felicity Hunt is a Research Associate in the Department of Education of the University of Cambridge. Her earlier paper on women bookbinders and printers was published in *Women's Studies International Forum* (1983). She is currently working on the development of a policy for girls' schooling between 1902 and 1944.

Angela V. John is a senior lecturer in History at Thames Polytechnic. She is the author of books and articles on women's employment in the coal mining industry past and present, including *By The Sweat of Their Brow. Women Workers at Victorian Coal Mines* (Croom Helm, 1980, Routledge and Kegan Paul, 1984) and *Coalmining Women* (Cambridge University Press, Cambridge, 1984). She has also written on Chartism in Wales, done an introduction to the Virago reprint of Lady Bell's *At The Works* (1985) and scripted and presented a B.B.C. Schools Radio Programme 'An Unsuitable Job For A Woman?' She has a doctorate from Manchester University.

Ellen Mappen is Director of the Junior Year in Women's Studies at Douglass College, Rutgers University, New Jersey U.S.A. She has a PhD on women workers and unemployment policy in late Victorian and Edwardian London and has written *Helping Women at Work: The Women's Industrial Council 1889–1914* (Hutchinson, 1985) and an Introduction to a reprint of Clementina Black's *Married Women's Work* (Virago, 1983).

Jenny Morris completed her PhD on the sexual division of labour and the origin of minimum wage legislation in 1982 and is currently teaching Housing at Tottenham College of Technology, London.

Nancy Grey Osterud teaches History and Gender Studies at Lewis and Clark College in Portland, Oregon, U.S.A. Since 1981, she has been doing research on relationships among women and men in a rural community in upstate New York during the transition to commercial agriculture.

Deborah Thom is currently a Research Associate on an E.S.R.C. project on 'Maladjustment and School Psychological Services in England and Wales, 1920–1972', at the Child Care and Development Group, Social and Political Science Faculty, University of Cambridge and is writing a book on mental testing and education and another on *Feminism and the Labour Movement 1860–1970* (Wheatsheaf). She has a doctorate from Thames Polytechnic on the ideology of women's work between 1914–24.

Meta Zimmeck is currently completing a PhD on the employment of women in the British Civil Service 1870–1939. She teaches part-time at the Institute of Education and also works as a tape transcriber for the Royal Courts of Justice.

Preface

This book has been conceived and developed alongside its companion volume, *Women's Experience of Home and Family, 1850–1940* (edited by Jane Lewis). Together, the volumes form a central axis around which to approach some of the major issues facing women over a period of 150 years.

In order to examine these issues in detail we have separated them into two books, one focusing on employment and the other on domesticity. At the same time we recognize that there can be no real distinction between the two and that work, if not always waged work, warrants as much attention in the volume on domesticity as in that on employment. By the same token, the structure of the labour force and attitudes towards women workers can only properly be appreciated by considering ideas about sexuality, childbearing and childrearing. The hierarchies of domination and subordination within the home, as well as the support systems within and beyond it, require analysis alongside the workings of industrial capitalism. Thus the volumes are mutually dependent and are intended to be read in conjunction with each other, as in the words of the final essay in Jane Lewis's book:

> Understanding women's position in society necessitates an understanding of the often complicated ways in which work, marriage and kinship are woven together in a perplexing intricate tapestry.

Angela V. John
Jane Lewis

The editor would like to thank the following: Sue Corbett at Basil Blackwell for constant support; Jenny Rudge; staff and students at Thames Polytechnic, especially the women's history group in the MA in Historical

Studies; Edith Stollery and Maggie Meadows for typing; Stella Reed and the Central Services Unit for photographic work; and Paul Stigant for reading the Introduction. Finally, but crucially, thank you to all the contributors for making this book possible.

Introduction

Angela V. John

This volume of essays seeks to fill a gap in the historiography of women's history. Whilst there have been studies of women's employment in different trades, professions and organizations in the 1800–1918 period, most have focused on single industries or institutions and although there now exist excellent collections of Victorian documents about women's work, the major historical study remains Ivy Pinchbecks's *Women Workers and the Industrial Revolution*, first published in 1930. A pioneering and stimulating book, it nevertheless subscribes to a somewhat unproblematic and optimistic interpretation of the effects of industrial capitalism on women, and anyway ends in 1850. Tilly and Scott's *Women, Work and Family* (1978) benefits from recent developments in feminist theory and effectively challenges those who argue that women were 'modernizing' at the same time and pace throughout the country. Jane Lewis's *Women in England* (1984) is a valuable synthesis of the post-1870 period though neither this nor Tilly and Scott's survey are intended to provide in-depth studies.[1]

The nine essays/chapters in this book exemplify and clarify some of the key issues in women's history. Each contribution is a detailed study (with bibliographical note for further reading) of an occupation, organization or historical approach to women's employment in the nineteenth and early twentieth centuries. Though free-standing, the essays are also part of a wider structure comprised of the three major areas of sex, skill and status; expansion and restriction in employment; and women and organization, thus enabling comparative analysis. The Celtic countries have been omitted as they require their own volumes and inclusion here would merely tag them onto a framework which is that of an industrializing and industrialized England. Yet England itself was experiencing change at different rates and with varying consequences. This book does not attempt a round-England tour but it does redirect us to some neglected areas and occupations such as metalliferous mining in Cornwall, recognizing that some women's work, for example in the Lancashire cotton trade, has (with good reason) received considerable historical attention.

Focusing on women's employment opportunities can minimize problems of unemployment. Though deplored in the late nineteenth century as a real social problem for men, it tended not to be so characterized for women whose waged work was presented as transient, a temporary pre-marital stage even though practice (reinforced by the imbalance in the sex ratio with close to one million more women than men in the population by the 1880s and by women's comparative longevity) cut across this. Whereas women were frequently described as 'invading' the public world of work, men who crossed the dividing line between the labour market and the private world of the home have still been portrayed as workers. Thus the daughter of a Lancashire ironworker describing how her father helped scrub the floor during his wife's confinements, explained that once the daughters were old enough to take over 'of course he *retired* from housework then' (my italics).[2] Although all women worked, this book concentrates on those who were 'gainfully employed' (2,832,000 by 1851 and 4,751,000 by 1901, a little under 30 per cent of the labour force) according to the Census (see Appendix). It also includes the many others who were not recorded as 'occupied' for one reason or another when the Census was taken but who worked for wages.[3] Waged work was not necessarily outside the home – as late as 1870 dressmakers outnumbered textile workers by nearly two to one, the majority of them working at home. The invisibility of many women workers and the need to view the family as a unit of production as well as of consumption are some of the recurring *leitmotifs* of these essays.

Most of the essays concern working-class women who formed the vast majority of female workers. Although there are clearly problems in defining a woman's class (determined by her father or husband), it is evident that as industrialization developed, so too did the ideal of the lady of leisure. Even though this was never matched by reality and shifted in emphasis during the nineteenth century, *lack* of work for a woman was seen as a defining characteristic of the successful late eighteenth and early nineteenth-century family. While the public world stressed male enterprise, profit and hard work – the word 'industry' had two meanings – a different role was marked out for women. Concern with observing and apeing appropriate social codes and conventions was at its most elaborate amongst those aspiring to gentility, but the aim of the respectable, skilled working-class husband to keep his wife at home in a lady*like* manner was also increasingly evident. As for women's own perceptions, the fervour with which so many middle-class women undertook philanthropic ventures speaks volumes about their constraints.

Many of the generalized categories used to define and describe employment – full-time/part-time, rural/urban, heavy/light, indoor/outdoor, adult/child – are inadequate, inappropriate and sometimes misleading when applied to women's experiences. Women frequently slipped in and out of such polarities, much of their work being casual and seasonal (such as hay-making, hop picking, market gardening or a temporary resort to prostitution). For married women in particular it might not even be perceived as employment since it did not necessarily involve going *out* to work. Many would have seen it in the same way as this Welsh woman recounting married life in the 1920s:

> No, never worked no more. Oh – I went out working in *houses* to earn a few shillings, yes, I worked with a family, my mother's and my sister's, and took in washing . . . And then when a shop would go idle and they were letting it to somebody else, I done it in several places, we'd have perhaps fifteen shillings – and I scrubbed 'em all . . . And I'd do *anything* to earn money![4]

The categories break down on close inspection. Though rural dwellers, the Cornish mine girls (Bâl Maidens) were industrial workers (and occasionally sought greater freedom in urban life).[5] Many urban employees were of rural origin – two-thirds of all domestic servants in England were daughters of rural labourers. In agricultural and fishing villages in Essex women did tailoring outwork at home, supplied work by firms in Manchester, Leicester and East London. In agriculture women are not very visible in historical representation yet throughout the period farmers' wives and relatives worked on small farms, female farm servants were hired by the year and women day-labourers performed a range of tasks though there were marked variations over time and place.[6] In pastoral farming dairymaids and farmers' wives made butter and cheese (the first cheese-making factory was only established in 1870 in Derbyshire). Yet from about 1750 in the areas of grain production in central and southern England there is evidence of women's employment being increasingly marginalised as their light sickle was replaced by the heavier scythe seen as a tool suitable only for males and taken up by a growing surplus of male labour. Once it was extended to the harvesting of wheat and rye, women were excluded from such work, increasingly becoming confined to lighter jobs such as hay-making and weeding corn. In some areas such as Norfolk (where the cottage textile industry was declining) they were in demand for this latter work, and were often hired with children in gangs. By the late nineteenth century Flora Thompson had witnessed the decline of women's fieldwork in her native Oxfordshire and the disappearance of the notorious gangs (regulated by an act of 1867). Tasks were now so gender-specific that the small number of women workers tended to be in separate fields from the men, engaged in their own special tasks of weeding, hoeing, stone-picking, topping and tailing turnips and mangel. When it rained they mended sacks in a barn.

Recent research into the size of the female agricultural labour force in arable and mixed farming areas in Gloucestershire does however suggest that, there at least, historians may have severely under-estimated the real size of the temporary yet regular female labour force on late nineteenth century farms. A number of female day labourers who worked for at least one third of the year were omitted from the Census returns for 1871 to 1891. In northern England women's labour in the harvesting of corn persisted well into the nineteenth century though contemporary illustrations reveal a gender division of tasks as men actually cut the corn into sheaves. Here too they were affected by the introduction of the scythe so that by about 1850 their work in the harvest field was restricted to gathering and making straw bands. Nevertheless, Northumberland women farmworkers remained in great demand in the late nineteenth century. On most farms there women workers known as bondagers were employed through the medium of the male labourer's contract and, where possible, were female relatives. The attraction of heavy industry in the north-east for men and the lack of alternative employment opportunites for women combined to ensure that women still performed a range of physically demanding agricultural tasks such as spreading manure and carrying sacks of grain. Here and elsewhere, women's heavy manual labour was conveniently ignored rather than targeted or deplored when it was seen to be necessary.

The work of a domestic servant carrying heavy buckets of coal in large houses might be more demanding than some of the sorting jobs performed by the Lancashire pitbrow woman at the colliery. The latter might work in the open air but her employment as an outdoor worker was considered by doctors to be preferable to the dusty, confined atmosphere of the mill and elderly women recall being sent to recuperate at the pit top. Some mill girls were *girls* though factory and education acts gradually ensured that full-time workers at least were women (even though historians have insisted on referring to them as mill girls or match girls). This connotes that other dichotomy of independent/dependent with its corollary of single/ married. In law, marriage and ideology, women were designated dependants. And Victorian writings were punctuated with attacks on the single, independent woman who did not fit the prescriptions of the dependent wife and mother. Many working-class women were portrayed as unsexed, a moral threat to society, whereas the middle-class, single woman was considered desexed and derided as being an old maid (being the opposite of the mill girl and ageing before her time). The potential duties of motherhood permeated considerations of women's employment yet although it was the mother's responsibilities rather than the parents', which were emphasized, it was the patriarchal authority of the father which was so applauded.

The divisions outlined above are clearly inadequate as tools of analysis yet they were powerful measurements for Victorian society and so cannot be easily dismissed. More valuable in understanding the circumstances which determined women's relationship to employment is an approach which incorporates changes in family and household size, composition and authority, the local economy and marriage market and the strength of ideological assumptions concerning the status and suitability of occupations in gendered terms.

The first three chapters address questions of sex, skill and status. Mechanization opened up a number of opportunities for working-class women but whilst many moved into the labour market, they remained essentially defined by their familial role and at the same time encountered sex antagonism in the workplace. Women's work was nothing new nor was a gender hierarchy of labour which accepted that women's work be accorded lower social and economic value than men's due to their primary association with reproduction rather than production and their responsibility for childcare and housework (with no economic value).[7] Capitalist employers incorporated and perpetuated this gender division of labour. Whilst on the one hand men could be seen as taking over some occupations traditionally associated with women (for example midwifery), for very many working women, industrialization witnessed their translation from an already unequal position into categories of unskilled or semi-skilled workers with low wages and status. The change was not necessarily immediate. For example, the early spinning jenny had positive benefits for women, increasing productivity and earnings though its adoption in the factory system signalled a breakdown of their control.[8] As industrialization developed, so men tended to become the specialized spinners and women were found in less specialized weaving. The close connection between domestic patterns and industrial structures can be observed in spinning. Women tended not to be employed as mule spinners even though they could handle the small automated spinning mules. Male union organization and an internal subcontracting system which gave spinners a supervisory role to exercise over their piecer assistants conspired to exclude effectively women who were seen as inappropriate for such positions.[9]

> Large-scale industry, by assigning an important part in the socially organised process of production, outside the sphere of the domestic economy, to women, young persons and children of both sexes, does nevertheless create a new economic foundation for a higher form of the family and of relations between the sexes.[10]

So ran Marx's theory. Yet in practice the latter part of his statement has not so much resulted in women shedding domestic responsibilities as juggling with a double bind made difficult by the physical separation of home and work. Nancy Osterud carefully charts the various processes by which this transformation was shaped in the Leicester hosiery trade, taking us from Marx's stage of manufactures or proto-industrialization which preceded the large-scale development in production, to the position of women operating knitting machines in factories. Here, in 'women's work' they were divested of recognized skill but assured of low wages and status.[11]

This essay shows how occupational segregation by gender was reinforced rather than introduced or relinquished with mechanization. The material relations of the family and the subordination of women to men were conveniently adapted and concretized. After much historical attention on the workplace and organized male labour (though, not until very recently, a focus on the meanings of masculinity) feminist historians stress that employment can only be understood in conjunction with analyses of patterns of domesticity. Joanna Bornat has emphasized the importance of recognizing how capitalism is reinforced within the family whilst Judy Lown has criticized artificial distinctions between the economy and the family, arguing that patriarchy requires conceptualizing in terms of the unequal power relations of gender and age 'forming a central axis of historical and social change'. Her work on the Courtauld silk weavers of Essex shows how a crucial part of the women employees' experience was the 'realignment of patriarchal interests' which structurally marginalized their status.[12] Even though women hosiery workers in Leicester underwent changes in the organization, nature and locus of employment, patriarchal interests were maintained.

Nancy Osterud highlights the diversity of patterns within a trade. Yet though the organization varied between town (Leicester) and country (surrounding Leicestershire villages), the consequences for the status of women's work were ultimately the same. Close reading of contemporary investigations warns us against a simplified notion of the 'family wage', that is, the belief that the male head of household should earn enough to keep his family and thus keep his wife out of waged work. Not all trade unionists were by any means opposed to married women doing some work. They were, however, concerned about the nature and status of that work *vis-à-vis* male structures of power and authority. Thomas Cooper, who was active in Leicester Chartism, decided to become the 'champion of the poor' after discovering stocking weavers at work late at night. Until corrected, he presumed that the 4/6d they earned was their daily wage:

> . . . 'Four and sixpence a week', I exclaimed. 'You don't mean that men have to work in those stocking frames that I hear going now, a whole week for four and sixpence. How can they maintain their wives and children?'
> 'Ay, you may well ask that', said one of them sadly.[13]

Despite the fact that women were an integral part of the hosiery trade, the knitters were clearly not challenging the assumption that they maintained those who were already legally dependent on them and who, as Cooper the Chartist was well aware, neither had a vote nor were being encouraged to demand one.

Women's protests were, however, occasionally heard. During the productive period of the Grand National Consolidated Trades Union in 1834 there was a short-lived female union of women stockingers at Leicester. And in the Chartist years some of the most ingenious tactics were developed by another group of Midland women, the Nottingham lacemakers.[14] More often, however, we hear the men's voices raised in protest and not infrequently the targets were women workers seen as colluding in men's loss of control through mechanization. In 1845 a Petition from the Potters outlined their fears of mechanization:

> To maidens, mothers and wives we say mechanization is your deadliest enemy . . . it will destroy your natural claim to home and domestic duties, and will immure you and your toiling little ones in overheated and dirty shops, there to weep and toil and pine and die.[15]

What was seen as a threat for the one sex was simply dismissed as inappropriate for the other. Male printers devised a rhyme entitled 'The Infernal Machine' which ridiculed female labour and warned of the adulteration of skill:

> To make the *matter* worse, I see,
> Females will be employed, 'tis hinted;
> Thus readers *miss*-informed will be,
> And every print will be *miss*-printed.[16]

Today at a time of computerized photocomposition and late twentieth-century struggles for control of work in the light of new technology, there is a familiar resonance in the tension in gender relations as women enter male printing preserves such as typesetting. Yet Felicity Hunt's essay shows that there has been a long history of struggle over male craft control, a struggle revolving round mechanization yet fundamentally concerned with the preservation of patriarchy and power. What can be interpreted as a nineteenth-century success story for male printers and bookbinders resisting loss of power through mechanization reads very differently when viewed from the perspective of women.

Felicity Hunt charts the restrictions on women's opportunities in printing from pre-industrial society. Zachariah Coleman in the novel, *The Revolution in Tanner's Lane* (1887),[17] summed up this elite, literate group when he commented that '. . . although he worked with his hands, printers were rather a superior set of fellows'. Nevertheless the nineteenth century was to witness an expansion in the number of women printers, reflecting the tension between capitalist enterprise and the union's restrictive practices. Cheap, unionized female labour in hand composing and machine operation encouraged their portrayal as undercutters of wage rates, colluding in downgrading men's skills. Yet, denied access to the union, the women could only earn below union rates.[18]

The early feminist movement did challenge the printers, though interestingly Emily Faithfull who ran the Victoria Press to train and use female compositors, justified the venture by emphasizing what she saw as inherently female and appropriate characteristics – 'chiefly a quick eye, a ready hand, and steady application'.[19] For 15 years the press produced about 80 pamphlets and books aided by an experienced senior compositor, significantly brought in from Limerick where she had carried on her father's printing business after his death. When the inveterate gentleman investigator of female labour, A.J. Munby, visited in 1860 he found about a dozen female compositors (three of whom were ex-governesses). Men read proofs and worked the presses (Emily Faithfull also believed in gender segregation).

Munby found a similar arrangement three years later and commented that 'this is little better than trifling with the female labour question . . . that which I want is, liberty for any woman who has the strength and the mind for it, to turn her hand to any manual employment'.[20] Yet as Munby knew, this was not what the majority of people wanted and it clearly did not accord with the wishes of the printers' union. Exclusion rather than organization and a commitment to equal pay characterized their approach.

In the sister trade of bookbinding there have been women pioneers in union and strike organization. Mary Zugg helped organize the 1849 Bible Dispute against wage cuts whilst in 1874 Emma Paterson a former bookbinder's apprentice founded the Women's Protective and Provident League to bring together women's trade societies. Though numerically more significant than women printers, Felicity Hunt shows how the women bookbinders were perceived as less of a threat to the trade. Their training and employment were clearly demarcated and restricted to certain processes. Clearly this had built-in disadvantages (not least payment by piecework) and it prevented direct comparison with male rates of pay (a feature only too familiar in the original wording of the 1970 Equal Pay Act). The introduction of machinery in the late nineteenth century altered the old occupational structure, with women now operating new casing and other machines, once again becoming associated with de-skilling in an expanding trade. Their earlier, relatively privileged position of assured areas of limited control was being broken down. Sidney Webb once remarked that 'for women's work the "gentility" of the occupation is still accepted as part payment',[21] a comment which seems particularly apposite for the 14,000 or so late Victorian women bookbinders.

The essays in Part I show some of the different ways in which women's skills have been effectively eroded. They also suggest the elusive meanings of such a term, the interpretation of which seems largely to depend on the sex of the person exercising it.[22] During the transition to factory production, extensive subdivision of labour processes, combined with technological change made craft-conscious male workers highly vulnerable and enhanced their resistance to the substitution of female labour. Their struggle to retain job control resulted in an emphasis on male exclusivity (already evident in customs such as meeting in public houses) and a stress on skill in the face of the breakdown of apprenticeship laws. Sanctions such as stopping female tile makers working if they began earning more than the male workers,[23] were accompanied by a stress on manly strength and female dexterity as appropriate complements. There were also small but significant assertions of control over space at the workplace. At McCorquodale's printing works in Lancashire a sign was erected in the waste room saying 'No woman allowed in here'.[24] Today in that most masculine of American bastions, mining, the recent entry of women coal-miners has revealed not only similar spatial appropriations but has also demonstrated that many skilled tasks are not, as presumed, beyond the ability and/or strength of women (the two are often confused). Rather it is a means of acquiring the knack, of having the opportunity to train, experiment and experience. This is not to say that such jobs are easy or overvalued but it does emphasize how women's access to knowledge and machinery design is, and has been, severely circumscribed.[25]

The very real threat which workers have faced (still face) in de-skilling via technology and the lower value traditionally accorded to female labour have helped ensure that when work has become feminized it has been seen as losing status. Paternalistic employment practices have enhanced these processes. Leeds clothing factories, described by the press as 'Palaces of Industry' were revealed by the middle-class socialist and feminist Isabella Ford to be strictly controlled regimes with elaborate systems of fines.[26] Yet at the same time the minority of male cutters retained a special presence within the factory which gave them a number of privileges in the cutting room.

Jenny Morris's essay on the tailoring trade provides another example of the subdivision of tasks by gender. She sees this as a key to sweated labour which was (and is) characterized by low wages and status. Her analysis widens the definition of sweating to encompass the factory as well as the home and workshop. In the words of one historian 'Sweating was as Victorian as the railroad and the music hall'.[27] Its first public scandal had been in 1843 and led to one of the most enduring images of sweating. A London tailoring business took a woman to court for pawning several articles she has been making up for them as a 'trouser hand'. Her case prompted Thomas Hood to write 'The Song of the Shirt' which appeared in the Xmas number of *Punch*.[28] Tailoring was one of many forms of sweated labour: dressmaking, nail and chain making, cabinet making, cigar and match making displayed similar complex hierarchies of subcontracting and low wages. In the London clothing trade the middleman (sometimes a middlewoman) became known as a 'sweater'. Here, lack of capital investment, high rates and rents produced exploitation of an available pool of cheap female labour which helped stave off provincial competition. The essay traces the history of tailoring from its early days as a handicraft trade, following the tailors' resistance to female labour.[29] By 1846 80 per cent of London's tailors were outworkers and women could be found in every branch outside the 'honourable' sector.

Women worked either as low-waged workers engaged by sweaters or as assistants for male relatives. They performed a host of carefully delegated separate tasks such as turning cuffs or making buttonholes and were effectively excluded from the better paid processes associated with skill. The very insecurity of the trade increased vulnerability and dependence on their employers. The London trade out of season might have as many as five slack months. As the Women's Industrial Council (See essay 8) commented, 'The vice of this business is irregularity'.[30] In Liverpool the Council found some women tailoresses working excessive hours for low pay in labour intensive work which tried to compete with factories. Clementina Black described the factories there as 'the centre of all that is evil' with women 'unwittingly helping to bolster up a rotten and pernicious system'.

As in the hosiery trade, a shift in location confirmed rather than disturbed the basis of gender relations. Hand sewing and machine work were similarly open to sweating at home, in workshops or in factories as Jenny Morris shows. Government contract work for uniforms demonstrates this well, from soldiers' widows making army shirts at home in Woolwich to the young Ada Nield working as a finisher on piecework in a Crewe factory in the 1890s and bringing home about 8/– a week for nine to ten hour days (though frequent fines and stoppages cut into this). When the Government Inspector visited, men were quickly switched to sewing in the sleeves of tunics, a task usually reserved for women at a rate of 5d per hour. The contractors' estimates were, however, based on male rates (1/5d per hour) which meant that the extra shilling was usually pocketed. Ada Nield's realization of such injustices led her to denounce publicly (though anonymously) our 'lingering, dying wage'. For this she risked her job and before long turned to trade unionism and the suffrage movement.[31]

The lack of opportunity for collective organization amongst tailoresses, especially the homeworkers, was something they had in common with the subjects of Edward Higgs's chapter, domestic servants. The chapters in Part II consider changing employment opportunities for Victorian women, examining three very different experiences, starting with the largest single employer of women. Between 1851 and 1871 the number of female domestic servants increased twice as fast as the population. It was primarily a job for the young – in the 1860s just under 40 per cent were under 20. It spelt out clearly the different implications of marriage for the two sexes. Domestic service shows how employment effectively *ended* with marriage for these working class women (perhaps partly explaining the high illegitimacy rate among servants). For many men, however, marriage signified a different kind of transition. For the middle-class man in particular it was often a recognition that he now felt himself sufficiently established in his job to keep a wife.

The term 'domestic service' covered an infinite variety of jobs and within very wealthy households there was a marked hierarchy of service representing a microcosm of stratified Victorian society. Although by mid-century two-thirds of servants were female, there was even a disproportionate number of men occupying the top jobs. Accounts written by servants illustrate the gradations throughout the occupation. The diary of that most extraordinary of ordinary servants, Hannah Cullwick (secretly married to Munby) reveals the variety of places in which one woman might serve.[32] From the age of eight when she entered service, Hannah's jobs included being nurserymaid, scullion, kitchen-maid, and maid of all work; she even briefly held the coveted position of cook. She lived in a variety of locations which included a public house, Aquelate Hall (a large country house), private residences in London and lodging houses there and at the seaside. In the process she not only acquired a number of survival skills but enhanced her acute powers of social observation. At one lodging house she was aware of being 'at the very bottom of service'. Not only was such a position unfortunate since the mistress was herself in a precarious economic position but Hannah was painfully conscious that her employer was *not* a true lady. This signified not so much social snobbery as an awareness of the complex and dependent symbiotic relationship between servant and employer.

Edward Higgs asks who employed servants and raises the difficulties in interpreting the sources on which we base our statistics. He neatly and provocatively demolishes some of the popular misconceptions and redirects attention towards an appreciation of the productive work of women in the home. Challenging the claim that having servants is a key to defining the middle class, he demonstrates via his sample of mid-century Rochdale households that the artisan and manual householders were quite likely to engage servants. The attraction of 'bargain basement' workhouse girls was noted by Mrs Nassau Senior in 1874 when she told the Local Government Board that the low wages paid to such girls made them sought after 'by too many people, who, a few years ago, would have done their own housework, whose income does not permit them to keep a superior servant, and who often look on their little servant as a mere drudge'.[33]

In demonstrating that there was not a straightforward relationship between class and servant-holding Edward Higgs (like Meta Zimmeck in the following chapter) argues for an approach which does not view its material solely via the prism of class. His study of Census enumerators' tables shows that the printed Census returns hide as much as they reveal though their very categorization betrays built-in perceptions of women that link them essentially to the family economy.

In practice, many of those returned as being in servant occupations were probably not contracted servants but relatives of the head of household, possibly day servants working outside their home or providing unwaged help as part of the family 'duty'. Autobiographies elucidate this latter relationship. Hannah Mitchell saw herself and her sister as little more than domestic drudges on the family farm in Derbyshire.[34] Selina Cooper gave up Lancashire mill work as a young woman to nurse her sick mother. She also took in washing part-time.[35] Indeed, when one of the founding Fabians, Sydney Olivier, was asked whether it was acceptable socialism to employ a servant he replied that 'the most wholesome and satisfactory solution in such cases is that the work should be done by unmarried relatives'.[36] Some girls got board and lodging and perhaps a little pocket money by gaining initial experience of service in the homes of distant kin who might be wealthier than their own family.

Edward Higgs alerts us to the variations behind the nomenclature and seeks recognition and clarification of the real productive labour power of all women engaged in domestic tasks.[37] It is not easy to demarcate neatly the domestic and market economy in nineteenth-century England. For example Lucy Luck's autobiography reveals how this workhouse girl was employed in a public house in Luton where 'I sometimes did housework, sometimes served in the bar, and other times did the finishing of straw hats'.[38] The seasonality of work such as straw-plaiting cut across regular full-time employment. Despite alterations in living-in patterns in farming, female servants might well be doing indoor farm work just as those working for shop keepers might also act as shop assistants.

Even the decline of domestic service can, argues Edward Higgs, be seen as less indicative of changing middle-class fortunes than as an indicator of how production was now moving outside the home. The days of domestic service on a large scale were numbered but it did remain a central experience up to the Second World War. Like sweating it did not fade away with the new century. Indeed it increased rapidly in the 1920s and the expansion of hospitals and other institutions ensured that cleaning would remain a necessary if often hidden component of twentieth-century life.[39]

Throughout the nineteenth century there was a mismatch between the representation of an occupation which was labelled eminently suitable for the female sex (William Greg even excepted servants from his description of 'redundant' or surplus women as 'they are supported by and they minister to, men')[40] but which ensured that contracted servants were kept at a distance from the comforts of the family which were so tantalizingly close to them. Charles Booth described domestic service as 'a relationship very similar in some respects to that subservience between sovereign and subject . . . there is demanded an all-pervading attitude of watchful respect, accompanied by a readiness to respond at once to any gracious advance that may be made without ever presuming or for a moment "forgetting themselves"'.[41]

Domestic service (which significantly was never investigated by Victorian Royal Commissions) was also conveniently urged as an antidote to the 'undesirable' elements of female employment. The chief instigator of the campaign against the pitbrow lasses (a group looked down upon by mill workers and domestic servants alike) told *The Times* his solution to the problems of their employment.

There is a great and constant outcry of a dearth of domestic servants. If the girls now being taught in our Board and other schools were instructed in the art of cooking, washing, sewing, etc. they would perhaps of their own free will, if able to exercise it, choose domestic service in preference to more degrading labour at the pit or elsewhere.[42]

Much of the controversy over the expansion or restriction of women's employment opportunities ranged around what was considered fit work for women. The Earl of Shaftesbury outlined in 1859 his idea of appropriate work: 'the instant that the work becomes minute, individual and personal; the instant that it leaves the open field and touches the home; the instant that it requires tact, sentiment and delicacy; from that instant it passes into the hands of women'.[43]

He was the first President of the Society for the Employment of Women! Such associations of women's work with what were regarded as women's special skills not only implied a lessening of respect for those men who did not work in 'manly' occupations but also recognized a secondary tier of skill linked to domestic virtues. Shaftesbury (as Lord Ashley) had piloted the 1842 Mines and Collieries Act through parliament, the first piece of gender specific legislation which removed all females from work below ground in mines. Children under ten were also banned (though female exclusion was the first clause of the Mines Bill despite the investigation having been into *children's* employment). Then, as today in many historical accounts, women and children were invariably linked, both lacking the vote and seen to be in need of protection. Women's employment in mining was actually centuries old and conditions were beginning to improve (though the sinking of deeper shafts posed new dangers for all mine-workers). What *was* new was the discovery of the moral and physical evils of such employment, now disseminated to an expanding and often prurient press, and rapidly legislated away.[44] Yet this protective legislation remained in practice partial legislation. It lacked efficient enforcement mechanisms (one man was appointed to cover two thousand collieries and he never went underground in his life!) so that for several decades women continued to work illegally and with greater vulnerability and dependence on employers than before. It was also partial in that it deliberately did not address all those employed in the industry. Yet the conditions of adult male miners left much to be desired.

The principle of protective legislation lay behind much

nineteenth-century law making.[45] Regulation of hours and times of work might not be as severe as total bans but they disadvantaged women workers who became less useful than men. For example women were not able to clean machinery after their day's shift once the Factory Act of 1844 had put a brake on their hours. Such laws were not necessarily interpreted by women workers as protective, especially when they were threatened with taking home a diminished wage. However, interference was nothing new in their lives. Working-class women were continually subjected to the searchlight of investigation by parliamentary committees and well-meaning middle-class ladies who would never have contemplated, let alone tolerated, being visited in their homes in the way they assumed they could descend on the poor.

Feminists and social reformers were divided on the wisdom of protective legislation. Some cynically criticized those wanting women to work all hours of the day and night in unsavoury conditions with which they were themselves unfamiliar. Others interpreted 'protective' as 'restrictive' and deplored the arrogant assumption that women were incapable of protecting themselves. Opportunities were narrow enough without the law intervening and such interference might encourage illegal, after hours work in shocking conditions. The 1891 and 1895 Factory and Workshop Acts may have helped drive production into domestic and other unregulated conditions of labour.[46] For some feminists, what was being protected (by an all-male parliament) was men's jobs. Lydia Becker used the word 'protection' to urge women's rights at a Whitehaven meeting to defend the pit women in 1886.

> When we have made a stand against further legislation against the industrial liberties of women, it will be time to make an effort to obtain the repeal of the protective legislation which now exists to the detriment of women . . . I believe the root of the matter is that the working women whose labour is threatened have not the protection of the Parliamentary vote.[47]

Certainly, the focus on women's employment seems to have prompted plans for *removing* women from certain occupations (sometimes with the blessing of trade unionists who subscribed to the idea of the family wage) rather than improving conditions for all. This led some to urge state benefits whilst others advocated unionization. It is not easy to discover what the women themselves felt. Some clearly worried that they were taking jobs which should belong to men and command a 'man's wage'. Responses would have depended on family circumstances, the nature of the work and its wages and whether their position could be construed as cheap labour in competition with men. Over 95,000 petitioned in favour of the Factory Acts Amendment Bill of 1984 with only 10,693 against.[48] Women were in a relatively strong position in textiles, however, and did not stand to lose their livelihoods. In contrast the pitbrow lasses facing opposition from union leaders as well as philanthropists and a frequently misinformed public opinion, protested vigorously against legislative attempts to ban their work and formed deputations to the Home Office in 1887 and 1911, supported by middle-class feminists.[49]

Many middle-class women faced obstacles within their own class. The opening up of professional work for women was slow and easily thwarted. By 1911 women accounted for only 6 per cent of the higher professions.[50] Although in the last years of the century a small number obtained senior posts in the Civil Service – Adelaide Anderson perhaps being the best known as Chief Woman Inspector of Factories from 1897 – they were exceptional and from highly privileged backgrounds. In this period they were in charge of women's affairs alone and despite their considerable responsibilities, men in less senior positions earned more. The Treasury made a clear distinction between women administrative officers – educated, socially acceptable and ambitious – and the woman clerk who was in contrast actively encouraged from the 1870s. These latter workers were generally from lower middle-class social origins and, though skilled, were cheap to employ.[51]

Meta Zimmeck's essay discusses the expansion of their work in the latter years of the nineteenth century. This period represented overall not so much a huge expansion of women's employment opportunities as a shift from one type of occupation to another as new areas of work became feminized with opportunities expanding in 'white blouse' jobs.[52] Such openings did not suddenly confer middle-class status but they did offer some form of liberation and respectability for those whose paths had previously led towards the restrictive world of domestic service. Describing late nineteenth-century rural Oxfordshire, Flora Thompson[53] explained how tradesmen's daughters known as 'home birds' keeping their father's accounts or helping mothers with lighter housework were less common than they had been. The new trend was for daughters to move away from home to become shop assistants in big London stores (by 1914 there were close to half a million women shop assistants in England and Wales, the largest single group of 'middle-class' women workers).[54] She saw others becoming schoolteachers and nursery governesses. By the First World War nearly three-quarters of all elementary schoolteachers in England and Wales were women in a rapidly expanding job which offered opportunities for social mobility.[55] Flora Thompson referred to one daughter who had become a book-keeper and receptionist at a boarding house and another who trained as a probationer in a London hospital. In nursing, like teaching, women were in a 'caring profession'. Here they ministered to others and performed chores which sometimes overlapped with domestic tasks. Not until 1891 did the Census introduce the term 'sick nurse' to differentiate between hospital nurses and household servants.[56] No longer, according to Flora Thompson, did tradesmen's daughters go into domestic service except as properly trained ladies' maids. Indeed the late nineteenth century witnessed a huge increase in the need to train for jobs and gain professional qualifications which provided yet more hurdles for ambitious women, eager to enter traditional male enclaves such as medicine.

One rapidly expanding area of women's employment was in the Post Office which was part of the Civil Service and was fast becoming the largest business organization in the country. The typewriter was in use from the last two decades of the century and was advocated as eminently suitable for women (it was compared to the piano and its letters named keys). The Post Office provided women with a range of clerical work which spelt unprecedented opportunities for the unmarried middle-class woman who might at last earn a respectable living. Interestingly the very constraints and restraints of such employment, such as the spatial segregation of the sexes, helped smooth the transition for young ladies from the familial basis of an overwhelmingly female daytime society to a public domain associated with men.[57] Meta Zimmeck shows us that just as the tailoress or woman hosiery worker laboured in an occupation divided by gender, so too were the status, pay and work patterns of women clerks separated from those of the men.

Some women Post Office employees worked in telegraphy as counter clerks and manipulators (transmitting). Rather superior in conditions of work, wages and social background were the first clerkships in the Savings Bank department of the Civil Service.[58] In contrast Flora Thompson tells of the country experience in Post Offices with their long hours for the resident learners (generally schoolmasters' or ministers' daughters).[59] Such work was markedly different from that of the women beginning to enter big city firms.

In 1863 Munby went to a public dancing room in London ('one of the few . . . which is frequented by respectable women and *not* by prostitutes'). To his delight he found a 23 year old woman who had come 'straight from business' after writing all day. He was fascinated by this bone fide copying clerk with three years' experience at a mercantile house. She knew of only three or four other firms with female clerks 'and it took a good deal of interest to get her her place'. She saw herself and her female colleagues as being 'instead of gentlemen' though none of them did accounting work. She claimed that the firm liked lady clerks best 'for they do the work as well as the "gentlemen", and are paid less'. She clearly valued her position, stressing the necessity of a 'good plain education'. For Munby, here indeed was a modern woman: 'she had spoken to me frankly at first, and now she talked soberly and gravely just as a young man might have done, about her affairs'.[60]

By 1891 there were 6,793 female commercial clerks in London. Yet this did not pass without protest. Then as now, the introduction of new office technology spelt fears of rationalization and replacement for the established male clerks. A letter to the press from the commercial and shipping centre Liverpool, expressed a male clerk's reaction to the suggestion that women should earn the same wages as men doing the same work:

> this is a gross piece of audacity on the part of the comparitively [sic] small, but bombastic section of clerical labour. Seeing that they are so fond of comparing the product of their labour as equal to that of the male clerk I would suggest that these intrepid 'typewriter pounders', instead of being allowed to gloat over love novels or do fancy crocheting, during the time they are not 'pounding' should fill in their spare time washing out the offices and dusting same, which you will no doubt agree is more suited to their sex and maybe would give them a little practice and insight into the work they will be called upon to do should they so far demean themselves as to marry one of the poor male clerks whose living they are doing the utmost to take out of his hands at the present time.[61]

The proletarianization which Meta Zimmeck correctly identifies as dominating most of the historical and sociological literature on clerks can in part be traced back to the fears and concerns of men such as this Liverpool clerk. The changing implications of technological development can only be fully understood by looking at the other side of the equation – identifying, as Meta Zimmeck does, the real opportunities developing for women. Though limited, she shows that they were less limiting then they had been and many would not have been impressed by being thus relegated to part-time office cleaners. One woman clerk wrote to *The Telegraphist* in 1885 emphasizing that although 'not Amazons, nor yet Miss Helen Taylors*',[62] they did as employees have the right to fair treatment.

Whilst opportunities were opening up for these women they were narrowing for others. Gill Burke's chapter looks at the Bâl Maidens employed in the copper and tin industries of Cornwall. Her study reminds us that diminishing job opportunities were not necessarily the direct or even indirect product of laws or union opposition. Nor did expanding horizons for men necessarily bring benefits for their wives. For the Cornish Bâl Maiden the end of mining work was set in motion by the fall in tin prices after 1873. The shift from copper to tin, changes in the work structure, and technological developments such as mechanized separating tables were crucial determinants of their fate. Yet whereas the coal-mining pitbrow lasses had something specific against which they could organize themselves (the Mines Bills of 1886–7 and 1911), the Cornish women faced more gradual decline without a focal point for organized pressure group resistance. Essential to an understanding of these changes is an appreciation of the international mine economy. Unequalled opportunities for men in the Rand goldfields of South Africa were accompanied by severely diminished chances for work for Cornish women. In the same way as matriarchal regimes characterized southern Italian villages in the 1930s as young men sought their fortunes in the United States, Cornwall had by the turn of the century many, many women dependent on precarious resources from overseas.[63] *The Cornishman* newspaper ran a weekly column entitled 'News from foreign mining camps'.[64] In neighbouring North Devon, in mid-century, there had been out-migration as many skilled woolcombers left when faced with the mechanization of their trade. There, women entered the trade in large numbers whilst it lost its image of skill and status.[65]

It is argued that the Bâl Maidens' lives now saw a 'communality of shared toil',[66] in contrast to their earlier more public work and lifestyles. The independent Bâl Maiden who married a Cornish miner was in a very different position from that of the late nineteenth-century woman divested of work and left behind as her husband sought his fortune. It is, however, difficult to piece together the daily lives of working-class women since they are so often refracted through the views of another class. Much of the

---

*Daughter of Harriet Taylor and step-daughter of John Stuart Mill.

literature which refers to mid-century independence and freedom for the Bâl Maiden, evoking a public world of fairs and festivals, was written after the event by middle-class writers of fiction for whom the temptation to romanticize a fast fading world must have been strong.

Gill Burke comments on the women's apparent love of fine clothes. Modern social historians have been slow to recognize the importance of dress for our understanding of society. Perhaps this in part derives from an association with older social history of the 'politics left out' variety. Maybe it has also been perceived (somewhat erroneously) as the concern of women and so set apart from 'serious' historical analysis. Yet Victorian society saw dress as one of the defining characteristics of respectable womanhood, especially since an initial impression based on outward appearance might be the closest that many observers got to the working class. And just as costume continued to display social rank and gender, particularly before the era of cheap, more standardized ready-made clothes, so too was a lack of a distinct female dress of particular concern. The bifurcation of society by sex should be expressed in separate costume and not in the dual garment! Thus the uproar over women wearing trousers at the pit top in Wigan – 'fustian unmentionables' – becomes comprehensible. In 1872 *The Times* described them clad in 'unseemly dress, and with those unseemly manners which indicate an unsexed mind'.[67] In the same year *The Ladies Journal* could write much more complacently about Bâl Maidens who did not submit to unisex clothing. The Children's Employment Commission 30 years earlier had, however, signalled its disapproval of their extravagant and flamboyant dress.[68] Yet this might have been an important way of expressing femininity in a largely masculine workplace. It was also a means of asserting independence, a gesture not available to the maid in service who had to display her badge of office, a starched uniform.

Yet as Gill Burke shows, not all contemporaries attacked the Bâl Maidens. The accounts written for *The Mining Journal* and *The Ladies Journal* are worth comparing, not least because they indirectly point up the class and gender of their readers. The former's middle-class, professional, male readership contrasted with a journal for ladies, produced at a time when women's job opportunities were beginning to expand and when it was thought appropriate to discover 'how the other half lives'. Suffrage journals and women trade union organizers would take further the right of all women to remunerative work.

The final part of the book considers women and organization. Much labour history has presented the female sex as a non-participating threat to unions or as a potential ally who does not always conform, contribution history *par excellence*. Yet a prior analysis of the nature of women's employment and the structure of domesticity is required before making such judgements. It is important to note what might have seemed the most relevant and urgent issues and structures for groups of working women. History is punctuated with instances where women have played major roles in protests concerned with the supply of food. Clearly here was something highly pertinent whether it be eighteenth-century food riots, exclusive dealing and price-fixing tactics in the Chartist period or Anti-Beef Tax Associations in the north-west and north-east towns in 1872.[69]

Jane Lewis has argued that 'women's passivity has probably been greatly exaggerated'.[70] Not only was it possible for Barbara Drake to write a 237 page book on women in trade unions in 1920 but women's protests have often been sublimated and are missing from historical accounts because they have not fitted into predefined notions of organization. Only recently has the strength of their networks and sex solidarity begun to be unravelled. Their involvement in the Ten Hour and Anti-Poor Law movements, in Owenite and Chartist organization is being pieced together, their particular expressions of protest often differing from those of the men but being especially effective in local communities. Nor have they been passive victims at work. Not only were there instances of unilateral strike action – for example the women tile workers' strike in Tunstall in 1907[71] – but women frequently shared struggles with fellow workers enmeshed in battles over control of work and at times they were able to exert some limited power of their own. Richard Whipp's study of the early twentieth-century pottery industry (where 50 per cent of the workforce were female in what was the sixth largest employer of women) argues that, in a trade where there was close interpenetration of work and home, women created pockets of influence and control.[72] He has reconstructed their role as collectors of union dues where they performed in the local community at an equal rate to the men. Evidence reveals one woman determining whether her son will join the union and another paying her husband's dues according to her domestic budget.

Nevertheless women pottery workers paid dues and received benefits at half or a third the rate of men. Union policy endorsed one week's notice for women yet two weeks to a month for male potters. Joining the union was no guarantee of status or power. When the

Kidderminster Power Loom, Carpet Weaving and Textile Workers' Association finally accepted women members during the First World War it ruled that the vote of 25 female members should be equivalent to one man's vote.[73] Over 80 per cent of the members of the Cardroom Workers' Association were women but they were largely excluded from positions as lay officers or permanent officials.[74]

Although it is easy to demonstrate the low participation of women in unions (3.2 per cent of women workers in 1900), not only did their rates of membership increase steadily over the last years of the nineteenth century but 75 per cent of the total labour force was not actively organized. It is interesting to note that two-thirds of women trade unionists in 1900 were in the textile trades (see Appendix E). In the Lancashire cotton industry women's union activity was aided by a centralized workplace (so different from the situation for many of the women examined in Parts 1 and 2), a sizeable workforce, close communities and an accepted tradition of married women's employment.

Joanna Bornat's chapter considers the textile trade of the West Riding where there existed the ingredients for a high degree of women's union activity. She asks why, in an area where numerous women did join the union (forming close to half the membership) and played key roles in strikes, did they somehow become 'Lost Leaders', not policy makers or even holders of significant positions? Since the union was led by supporters of suffrage, one of whom had a wife (Elizabeth Turner) who was herself an activist, this was not a straighforward case of male antagonism. Joanna Bornat penetrates behind the male union leaders' official pronouncements to reveal a disjuncture between their formal support for women's rights and their underlying paternalism. Add to this the structure of women's employment within the wool and worsted trades, and the strength of domesticity in defining women's economic as well as social role becomes apparent as does the fact that the union was not of central importance to the majority of women. Employers sanctioned gender differentiation within the mills which mirrored wider familial assumptions about women's place and helped to institutionalize their marginality and block social mobility in public life.

What was this work organization?[75] Woollen and worsted trades, although organized differently, reveal distinctions by age and sex which paralleled wider social configurations. The scene was set from an early age. What were perceived as 'blind alley' jobs in textiles for boys were never described as such for girl entrants. The shaping of prospects and hierarchy of positions branched sharply. Men were the supervisors and occupied the most highly skilled jobs. In both wool and worsted there were preparatory stages which depended on women's labour. In the trade in recovered rags (Dewsbury and Batley) women sorted rags while men blended the resulting material. Pure raw wool was sorted into different qualities by skilled men but in both wool and worsted mills, preparation for spinning was a woman's job. In Colne Valley women were increasingly replacing boy piecers. And in weaving more women were working in warping (the intricate preparation of the long warp threads for a loom). Whereas weaving in the woollen trade might be done by men or women, worsted weaving in Bradford was a woman's occupation. Finishing processes (for example dyeing) were mainly men's jobs though mending a finished piece might be done by women (supervised by men). This was a popular and well-paid job. Burling and knotting (removing lumps and knots from cloth) was designated women's work.

Thus although there were signs of improvement for women (resented by the men) women were, in the main, excluded from the most skilled jobs and tended to be found in subsidiary, servicing and casual work. Variations between and within regions and jobs make it very difficult to establish wages. In 1906 a supervisor might earn £2 but some adult spinners got only 10/– weekly. On average women's earnings were about half those of men. In 1883 Clementina Black noticed that in Huddersfield and Colne Valley men were the standard weavers and women paid something *less* than the men's scale. Thirty years later women had become the standard weavers with men paid rather *more* than the women's scale (my italics).[76] Although in Huddersfield it was not uncommon for men and women to be weaving side by side, the latter were consistently paid 10 per cent less than the men. The origin of such a practice needs to be sought beyond the point of production. Women, as Deborah Thom also argues, were defined as women first, as workers second, if at all, and in the context of the 1890s depression in wool and worsted when employers reduced wages, especial concern was voiced about the employment rights of married women.

For some trade unionists the ideal state was for them to earn a family wage. The origins of this demand can be traced back to the early unions. In 1843 the Chartist paper *The Northern Star* put the position of the newly formed Miners' Association: 'Keep the women at home to look after their families; decrease the pressure on the labour market and there is then some chance of a higher rate of wages being enforced'.[77] This was prompted by class as well as gender – in this instance the belief that miners' wives should be entitled to the same home comforts as the wives of their employers and an assertion of control from the first national miners' union seeking improvements in the industry on the men's terms rather than those of government officials. Traditionally payment had been via a family wage in the sense that the hewer was paid a wage which was supposed to cover the employment of his assistants. Until 1842 they had tended to be his wife and daughters.

Much has been written about the family wage which was never more than an ideal.[78] Men's wages, even for those in regular employment, were not high enough to maintain families with only one worker (as essay 3 shows). The single/married dichotomy is, as we have seen, inadequate to describe the variety of domestic arrangements which existed. Not only did not all men have dependants but many women had relatives who lived off their earnings and household labour. The unemployment of men ensured that wives had little option but to work for wages especially at times in the family cycle when children were too young to earn. Not only was there no evidence that higher wages would result from women staying at home, but the argument seems to have been divisive for the labour movement. The issue underlines the ways in which family responsibilities were always gender-linked, earning and providing being masculine virtues whilst the dependence of women was applauded even if the practice cut across the theory that the man kept the family whilst the woman kept it together.

Familial influence permeated work organization. In the Lancashire cotton trade employers frequently told men to bring their wives too if they wanted work and in early spinning and weaving (before the power looms) families had been able to work together within factories. In the second half of the nineteenth century between half and two-thirds of married women cotton operatives had husbands working in the trade and at collieries and pot banks, sons and daughters followed fathers, brother and sisters, sustained by paternalistic structures of employment. As Patrick Joyce has observed, 'There is, perhaps, no more suggestive conjunction than the paternalism of the factory regime and the employer dynasty and the paternalism of the operative family'.[79] Yet it is from Lancashire that we see the emergence of that remarkable group of women trade unionists and radical suffragists, such as Selina Cooper.

In 1913 the Yorkshire textile leader Ben Turner moved a TUC

resolution for a minimum wage for 'all adult workers and especially women . . .'. It was passed unanimously. However, the same Congress approved another resolution for a minimum wage for adult *male* workers alone, 50 per cent higher than that asked for all workers.[80] Ellen Mappen's chapter focuses on the minimum wage issue, comparing the attitudes of Clementina Black and Margaret Gladstone MacDonald in the years leading up to the Trade Boards Act of 1909 which established four Boards to fix a minimum hourly wage for approximately 250,000 workers in the ready-made clothing trade, chain-making, lacemaking and finishing and box making. As Jenny Morris notes, this institutionalized a gender division of labour by setting different rates for men and women. It confirmed the connection between low wages and women's work and a belief in women's inferior productive capacity. Nevertheless it was a landmark in the development of state intervention though it has received far less historical attention than the social welfare reforms (such as provision of school meals and non-contributory old age pensions) of the Liberal government elected in 1906. Trade Boards were intended to put a brake on employers' power and on the forces of supply and demand in determining workers' wages. Renamed Wages Councils they expanded to 26 by 1985.[81].

The idea of a state legislated minimum wage can be traced back into the nineteenth century. Indeed a fixed minimum wage subsidized by poor rates lay behind the Speenhamland system of poor relief in 1795. The labour movement's concern (especially in trades where it was difficult to provide wage protection via unions) grew in the late nineteenth century as did that of workers – East London tailoresses appealed to the London County Council for a government enforced minimum wage.[82] Ellen Mappen traces the development of the minimum wage issue and its advocacy by Clementina Black who deplored the scandalously low pay of married women workers. Ellen Mappen and Deborah Thom show how the Sweated Trades Exhibition of 1906 and the creation of the Anti-Sweating League were important formative experiences for such women as well as highlighting concern about low pay and the sweated trades. In the mid-nineteenth century Mayhew had revealed links between seasonal unemployment in tailoring and prostitution. Moral fears permeated the later debate, given new fervour by concern with motherhood and the future of the race. The metaphor of disease which had been so prominent in descriptions of the urban working class was now extended to the evils of sweated labour. The chairman of the Anti-Sweating League declared at the opening of the 1906 Exhibition that sweating was seen to be: 'not an excrescence on the body politic, having no bearing upon its general health, but an organic disease . . . a running sore, a morass exhaling a miasma that poisoned the healthy elements of industry'.[83]

Ellen Mappen shows how Clementina Black's views diverged from those of her contemporary Margaret MacDonald. The latter saw Trade Boards as diversionary tactics, preferring the licensing of home workshops. Her views need to be set in the context of the early Labour Party's policies, voicing fears about evasion of the law and the minimum wage becoming the standard wage. She was more concerned with collectivist remedies linked to better educational opportunities to help eradicate child labour, pensions for the elderly and employment protection legislation. She hoped that '"A Right to Work" Act for Men would be a Charter to the "Right to Leisure and Home Comfort" for their wives'. Having witnessed low-paid work such as that of the laundress, she concluded that the double load of laundry work and housework was disastrous.[84] For still others, minimum wage legislation was sought precisely *because* women were seen to keep wages down. By protecting male incomes, married women's work might be reduced. This attitude made assumptions about the permanency of the married state and about men's willingness to hand over increased wages. Regarding women as secondary breadwinners to be considered only in relation to their families both perpetuated inequality in the home and strengthened it outside.

Ellen Mappen reveals how middle-class women, concerned to improve the lot of working women and influenced by feminism, nevertheless did not reject a framework of domesticity. Their exploration of wretched conditions, far removed from their own backgrounds and in which the social and sexual contours of sweated workers' lives militated against the likelihood of change emanating from the men, doubtless encouraged this. So these women, like the women trade unionists examined by Deborah Thom, ultimately subscribed to the primacy of the wife and mother's role for working-class women, yet, interestingly, many of them rejected it in their own personal lives.

Deborah Thom's challenging essay reminds us of the dangers of compartmentalizing history into rigid periods. The extraordinary years of wartime, subject to intense scrutiny by contemporary investigators and later historians can, she argues, deflect attention from peacetime, making it difficult to determine continuities and discontinuities in attitudes and policies. Yet the pre-war years of Suffragette militancy and struggle over the minimum wage were crucial determinants for the wartime policies of the leaders she considers, Mary Macarthur and Julia Varley. Moreover, the experience of war itself was to prove less influential in emancipating women workers than longer-term changes in employment opportunities and women's own demands.[85] To some extent war institutionalized a sense of women's unequal capacities by building into the structure of work, processes of dilution and substitution which acknowledged women as emergency workers and their war-work as women's work. The ultimate acceptance of their position as temporary, and the validation of motherhood as their most valuable work was accepted by women as well as men.

Lady Bell, the writer and social investigator recognized that war had brought a sense of freedom, something which, though soon a memory for women, could not be lost. Writing in 1919 she recognized that the immediate post-war period was the difficult time when women had to go back into their houses and piece together 'ordinary Life', some with 'untold relief, others with courage, many many more with inward revolt'. Her final message, however, confirmed 'familism rather than feminism' as she appealed to the 'common experience of motherhood' at a time when the reconstruction of family life represented the ultimate expression of a return to normality.[86] War had helped stimulate eugenist ideas whilst the absence of husbands both increased many women's responsibilities and created concern which underlined the strength of pronatalist ideas. Despite real attempts to organize women in 1916–18, Deborah Thom argues that women union leaders were accepting the loss of large numbers of women workers at the end of the war. Moreover, gender had always been the determining factor in women's employment with women union leaders paying more attention to women's special problems such as gynaecological issues than to questions which cut across gender and affected all workers.[87]

The chapter raises fundamental questions about leadership and about the way movements are interpreted historically. The temptation to present accounts of women trade union leaders such as Mary Macarthur which are little more than hagiography is enhanced by two factors. One is the need for historians to recognize women's leadership alongside male organizers and so combat andro-centrism. Trade union history has elevated and celebrated its heroes, many of whom have recorded their achievements in autobiographies. Providing similar treatment for women is possible but it runs the

danger of collapsing women's goals into those of men and at the same
time ignoring the experiences of ordinary women members.
Secondly, the success story of a pioneer such as Mary Macarthur
encourages such an approach. In Margaret Bondfield's words she
'lived a short life; but it was crowded and thrilling'.[88] J.J. Mallon,
secretary of the Anti-Sweating League put it this way:

> She has the habit of passing everything through heroic moulds.
> She shares in historic councils and earth-shaking debates, and
> sees world movements come to birth. Breathlessness is her
> dominant characteristic. She is always at top speed. She whirls
> from meeting to meeting, strike to strike, congress to congress:
> the street shouting behind the dust and rattle of her car.[89]

Deborah Thom avoids a simple recounting of the drama of this
woman's life and instead reminds us of the invisibility of the
majority of women workers and of the complex relationship between
them and their leader. Individuals such as Mary Macarthur could
shape and dictate policies which had more long-term impact on
history than they necessarily had on their contemporaries. Yet how
can the historian penetrate behind the Mary Macarthurs and Julia
Varleys? Integral to Deborah Thom and Joanna Bornat's studies has
been oral history. Such a technique can, like all sources, be fraught
with contradictions, not least that of being removed in time from the
events and perhaps is most revealing about how memory is
constructed and the ways the present reshapes the past. Nevertheless
it is one of the most rich and potent approaches for the feminist
historian seeking to reconstruct the daily negotiations, compromises
and patterns of women's lives in the not too distant past. It can,
amongst other things, point to distinctions between what middle-
class women might perceive as most advantageous for their sex and
what women as workers might opt for in the short term.

Deborah Thom's essay reminds us how, despite the opening up of
opportunities, the inequalities of women's labour ultimately
predominated. The nineteenth century had witnessed a number of
advances for women. There clearly were unprecedented work
opportunities for middle-class women late in the century and
conditions of work for both men and women very gradually
improved over the years. And despite the disadvantages under which
women laboured, it should not be suggested that working-class men
faced unlimited chances. Their prospects were frequently grim
but the total acceptance of their role as paterfamilias (bolstered
in law) gave them a grave responsibility to shoulder. Nor have
'unequal opportunities' given way to equality for all. Not only are

there reminders of continuing 'Victorian values' – an estimated two thousand unregulated workshops exist in the East End of London alone – but despite the winning of the vote for women over 30 in 1918, Equal Opportunities legislation was deemed necessary over 50 years later. This demonstrates the continuing gap between theory and practice and the dangers of a Whig version of women's history. Ten years after the implementation of the Equal Pay Act (1970) with more women than ever in the workforce (40 per cent), half were estimated to be receiving wages below the poverty line.[90] Only in its amended form in 1984 did the Act accept the principle of equal pay for work of equal value. Clara Collet's remark of 1902 still has a depressingly familiar ring:

> There is no hardship in women working for a living, the hardship lies in not getting a living when they work for it. [91]

Notes

Place of publication throughout the book is London unless otherwise stated.

1 Ivy Pinchbeck, *Women Workers and the Industrial Revolution* (Virago edn, 1969); Louise A. Tilly and Joan W. Scott, *Women, Work and Family* (Holt, Rinehart and Winston, 1975); Jane Lewis, *Women in England 1870–1950 (Wheatsheaf, Brighton, 1984)*. For documents see especially Patricia Hollis, *Women in Public, The Women's Movement, 1850–1900* (George Allen and Unwin, 1979) and Janet Horowitz Murray, *Strong-Minded Women* (Penguin, Harmondsworth, 1984).
2 Elizabeth Roberts, *A Woman's Place* (Basil Blackwell, Oxford, 1984), p.116.
3 For a useful mid-nineteenth-century breakdown of occupations and wages of women and men see Jules Ginswick (ed.), *Labour and the Poor in England and Wales 1849–51*, vol.1 (Cass, 1983). See Appendix D.
4 Diana Gittins, *Fair Sex* (Hutchinson, 1982), p.115.
5 Plymouth magistrates told the 1871 Royal Commission on the Administration of the Contagious Diseases Acts that police sent back home mining girls who sought freedom in Plymouth. Judith R. Walkowitz, *Prostitution and Victorian Society* (Cambridge University Press, Cambridge, 1980), p.158.
6 For agriculture see Pamela Horn, *The Rural World 1700–1850* (Hutchinson, 1980), S. Alexander, A Davin, and E. Hostettler, 'Labouring Women' *History Workshop Journal*, no.8 (Autumn 1979) and K.D.M. Snell, 'Agricultural Seasonal Unemployment: the Standard of Living and Women's Work in the South and East 1690–1860', *Economic History Review*, vol.xxiv, no.3 (1981). Eve Hostettler, 'Gourlay Steell

and the Sexual Division of Labour', *History Workshop Journal*, no. 4, (Autumn, 1977). Jennie Kitteringham, *Country Girls in 19th Century England*, History Workshop pamphlet, (1973) and C. Miller, 'The Hidden Workforce: female field workers in Gloucestershire, 1870–1901', *Southern History*, no. 6 (1984).

7 For pre-nineteenth-century employment see Alice Clark, *Working Life of Women in the Seventeenth Century* (Routledge and Kegan Paul edn, 1982); Bridget Hill, *Eighteenth Century Women: An Anthology* (George Allen and Unwin, 1984); R. W. Malcolmson, *Life and Labour in England 1700–1780* (Hutchinson, 1981) ch. 2; E. Richards, 'Women in the British Economy since c1700. An Interpretation', *History*, vol. 59, no. 197 (1974). In this introduction I use the term 'gender division of labour' to denote social construction (rather than the biological category of 'sex').

8 Maxine Berg, 'Responses to Machinery in Eighteenth Century England', *Bulletin of the Society for the Study of Labour History*, no. 49 (Autumn 1984), p. 12. See too Maxine Berg, *The Age of Manufactures, 1700–1820*, Fontana, 1985), ch. 6 for a valuable discussion of domestic industry. Spinning remained an exclusively female (low paid) trade until the introduction of larger spinning jennies.

9 William Lazonick, 'Industrial Relations and Technological change: the case of the self-acting mule', *Cambridge Journal of Economics*, vol. 3, no. 3 (September 1979).

10 Karl Marx, *Capital*, vol. 1 (Pelican edn, Harmondsworth, 1976) pp. 620–1.

11 For proto-industrialization see M. Berg, D. Hudson, and M. Sonescher (eds), *Manufacture in Town and Country before the Factory* (Cambridge University Press, 1983), ch. 5, Pat Hudson, 'From Manor to Mill: the West Riding in Transition'.

12 Joanna Bornat, 'Home and Work: A new Context for Trade Union History', *Oral History* vol. 5, no. 2 (Autumn 1977), pp. 102. Judy Lown, 'Not so Much a Factory, More a Form of Patriarchy: Gender and Class during Industrialisation', in E. Garmarnikow et al. (eds), *Gender, Class and Work* (Heinemann, 1983), p. 29.

13 T. Cooper, *The Life of Thomas Cooper By Himself* (Leicester University Press edn, Leicester, 1971), p. 139.

14 Barbara Taylor, '"The Men Are as Bad as Their Masters . . .": Socialism, Feminism and Sexual Antagonism in the London Tailoring Trade in the 1830s' in Judith L. Newton, Mary P. Ryan, and Judith R. Walkowitz (eds), *Sex and Class in Women's History* (Routledge and Kegan Paul, 1983) pp. 198–9. James Epstein, 'Some Organisational and Cultural Aspects of the Chartist Movement in Nottingham', in *The Chartist Experience*, eds James Epstein and Dorothy Thompson (Macmillan, 1982), pp. 236–242.

15 Quoted in E.H. Hunt, *British Labour History 1815–1914* (Weidenfeld and Nicholson, 1981), p. 25.

16 Quoted in Felicity Hunt, 'Women in the Nineteenth Century Bookbinding and Printing Trades 1790–1914 with special reference to London', MA (University of Essex, 1979), p. 36.

17 Mark Rutherford, *The Revolution in Tanner's Lane* (Hogarth Press, 1984), p. 38.

18 For comparison with the United States where women learned the trade in New York only by working in non-union shops or strike-breaking see H. Hartman, 'Capitalism, Patriarchy and Job Segregation by Sex' in *Capitalist Patriarchy and the Case for Socialist Feminism* ed. Zillah R. Eisenstein, (Monthly Review Press, 1980) pp. 226–7. See also Cynthia Cockburn, *Brothers* (Pluto Press, 1983) ch. 6 for women strike-breakers in Edinburgh. In Nottingham Letter Press Printers banned women from working rotary machines where the higher wages were earned and refused to print rules set up by women. *Women's Suffrage Journal*, vol. 17, no. 197 (1 May 1886).

19 Horowitz Murray, *Strong-Minded Women*, p. 288. See also K. Sarad 'Family Faithfull and the Victorian Press', in *Studies in the History of Feminism (1850s–1930s)*, Fawcett Library Feminist History Class, 1981–2 (1984).

20 Munby MS Wren Library, Trinity College, Cambridge. Diary 6, 7 September 1860; Diary 19, 16 May 1863. In 1984 the major print union SOGAT 82 elected a woman General Secretary whose votes doubled those of her nearest rival.

21 Quoted in Lewis, *Women in England*, p. 192

22 For notions of skill see Anne Philips and Barbara Taylor, 'Sex and Skill: Notes Towards a Feminist Economics', *Feminist Review*, no. 6 (1980) pp. 79–88; Cockburn, *Brothers;* and Idem, 'The Material of Male Power' *Feminist Review*, no. 9 (Autumn 1981), pp. 41–58. For a summary of the deskilling debate see John Benson (ed.) *The Working Class in England 1875–1914* (Croom Helm, 1985).

23 Patrick Joyce, *Work, Society and Politics* (Harvester Press, Brighton, 1980), pp. 112–3.

24 *Wigan Observer*, 14 February 1880.

25 Angela V. John in *Spare Rib*, no. 123 (October 1982) pp. 24–5.

26 June Hannam, 'Socialism, Feminism and Labour Politics: Isabella Ford and the Leeds Labour Movement, 1890–1914', Paper given at the 1985 Social History Conference on Sex and Gender.

27 James A. Schmiechen, *Sweated Industries and Sweated Labor* (Croom Helm, 1984), p. 2. See also Sally Alexander, *Women's Work in Nineteenth-Century London* (Journeyman Press, 1983).

28 David Goodway, *London Chartism, 1833–1848* (Cambridge University Press, Cambridge, 1982) p. 171.

29 See B. Taylor 'The Men are as Bad As Their Masters'. As early as 1800 women were being brought in as strike-breakers. I am grateful to Rodney Dobson for this information.

30 Clementina Black, *Married Women's Work* (Virago, 1983 edn), p. 183; for the impact of the sewing machine see Maxine Berg, *Technology and toil in Nineteenth Century Britain* (CSE books, 1979, ch. 7) 'Confection' (ready-made clothing) had a dramatic effect on women's employment in the French Tailoring trade. Jane Rendall, *The Origins of Modern Feminism* (Macmillan, 1985), p. 156. See also Barbro Hoel, 'Contemporary

Clothing "Sweatshops", Asian Female Labour and Collective Organisation', in *Work, Women and the Labour Market*, ed. Jackie West (Routledge and Kegan Paul, 1982).

31 Doris Nield Chew, *Ada Nield Chew, The Life and Writings of a Working Woman* (Virago, 1982), pp. 13, 76.

32 Liz Stanley (ed.), *The Diaries of Hannah Cullwick* (Virago, 1984).

33 Frank Prochaska, 'Female Philanthropy and Domestic Service in Victorian England', *Bulletin of the Institute of Historical Research*, vol. lix no. 129 (May 1981), p. 83

34 Hannah Mitchell, *The Hard Way Up* (Virago, 1984 edn).

35 Jill Liddington, *The Life and Times of a Respectable Rebel* (Virago, 1984), p. 22.

36 Quoted in *The Guardian*, 9 March 1984.

37 For new ways of looking at work within the household today see R. E. Pahl, *Divisions of Labour* (Basil Blackwell, Oxford, 1984).

38 In John Burnett, *Useful Toil* (Penguin, Harmondsworth, 1984 edn) pp. 67–77.

39 See Pam Taylor, 'Daughters and Mothers – Maids and Mistresses: Domestic Service between the Wars', in *Working Class Culture* ed. J. Clarke, C. Critcher and R. Johnson (Hutchinson, 1979).

40 Quoted in Martha Vicinus, *Independent Women. Work and Community for Single Women 1850–1920* (Virago, 1985) p. 4.

41 Quoted in Leonore Davidoff, 'Mastered for Life: Servant and Wife in Victorian and Edwardian England', *Journal of Social History*, vol. 7 no. 4 (Summer 1974), p. 424.

42 *The Times*, 16 May 1883.

43 Quoted in Rendall, *The Origins of Modern Feminism*, p. 185.

44 See Angela V. John, *By the Sweat of their Brow. Women Workers at Victorian Coal Mines* (Routledge and Kegan Paul, 1984 edn).

45 For protective legislation see Olive Banks, *Faces of Feminism* (Martin Robertson, Oxford, 1981) ch. 7. For modern implications see Angela Coyle, 'The protection racket?', *Feminist Review*, no. 4 (1980), pp. 1–14.

46 Schmiechen, *Sweated Industries*, ch. 6.

47 *Women's Suffrage Journal*, vol. xvii, no. 197 (1 May 1886).

48 Linda E. Walker, 'The Employment question and the Women's Movement in late Victorian and Edwardian Society with particular reference to "The Englishwoman's Review", MA (University of Manchester, 1974), p. 81.

49 John, *By the Sweat of Their Brow*, ch. 5.

50 Lewis, *Women in England*, p. 195, for middle-class women; see this and Vicinus, *Independent Women*, also Leonore Davidoff and Catherine Hall, *The Domestic Enterprise: Men and Women in the English Provincial Middle Class, 1780–1850* (Hutchinson, 1987), ch. 6.

51 Meta Zimmeck, 'Strategies and Stratagems for the Employment of Women in the British Civil Service, 1919–1939,' *Historical Journal*, vol. 27, no. 4 (1984).

52 Tilly and Scott, *Women, Work and Family*, p. 151. For the impact of modern technology see Janice Morgan, 'Typing our way to freedom: is it

true that new office technology can liberate women?, in *The Changing Experience of Women*, E. Whitelegg et al. (ed.), (Martin Robertson, Oxford, 1982).

53 Flora Thompson, *Lark Rise to Candleford* (Penguin, Harmondsworth, 1984 ed), p. 499.

54 See Lee Holcombe, *Victorian Ladies at Work* (David and Charles, Newton Abbot, 1973). See H. Granville Barker's 1911 play, *The Madras House* (Eyre Methuen, 1977 edn) for an indictment of the shop assistants' living-in system. The separation of home and work and the development of a gendered middle-class spelt a decline in women's direct involvement in family business though many still played an essential role in financing ventures via marriage settlements. Catherine Hall, 'The Butcher, the Baker, the Candlestickmaker: the shop and the family in the Industrial Revolution', in Whitelegg, *The Changing Experience of Women*.

55 See Frances Widdowson, *Going Up Into the Next Class. Women and Elementary Teacher Training 1840–1914* (Hutchinson, 1983 edn).

56 For a discussion of the huge variation in opportunities and conditions within nursing, see Ann Simnett, 'The Pursuit of Respectability. Women and Nursing 1840–1901', MA (Thames Polytechnic, 1983) which contrasts recruits to St Bartholemew's hospital with workhouse nurses in Essex.

57 See C. Dyhouse's essay in Lewis, *Women's Experience* for an excellent description of the 'female' daytime.

58 Anna Davin, 'Telegraphists and Clerks', *Bulletin of the Society for the Study of Labour History*, no. 26 (Spring 1973) p. 9

59 Thompson, *Lark Rise*, p. 41

60. Munby MS, Diary 18, 10 April 1863.

61 *Liverpool Echo*, 1911, quoted in Linda Grant, 'Women's Work and Trade Unionism in Liverpool 1890–1914' in *Bulletin of the North West Labour History Society (Women and the Labour Movement)*, no. 7 (1980–1), pp. 76–7.

62 Quoted in Annmarie Turnbull, '"So extremely like Parliament": The Work of the London School Board, 1870–1914', in London Feminist History Group, *The Sexual Dynamics of History* (Pluto Press, 1983), p. 132.

63 See Carlo Levi, *Christ Stopped at Eboli* (Penguin, Harmondsworth, 1982 edn), p. 102.

64 See Gill Burke, 'The Cornish Miner and the Cornish Mining Industry 1870–1921', PhD (London University, 1982), ch. 9.

65 See D. Gittins's essay in Lewis, *Women's Experience*.

66 Burke (thesis), chs 7 and 8. Although civil marriage had been popular in the mining areas of Cornwall, depression in the trade led to a massive shift to chapel marriage (three times more common than in the country generally by the end of the century). Olive Anderson, 'Civil Marriage in Victorian England and Wales', *Past and Present*, no. 69 (1975), pp. 80–1.

67 *The Times*, 27 June 1872.

68 Children's Employment Commission, PP. 1842, Cmd. 380, XVII, p. 832.

69 John, *By the Sweat of their Brow*, ch. 4.
70 Lewis, *Women in England*, p. 183.
71 Richard Whipp, 'The Subject or the Subject of History?: Women and the Social Organization of Work in the early twentieth century Pottery Industry', unpublished paper, 1985. I am grateful to Richard Whipp for letting me read this. For Welsh women's protests see Angela V. John, 'A Miner Struggle? Women's Protests in Welsh Mining History', *Llafur*, (Society for the Study of Welsh Labour History), vol. 4, no. 1 (1984).
72 Richard Whipp '"Plenty of Excuses, No Money": The Social Bases to Trade Unionism, as illustrated by the Potters', *Bulletin of the Society for the Study of Labour History*, no. 49 (Autumn 1984); see too Arnold Bennett, *Anna of the Five Towns* (Penguin, Harmondsworth, 1982 edn), p. 121.
73 Sheila Lewenhak, 'Women at Work: Sub Contacting, Craft Unionism and Women in England with special reference to the West Midlands 1750–1914', in Anthony Wright, Richard Shackleton, *Worlds of Labour. Essays in Birmingham Labour History* (University of Birmingham, Birmingham 1983), p. 12.
74 Benson, 'Work'; p.78: Sheila Lewenhak, *Women and Trade Unions (Ernest Benn, 1977), pp. 92–3.*
75 See *Joanna Bornat, 'An Examination of the General Union of Textile Workers 1883–1922', PhD (Essex University, 1980).*
76 *Black, Married Women's Work*, p. 129. In Lancashire weaving men and women in theory earned the same rates. Yet they tended not to take home the same amount. Ada Nield Chew's story of Mr and Mrs Bolt, Lancashire weavers with four looms apiece in the same weaving shed illustrates this. At the end of the week Mrs Bolt brings home 20/-, Mr Bolt 26/-. The allocation and tuning of looms and the criteria by which weavers' piece rates were calculated affected this. Nield Chew, *Ada Nield Chew* p. 163 and Jill Liddington, *Working Class Women in the North West*, ii, *Oral History*, vol. 5, no. 2 (Autumn 1977), p. 33.
77 *Northern Star*, 7 October 1843.
78 For the 'family wage' see Michèlle Barrett and Mary McIntosh, 'The "Family Wage"', in Whitelegg, *The Changing Experience of Women'* Jane Humphries, 'Protective Legislation, the Capitalist State and Working Class Men: The Case of the 1842 Mines Regulation Act', *Feminist Review*, no. 7 (Spring 1981) and reply by Angela V. John in *Feminist Review*, no. 9 (Autumn 1981), pp. 106–9.
79 Joyce, *Work, Society and Politics*, p. 115; see also Jill Liddington and Jill Norris, *One Hand Tied Behind Us* (Virago, 1978).
80 Lewenhak *Women and Trade Unions*, pp.140–1.
81 Although the TUC and Labour Party have moved towards the adoption of a *national* minimum wage and although (according to the Low Pay Unit) 40 per cent of employers already pay *below* the approximately £70 weekly minimum wage, the Conservative government's belief in the free market has spelt the probable death knell for wages councils.
82 Schmiechen, *Sweated Industries*, p. 163.

83 E. P. Thompson and Eileen Yeo (eds), *The Unknown Mayhew* (Pelican, Harmondsworth, 1973 edn), pp. 175–216. Quoted in Lewis, *Women in England*, p. 34.

84 Ellen Mappen, *Helping Women at Work, The Women's Industrial Council 1889–1914* (Hutchinson, 1985), pp. 26, 79.

85 See Deborah Thom, 'The Ideology of Women's Work in Britain 1914–1924; with special reference to the NFWW and other Trade Unions', PhD (Thames Polytechnic), 1982.

86 Lady Bell, 'Women at the Works – and Elsewhere', *Fortnightly Review*, vol. 106 (1919), pp. 909–20.

87 Thom (thesis), p. 146, 231.

88 Mary Agnes Hamilton, *Mary Macarthur, A Biographical Sketch* (Leonard Parsons, 1925), Introduction.

89 Quoted in TUC Exhibition, 'Women in Trade Unions' (1983).

90 *The Guardian*, 6 March 1985.

91 Clara Collet, *Educated Working Women: Essays on the Economic Position of Women in the Middle Classes* (P.S. King and Son, 1902), p.23. After a long struggle in tribunals and courts a canteen cook finally won the first test case in England concerning equal pay for work of equal value in May 1988.

Appendix A

TOTAL POPULATION OF ENGLAND AND WALES
(In thousands)

Year	Total	Male	Female
1801	8,893	4,255	4,638
1851	17,928	8,781	9,146
1881	25,974	12,640	13,335
1911	36,070	17,446	19,625

The figures for this tabel (see opposite) are based on the 1911 Census categories. Bearing in mind the need for caution stressed in the Introduction and elsewhere in this book, it will be appreciated that the Census returns severely under-represent the number of 'occupied' females over ten during the period just as the 'unoccupied' category (5,192,000) in 1851 and 11,432,000 by 1911) camouflages the actuality and fluctuations of work. For example many women did seasonal jobs such as helping in the grain harvest. As the Census was usually taken in March or April this work would have been missed. Much outwork, for example dressmaking, was done not by one women but by women relatives and children sharing

Appendix B

MAIN OCCUPATIONS OF FEMALES OF ALL AGES IN GREAT
BRITAIN IN 1851, 1881, AND 1911 (In thousands)

Occupation	1851	1881	1911
Agriculture, horticulture and forestry	229	116	117
Textiles	635	745	870
Metal manufacture, machines, implements, vehicles, precious metals etc	36	49	128
Building and construction	1	2	5
Transport and communications	13	15	38
Clothing	491	667	825
Mining, quarrying and workers in the products of mines and quarries	11	8	8
Food, drink and tobacco	53	98	308
Domestic offices and personal services	1,135	1,756	2,127
Professional occupations and their subordinate services	103	203	383
Wood, furniture fittings and decorations	8	21	35
Commercial occupations	—	11	157
Bricks, cement, pottery, glass	15	27	42
Public administration	3	9	50
Paper, printing, books, stationery	16	53	144
Chemicals, oil, soap, resin	4	9	50
Total occupied	2,832	3,887	5,413
(Total occupied males)	6,545	8,852	12,927

tasks. Many women worked in family businesses yet were not
recorded as being in active employment. The problems of
quantifying domestic service are discussed in Edward Higgs's essay.
It is even possible that as many as one-third of all women workers
were not counted in the occupational categories. From 1841 every

householder was handed a schedule by an enumerator. Yet not only is the evidence in this Census incomplete and difficult to compare with later occupational categories (so the above table begins in 1851) but instructions then and later were not clear so that responses were not uniform. Householders' schedules excluded the work of women within the family economy. Male householders and male enumerators saw occupations in terms of male heads earning wages in the labour market. Not only did enumerators follow different conventions but the efficiency of enumeration changed over time. There were radical changes in 1911 when tabulation was done directly from the householders' schedules (by machine) for the first time.

Appendix C

SEX RATIO OF THE LABOUR FORCE IN 1851 BY OCCUPATIONAL CATEGORY (in thousands and using the same categories as B)

Occupation	% of all females	% of all females in each occupation
Agriculture etc.	8.1	11.4
Textiles	22.4	49.0
Metal manufacture	1.3	6.3
Building and construction	0	0.2
Transport and communications	0.5	2.9
Clothing	17.3	54.0
Mining etc.	0.4	2.8
Food etc.	1.9	13.2
Domestic offices etc.	40.1	85.5
Professional etc.	3.6	38.9
Wood etc.	0.3	5.0
Bricks etc.	0.5	16.7
Public admin.	0.1	4.5
Paper	0.6	20.5
Chemicals	0.1	8.7
Totals	100.00	30.2

Appendix D

SOME AVERAGE WEEKLY WAGES IN SECONDARY INDUSTRY:
ENGLAND 1849–51*

Location and Trade	Sex	Wage	Job description	Additional
Yorkshire (woollen and worsteds)	male	25/– to 27/–	wool sorters	for fine cloths 15/– to 20/– for less fine
	female	6/– to 7/–	picking and boiling	
	female and male	12/–	power loom weavers	
	male	18/– to 20/–	finishers	
	male	30/–	hot pressers	
	female	7/– to 8/–	burling	for domestic work
Leicester (hosiery)	male	20/–	fancy trade	children 5/–
	female	10/–	fancy trade	
Birmingham (brass)	male	35/– to 40/–	brass metal maker	
	male	35/– to 50/–	brass modeller	
	male	30/–	brass moulder	
	female	10/–	lacquerer	girls 4/– to 7/–
	female	7/– to 8/–	brass nails, stamper, burnisher, weigher, packer	
	male	15/– to 21/–	brass thimble maker	
	female	7/– to 9/–	brass thimble maker	
Potteries	male	42/– max	dipper	but pays boy asst. 4/–
	male	30/– to 40/–	thrower	
	male	30/– to 35/–	dishmaker	
	male	20/– to 50/–	painter	varies according to skill
	female	9/– to 12/–	painter	

cont.

Appendix D *cont.*

Location and Trade	Sex	Wage	Job description	Additional
South Staffs. (coal)	male	4/4½d per day	colliers	
	female	10d to 1/– per day	bankswomen	
(iron works)	male	18/– to 25/–	blast furnacemen	wages fluctuate with state of trade
	male	25/– to 30/–	forgemen	
	male	7/6d to 10/–	underhands	
	female	4/– to 6/–	about blast furnaces and coke ovens	
Derbyshire (lace)	male	21/– to 30/–	tenters of machines	
	female	5/6d to 9/–	wooden bobbin winders	
Lancashire Manchester (spinning)	male	40/– to 50–	spinner	
	male	13/– to 15/–	card room hands	
	female	7/– to 11/–	drawing room tenters	depends on type of frame (less than figs. quoted if coarse yarn)

*Based on *The Morning Chronicle* surveys.

Appendix E

WOMEN'S TRADE UNIONISM IN GREAT BRITAIN

Trade	1876	1906	1918
Textiles	19,000	143,000	423,000
Clothing	100	5,082	119,000
Printing	300	977	39,000
Pottery	—	530	20,000
Food and tobacco	—	2,447	7,000
Distributive	—	4,920	62,000
Clerical	—	5,315	83,000
General labour	100	2,674	216,000
Metal unions		484	11,000
Others	—	996	34,000
Total	19,500	166,425	1,014,000

Sources for Appendix based on B. R. Mitchell and P. Deane, *Abstract of British Historical Statistics* (Cambridge University Press, Cambridge, 1971 edn), p. 60; Hollis, *Women in Public*, p. 53; Ginswick, *Labour and the Poor*, pp. xxxvii–xlv; Hunt, *British Labour History*, p. 29; R. Floud and D. McCloskey, *The Economic History of Britain since 1700*, vol i. *1700–1860* (Cambridge University Press, Cambridge, 1984 edn), p. 208; Drake, *Women in Trade Unions*, table 1.

Part I

Sex, Skill and Status

A narrow frame knitter of the 1830s

1

Gender Divisions and the Organization of Work in the Leicester Hosiery Industry

Nancy Grey Osterud

In the early nineteenth century, Leicester was the centre of the woollen and worsted branch of the hosiery manufacture in England. The largest market town in its county, Leicester not only served as an organizational centre for a widespread rural industry, but also employed a large proportion of its population directly in the staple trade. The hosiery industry had been established on a capitalist basis from the beginning in the Midlands, with merchant-manufacturers employing wage-labourers from the late seventeenth century on. Production was organized on the putting-out system. Merchants owned the raw materials and sold the finished product, while workers were paid by the piece for the goods they produced. They used relatively sophisticated hand-operated machines, called knitting frames, but did not own them; frames were rented, and the charge was deducted from the workers' earnings. As in other putting-out industries, the household was the basic work unit, and all family members participated in income-producing labour. Jobs were allocated on the basis of age and sex. In a typical family, the husband and father would work the knitting frame while children wound bobbins and the wife and mother seamed the stockings; in large families, older daughters might help with the seaming while the wife or an older son might work a second frame.

By the end of the nineteenth century all this had changed. Leicester had become a large manufacturing town. Two staple industries – the manufacture of hosiery and knitted fabrics, and the manufacture of boots and shoes – dominated the economy, and there were a number of important subsidiary industries as well. In the hosiery industry, women workers were in the majority, comprising two-thirds of the labour force in 1891. They tended automatic knitting machinery and finished garments on sewing machines in large steam-powered factories, while men worked as overseers and mechanics. The boot and shoe industry, by contrast, employed predominantly male labour. In 1891, two-thirds of its workers were men. They cut out, lasted, and finished the shoes; women were employed only in stitching together the uppers. The town's labour force was thus strongly segregated by sex, both within and between industries.

The transition from outwork to factory production in Leicester did not involve the displacement of women from wage labour. Even married women continued in employment as household and workplace diverged. The segmentation of the labour force was replicated within individual families, as men and women, adults and young people, found jobs in different workplaces and different industries. There was no family wage, no provision that working men would earn enough to support their wives and young children; the working class and its employers assumed that there would be more than one wage-earner in each household. Although the nature and amount of each person's contribution to the family income depended upon his or her family position and employment opportunities, wives as well as sons and daughters worked for wages outside the home.

While industrialization did not displace women from the labour force, neither did it transform the familial definition of their work. In 1900, as in 1800, women's labour-power was a resource working-class families relied upon to ensure economic security or simple survival; women worked for pay when their families required it. The change in the authority relations of work, the shift from working with their husbands to working for bosses, did not provide women with any basis for autonomy from familial roles. Family and work emerged from their proto-industrial unity, but as far as women were concerned this separation was more apparent than real. Women's lives at work were controlled by their lives at home, and their position in the factory reinforced their position in the family. Women's domestic roles and their paid employment defined and supported one another.

Tracing the connections between family and work illuminates the contours of the gender system, the socially and culturally constructed set of relations among women and men that underlay both the domestic and the public domains. Biologically-based sex differences cannot explain the distinction between women's and men's activities, the inequality of their social positions, and the asymmetry in their personal relations, that are found in modern society. This case study contributes to the understanding of the history of the modern gender system by tracing the simultaneous and linked development of gender divisions within working-class families and industrial workplaces. Beginning with the transformation in the meaning of women's work that came with the reorganization of production in the early nineteenth century, it examines both working-class attitudes toward women's labour and the emergence of occupational segregation and wage differentials between women and men. It demonstrates how those led to the recomposition of the labour force during the late nineteenth century, when hosiery became a women's industry. This decisive separation between household and workplace for women only confirmed their status as secondary wage-earners in working-class families. An understanding of the development of gender divisions during the process of industrialization in Leicester clarifies the way in which working-class family relations and the social relations of capitalist production shaped one another.

The Transformation of the Labour Process

The process of framework knitting, as it was performed at the turn of the nineteenth century, involved considerable skill. Rather than being knit one stitch at a time upon a continuous needle, as in hand knitting, fabric was knitted a row at a time upon multiple needles. The frame itself held the loops in place, and the mechanism pulled each row of loops over the previous one. But the knitter controlled the process, laying down the thread by hand, stepping upon a treadle to form the loops, and pulling several levers in succession to knit the row, while lifting the entire frame up and down at the same time. The evenness of the fabric depended upon the worker's timing; experienced knitters developed a rhythm which ensured accuracy and uniformity in the operation of their frames. In addition, the worker was responsible for shaping the stocking by adding or binding off stitches at the end of each row. Without the aid of patterns or counting devices, the knitter was expected to fashion a flawless stocking. The best description of the worker's control over the process is that of William Felkin: 'While the hands are thus busy, and the feet moving at the rate of one hundred yards in a minute, the eyes must keep watch over the needles as to their soundness and uniformity, and upon the work, that it be free from blemish and irregularity in the line of loops traced down its length'.[1] Knitters were supplied with thread wound on to bobbins by the children who worked with them; bobbin-winders resembled the simple tools used in household spinning. Seaming was a more complex process. Knitted fabic had to be linked rather than sewn; each loop had to be joined to the parallel loop on the opposite edge if the seam were to be sound and lie flat. Ordinarily a woman seaming could just keep up with a man knitting.

The transition to factory production in the hosiery industry was not complete until the end of the nineteenth century, and even then some work continued to be given out to women who did hand sewing at home. The persistence of the putting-out system was not the result of technological difficulties that retarded mechanization, nor was it the consequence of a limited demand for knitted goods. Hosiers continued to conduct their business on the basis of the putting-out system because it remained a rational and profitable way of organizing the manufacture, at least until the last quarter of the nineteenth century. The market for stockings, gloves, undershirts and drawers, and other knitted articles was extensive, but it was also very unstable; some branches of the trade were seasonal, while others were sensitive to national economic fluctuations. The putting-out system allowed hosiers to pass on many of the capital costs of the industry to the workers. In good times, the framework knitters paid high rents for the machinery they used. At the first sign of declining demand, the hosiers could simply stop giving out work to their frames, and the knitters would be unemployed until trade revived. Depressions cost the hosiers very little; they had no large buildings or expensive machinery to maintain, and they could hold on to their stocks until the market improved. As one contemporary observer put it:

> The effect, it is evident, is that of throwing upon one class engaged in the trade the whole of the burthen under circumstances of depression, which ought at least to be equally borne by all. It is, in fact, a means of forcing the workman to furnish to the frame-owner an indemnity from the consequences of the depression of trade.[2]

The putting-out system meant that the hosiers did not have as much control over the process of production as they would have had under the factory system, but it also gave them a crucial margin of flexibility in an industry characterized by economic uncertainty.

The putting-out system was compatible with the rationalization of production. Technological innovations and changes in the labour process generated entirely new branches of the trade during the second quarter of the nineteenth century. The first major change in the labour process was the introduction of wide frames. These turned out lengths of knitted fabric, rather than shaped or fashioned stockings; some could make several straight-down stockings at a time. Articles made on wide frames had to be cut with scissors and stretched into shape before being sewn together. Because a cut edge on knitted fabric tends to unravel, the products of these frames were regarded as inferior. Workers expressed their hostility to the debased branch of their trade in the Midland Luddite riots, as well as in numerous petitions to parliament for the prohibition of cut-up goods. This agitation was unsuccessful. Hosiers paid wide-frame workers piece-rates which, although lower than those paid on the old narrow frames, yielded higher earnings. Wide frames became more and more common, especially in the town.

At the same time, hosiers began to gather their hand workers together into workshops, small buildings distinct from residences in which a number of knitters worked in close proximity. This made it easier for employers to give out and take in work, and enabled them to exercise greater control over the work process itself. It also facilitated the increasing division of labour which the wide frames made possible. Some wide frames were used to make stocking legs, which were then transferred to narrow machines to have the feet and tops added by other workers. Employers continued to collect rent for the frames and increased their profits by charging workers for standing room, heat, and light. In contrast to developments in other industries, however, the trend toward workshop organization was not accompanied by stricter work discipline. Knitters in workshops did not keep fixed hours, and the irregularity of their work habits was notorious. Well before the application of power to the work process, then, knitters began to perform their labour outside the household. Both the proportion of knitters working in shops and the average size of workshops themselves increased steadily during the middle of the century.

This transformation of the production process affected women and men very differently. While knitting moved into workshops, seaming remained a domestic occupation. The amount of sewing actually increased, for the new wide frames were more productive than the old narrow ones and cut-up garments had to be stitched together by hand. Technological development in the men's branch of the trade, then, increased the amount of hand work available for women.[3] Household and workplace remained synonymous for women, while they diverged for men. The division of labour within capitalist production also meant that family members worked as individuals rather than as members of a household work unit. Women no longer seamed the stockings that their husbands knitted. Men and women were paid separately for the labour they performed, and often they were employed on different types of products and even by different hosiers. The hosiery industry in the town thus became more sharply divided along gender lines; men knitted in centralized workshops, while women seamed stockings and stitched garments at home.

This division of labour was based upon the customary practices of working-class families, but its incorporation into the social division of labour changed its meaning. As long as tasks were allocated within the household, gender divisions remained flexible; jobs had to be distributed among the available workers so as to produce the maximum quantity of knitted goods. Depending upon the composition of the household, women and/or older girls might work a knitting frame, while younger boys might seam and old people wind bobbins. This flexibility was lost when the scale and location of work changed in the nineteenth century. Once jobs were assigned by employers the gender division of labour became more rigid. In Leicester, women gradually moved out of knitting and became almost entirely concentrated in seaming by mid-century.

This did not occur through a simple process of exclusion; employers did not actually refuse to give out knitting to female workers. It resulted, rather, from the interaction between the customary division of labour within working-class families and the transformation of the labour process. As new knitting machines were introduced into centralized workshops, women did not leave their households to find employment as knitters in the expanding branches of the trade. Contemporary evidence suggests two important reasons why. First, the definition of knitting as men's work was reinforced by the heaviness of the physical labour involved in the operation of wide frames. While this definition was primarily an ideological one, it had just enough basis in immediate experience to give it added power at this juncture; strength was at least as important as sex, for neither young nor ageing men were employed in wide frames. Secondly, the location of the work outside the household would have interfered with women's continued performance of their domestic labour.

When women knitted at home, their work was often interrupted. They cared for infants, supervised the work of children, prepared meals, and did the weekly washing while their husbands observed St Monday by rambling in the fields or drinking in neighbouring beer houses. Difficult as it must have been for women to allocate their time, to respond both to their families' immediate demands for attention and to their families' equally pressing need for the small sums they could contribute to their families' income, women managed to combine both kinds of labour as long as they could work at home. Those women who continued to work in their households as knitters in the older branches of the trade eventually earned less than those employed as seamers and stitchers in the expanding branches, so many shifted to the better-paid occupation. The movement of women out of knitting into seaming was essentially complete in Leicester by 1851.

These changes occurred primarily in the town. The manufacture of wrought hose, which was shaped to fit the leg, continued in the countryside along traditional lines. Women in rural Leicestershire villages worked as members of family groups, and knitted, seamed, or wound as the composition of their households dictated. At the same time, this branch of the manufacture was affected indirectly by developments taking place in Leicester. Urban and rural framework knitters generally made different products; cheap unfashioned stockings for the mass market were produced in the city, while more expensive full-fashioned stockings were made in the countryside. There was some competition between the two branches, as hosiers cut wages in the wrought-hose trade in order to bring the price of their product closer to that of straight-down hose. But the complementary relationship between the two branches was more important in the long run in reducing the earnings of rural hosiery workers. The cheaper hose made in the town dominated the most stable portion of the market, while the higher quality hose made in the countryside met with uncertain and fluctuating demand. This entire branch of the industry became more marginal. By the middle of the century, the narrow frames in rural villages were fully employed only at moments of peak demand, and were underemployed or unemployed for protracted periods.

The increasing economic instability of the wrought-hose trade was accompanied by the employment of an increasing proportion of women in narrow knitting frames. This trend seems to have been primarily the result of the response of rural families to declining wages and intermittent employment; without access to other opportunities, they brought additional family members into the trade when work was available in order to maintain family income. The system of frame-renting meant that manufacturers did not suffer when frames were unemployed and actually profited from their partial employment. This facilitated the proliferation of knitting machinery in rural areas. By mid-century, 40 per cent of the knitting frames in many hosiery villages were in the hands of women.

The transformation of the labour process that took place during the early nineteenth century changed the meaning of women's work within the putting-out system. While the actual jobs women did in the country and the town diverged, their place within capitalist production was similar: they were increasingly employed in the lowest-paid and most casualized forms of labour. In Leicester, women were relegated to seaming, which was auxiliary to the process of knitting in the expanding branches; in Leicestershire, they moved into knitting just as this entire branch of the trade was becoming more marginal. Women's place on the periphery resulted from the interaction between the division of labour within the family and changes in capitalist production. In Leicester, where household and workplace began to diverge with the transformation of the labour process, the primacy of women's domestic responsibilities meant that they concentrated on paid jobs which were different from and subordinate to those held by men. In Leicestershire, where families remained the primary work unit but came under intense economic pressure, the family's need for cash income meant that women increased their commitment to paid labour, but did so under circumstances which ensured that their contributions would remain marginal. In both cases, although women continued to combine paid with unpaid labour in the household, the shifting economic context of their work changed its significance.

Gender Relations in Working-Class Families

Some insight into what these developments meant for working-class families may be gleaned from the testimony framework knitters gave before the various parliamentary committees and commissions which investigated their grievances during the nineteenth century. This evidence must be used very carefully, for the middle-class investigators made assumptions which reflected their own views of family life, and the knitters' representatives were almost entirely men, but it does provide a record of working men's attitudes toward gender issues. The framework knitters, unlike their bourgeois interlocutors, assumed that their wives would contribute to the family income in whatever way it was possible for them to do so; what was open to question was only the optimal form their contribution might take. This exchange between Richard Muggeridge, the commissioner who investigated the condition of the framework knitters in 1845 and who came to share their ideas about women's work, and Lord Manners, the Leicestershire MP who served on the 1854 committee, illustrates the disparity between the two points of view.

> Lord Manners: Speaking generally from your experience, and with the knowledge you possess of the labouring classes, are you of the opinion that it is a beneficial thing, with a view to the management of a family and the domestic economy of a cottage, that the female head of that family should be employed . . . in manufactures?
>
> Richard Muggeridge: No, certainly not. I do think that the mother of a family ought always to find enough to do without being employed at frame work. There are many things which she might do to assist the family, such, for instance, as seaming, which is quite a woman's work.[4]

Lord Manners deplored married women working for wages outside the home. Muggeridge's answer, by contrast, assumes that married women must work for wages, and maintains that while framework knitting is inappropriate for them, seaming is 'quite a woman's work'. Acceptance of the fact that married women must engage in paid labour is here joined to the assertion of a strict segregation of labour along gender lines. The working-class version of this position is perhaps William Wingell's forthright statement, 'I should not be able to live at all if it was not for the little that my wife gets'.[5]

Although working-class men shared neither the bourgeois view of the family nor the tenets of bourgeois political economy, they nonetheless almost unanimously concluded that the earnings of married women were secondary to those of their husbands, and that women should be employed on tasks which were clearly subordinate and/or auxiliary to those performed by men. The parliamentary investigators feared that if women worked at the same jobs as their husbands they would undercut the men's earnings. Working-class men did not worry about their wives competing with them for employment nor presenting a threat to their wage-rates. They regarded women and men as members of families who shared their earnings with one another, and approached the question of women's work and wages with the objective of maximizing the family's income. Yet they came to the same conclusion as the parliamentary committee about the appropriate employment for women and the subordinate place of women's work in the family economy.

The logic of traditional working-class family relationships, combined with the changing conditions of labour in the hosiery industry, led men to adopt that perspective. How did it happen that women's employment, although still recognized as essential to family survival, came to be regarded as secondary to that of men? The shift from a flexible division of labour within working-class families to a rigid gender division of labour had already taken place in Leicester by the middle of the nineteenth century. The hosiery industry in the town was divided into two sectors which corresponded to the sex of the workers; men worked at knitting in workshops, while women seamed stockings by hand at home. The division of labour was becoming more uniform and visible, and the work that women did was increasingly determined by their sex. In the parliamentary hearings of 1854, the framework knitters' spokesmen argued that this same shift ought to take place in the countryside as well. They contended, in fact, that the dissolution of the family work unit would benefit the family as a whole.

Thomas Winters, a Chartist and trade unionist who had worked all his life as a framework knitter – first in the wrought-hose branch in a Leicestershire village and then in the glove branch in Leicester – engaged in perhaps the most sustained dialogue on the question of family work patterns with the parliamentary committee of any of the knitters who were interviewed. The committee was considering the legal prohibition of the frame-renting system, which the knitters had requested. One of the leading manufacturers told the committee that if rents were abolished fully one-third of the wrought-hose hands in the countryside would be put out of work. Hosiers would furnish employment only to those workers from whose labour they could make a profit, and knitters who produced little – who were, indeed, employed only for the sake of the rent they paid – would have to leave the trade. Winters, who had been fighting for the abolition of rents for a decade, conceded that this might be the case, but contended that it would not be harmful to the hosiery workers. 'We have a right to suppose,' he argued, 'that the persons thrown out of employment would not be the heads of families.' They would, instead, be women and children, who did less work each week than the male heads of household. If the work now performed by the family as a whole were concentrated in the hands of the adult man, Winters continued, 'they would receive the same amount of money in the family, and save the expense of rent and charges, which would add more money to the general income of the family, and therefore they would be benefitted by being out of work rather than by being in work.'[6] When a concerned Member of Parliament asked Winters, 'And how would you dispose of those who were not employed?' he replied:

> They would be placed in a much superior position to what they are in now, because they are all labouring together for a certain sum; and that certain sum would then come into the hands of one person, and supposing that to be the case, there would be a benefit . . . in the shape of rents and charges, which would go some way towards supporting the family; but in addition to that, it would give those other parties an opportunity of getting employment elsewhere, and so of increasing the comforts of the family from that source also.[7]

Given the terms of the argument, the logic is impeccable. The concentration of the family's labour in the hands of one member would free the other members to find alternative employment. The family would no longer work together, but its total income would be increased.

This analysis presumes that it would be women (and children) who would no longer be employed as knitters, and that alternative employment would be available to them which was appropriate to their gender (and age). To ascertain why Winters was so confident of these things is a difficult matter. But the evidence that exists about the division of labour within working-class families suggests that women's labour was regarded as less valuable than that of men. Most women who knitted at home produced less each week than their male counterparts. The framework knitters' testimony before parliamentary committees from 1812 on is filled with complaints that their wives' domestic responsibilities constantly interfered with their paid labour, limiting the hours they spent at the frame, the quantity of work they turned out, and the amount of money they earned. The manufacturers also explained many women's relatively low earnings in terms of their having to attend to household affairs. Still, while the hosiers were apt to regard women workers as less skilled than men because they produced less in any given week, the framework knitters recognized that the work women did was equal in quality, if not in quantity, to that performed by men. As long as stockings were completed within the household, hosiery workers were paid as members of families rather than as individuals, and there were no separate rates for different tasks or for men, women, and children.

At the same time, there is some evidence that male heads of household deliberately gave their wives jobs which carried lower piece-rates and reserved the better-paying jobs for themselves. Walter Upton, a framework knitter in the children's sock branch, explained to the commissioner who investigated the trade in 1844 that 'our branch varies from the highest prices of fancy work down to the smallest. There is not a branch of labour that is so unequally paid for . . . It so happens that women and children fall into the bad jobs; men will not work at them if they can get anything that will beat them.' In response to the commissioner's inquiry as to whether women were generally employed in the lowest-paid types of work and, if so, how this happened to be the case, Upton replied:

> This is the way I take it, and I give it from my own opinion of things – the course I should take myself – that is, I should apply of course for the best work for my own hands, because I am the most expert in the business, and if my wife worked, she could not work more than half her time, and the children the same. They are not so much consequence as we, therefore it is in that way that we look out for the best jobs for ourselves, and make the best we can of the thing.[8]

In the sock branch, women generally made the straight-ribbed tops, while men added the fashioned heels and feet. In other branches, women were put to work footing the straight-down hose that their husbands had legged, or making low-priced goods on coarser frames while their husbands worked on finer ones. When different types of work were available, it made sense to the male head of household to allocate the lower-paying jobs to women.

At first, this practice probably carried no imputation that women's work was less valuable than that of men. But in a piece-work industry, skill and labour-time are easily conflated, and individual output and earnings are readily measured. When the amount that each family member earned was computed individually and their relative contributions to the family income could be assessed in cash terms, the difference in the earnings of husbands and wives became clearly visible. The services that married women performed within the household were crucial to the family's well-being, but they carried no cash value. Male knitters recognized that such domestic responsibilities limited women's earnings, but that did not prevent them from regarding women's labour as less valuable than their own. The problem of most working-class families in nineteenth-century Leicester was to stretch the week's income to cover the past week's expenses. The provision of services took second place to wage-earning, and could substitute for cash only to a limited extent. The fact that women performed their paid labour at home and also kept the family budget may have made their contribution to the family income even less visible to their husbands. Men regarded their wives' work as supplementary to their own. It was only fitting, in their eyes, for women to be employed in an auxiliary and/or subordinate capacity within industry.

The relationship between the traditional working-class family economy and the division of labour in capitalist industry is complex. The gender division of labour within working-class families under the putting-out system was clearly asymmetrical. Women held primary responsibility for childcare and household chores, so they did not participate in paid labour on equal terms with their husbands. Their power within the family was also clearly less than that of men. Although women managed the family's transactions with landlords and shopkeepers, they were not responsible for the family's contracts with employers, and they controlled the labour power of only the smallest children. At the same time, as long as the family work unit remained intact, these asymmetries did not result in any real inequality in men's and women's relationships to capitalist production. Both were wage-earners, and both worked for the good of the family as a whole.

The incorporation of the gender division rooted in the family into the social division of labour confirmed, reinforced, and extended the subordinate position of women both within the family and in the labour process. By distinguishing between paid and unpaid labour and subordinating unpaid to paid labour within civil society, while preserving the primacy of unpaid domestic labour for women, the development of industrial capitalism placed women in an impossible position. Their participation in activities that were seen as valuable was constrained by activities that were absolutely necessary yet seen as without value. The result was not the exclusion of women from income-producing labour, but rather their participation in that labour on unequal terms. To apply to this case the argument outlined by Sally Alexander in 'Women's Work in Nineteenth-Century London', the traditional working-class family economy provided the conditions for the hierarchy of labour-powers along the lines of sex, 'but it was the transference of the sexual division of labour from the family into social production which ensured that it was women who moved into the subordinate and auxiliary positions within it'.[9]

Patterns of Women's Employment

A very different kind of evidence, drawn from the manuscript enumeration books of the 1851 and 1871 censuses, places hosiery workers in the context of the town's population and illuminates the pattern of female employment. In Leicester, 40 per cent of all women were recorded as engaged in paid labour in both 1851 and 1871. While 43 per cent of all single women and 58 per cent of all widows were employed in both years, so were a significant proportion of all married women – 32 per cent in 1851 and 28 per cent in 1871. These rates of female labour force participation are high, compared with those of other English towns; only the cotton textile manufacturing districts of Lancashire equalled them. The hosiery and boot and shoe industries were the primary employers of female labour. In 1851, fully 40 per cent of all women workers, and 48 per cent of married women workers, were employed in hosiery. In 1871, 22 per cent of all working women, and 28 per cent of married working women, were employed in hosiery, while another 11 per cent of all working women, and 16 per cent of married working women, were employed in boot and shoe making. A significant number of women tended machinery in the factories that prepared yarn for knitting. The town's staple industries employed 54 per cent of the female labour force in both 1851 and 1871. The traditional occupation of dressmaking employed just 10 per cent of the female labour force, and only 25 per cent were domestic servants. Smaller numbers kept retail shops, taught in schools, and assisted their husbands in family businesses. What made Leicester distinctive, then, were its female-employing staple industries.[10]

Women's employment was remarkably continuous over the life course. Wives continued to work for pay during the early years of marriage. In 1851, nearly 40 per cent of wives in their twenties and 30 per cent of those in their thirties and forties were in the labour force; in 1871, 30 per cent of wives in their twenties and 20 per cent of those in their thirties were employed. Working wives retired only at advanced ages; in 1851 and 1871, more than 20 per cent of wives in their sixties remained in the labour force. The relationship between women's employment and the family cycle was quite different from twentieth-century patterns. Instead of leaving the labour force during their childbearing years and returning when their children were older, as many women do now, wives in nineteenth-century Leicester remained in the labour force when their children were young and stopped working for pay when their children were old enough to replace them as contributors to the family income. Thus in 1851, 30 per cent of wives with children under the age of seven were employed, but only 20 per cent of those whose children were all over seven were. The pattern was even clearer in 1871. Over 20 per cent of those with children under seven were employed, but only 10 per cent of those with older children worked for pay. When children left home, however, some wives had to return to the labour force.[11]

The domestic location and casual nature of women's work in Leicester's staple industries made this pattern possible. In 1851, over 40 per cent of all employed women worked at home; in 1871, this proportion was still over 35 per cent. Married women workers were especially likely to work in their own households; 60 per cent of employed wives worked at home in 1851, and 50 per cent did so in 1871. This pattern both reflected and reinforced the close connections between women's employment and their familial roles. Working-class wives engaged in paid labour quite literally to feed and clothe their children. They worked for wages most often during the years in which their dependent children were most numerous, and in which their burden of unpaid domestic labour would also have been heaviest. These women took in seaming when their children needed commodities such as shoes, and sat up late at night until they finished the number of stockings that would provide enough cash to cover the anticipated expense. If a child's dress could be made over from an old garment of her own, a woman might spend her time sewing for her family rather than seaming for wages in order to purchase new fabric. The form that women's labour took – of waged work, or of unpaid domestic work – mattered little, for both were means to provide for the immediate needs of their families. Women's waged labour was assimilated to their role as domestic managers. Wives were responsible for the family budget, and they took in paid work whenever the budget would not balance unless they made a cash contribution.

This pattern of married women's employment was not universal in Leicester, even among the working class. It was, rather, distinctive of the hosiery and footwear industries' labour force. Women whose husbands worked in the staple industries were twice as likely to be employed as women whose husbands worked in the artisan trades, commerce, or general labour. In 1851, 40 per cent of the wives of hosiery workers were employed, compared to 20 per cent of the others. In 1871, 30 per cent of the wives of hosiery and footwear workers were in the labour force, while the labour force participation rates for other married women ranged from 15 per cent to 20 per cent. The continuity in women's employment over the life course was also more marked in the families of hosiery and footwear workers. In 1851, the proportion of wives of hosiery workers who were employed never fell below 30 per cent, even when older children were working, and was as high as 54 per cent when there were numerous young children to support. Women whose husbands were in the artisan trades, on the other hand, often withdrew from the labour force when they bore children, and only 20 per cent were employed thereafter. Similarly, no more than 20 per cent of the wives of men in commerce were employed, and just 13 per cent of them worked for pay when they had young children. In 1871 the levels of married women's labour force participation were slightly lower, but the patterns were similar. Hosiery and footwear workers' wives did not stop working for pay when they had young children; at least 20 per cent of those with children under seven remained employed. Less than 20 per cent continued to work for pay after their children were older, however. The withdrawal of artisans' wives from paid labour with the onset of childbearing was as marked in 1871 as in 1851. The wives of men in commerce, however, had reduced their level of labour force participation at all stages of the family cycle. This was a middle-class trend. During the third quarter of the nineteenth century, the families of capitalists and businessmen moved from their homes in the town centre, which had often been next to their offices and shops, into new residential districts on the edges of the town. Fewer middle-class women were actively involved in their families' enterprises or continued to practice their own professions after marriage.

By 1871, therefore, there were three distinct patterns of married women's employment in the town. Middle-class women rarely worked for pay after they married. The wives of skilled artisans and tradesmen, such as carpenters, iron-workers, and tailors, tended to leave the labour force when they had children. This was not the case among the families of framework knitters and others employed in the town's staple manufactures; these women remained at work when their children were young, and withdrew from the labour force only when their children entered it. The difference in the experiences of middle-class and working-class women, and in the expectations of middle-class and working-class men, was responsible for some of the miscommunication that occurred in the parliamentary hearings. The difference within the working class in the pattern of married women's employment was perhaps responsible for a certain ambiguity in the testimony of framework knitters on the question of whether or not married women should be employed. When they were trying to enlist the sympathy of the middle-class members of the investigating committees, framework knitters complained that their wages were so low that they could not support their wives and children, and their wives were forced to work for pay as well as to care for their households. On the level of abstraction, they seemed to believe that working-men should earn a family wage. When they spoke concretely about their individual family situations and common industrial conditions, however, they assumed that their wives would be employed; the ideal did not apply to them. This ambivalence in their testimony may reflect the perception that framework knitters had of their position within the working class. Although their wives generally engaged in paid labour, they knew that there was another group of workers within their class whose wives did not have to work for wages once they had become mothers.

The prevalence of married women's employment among the families of Leicester's hosiery and footwear workers meant that women's paid labour was integrated with and controlled by women's familial roles as mothers and domestic managers. The fact that married women worked for wages, and increasingly made independent labour bargains rather than working with their husbands, did not give them autonomy from or power within their families. Instead, it permitted the maintenance of traditional family relationships in a new work situation, and perpetuated a pattern which set women to work when their families needed the money their employment would bring. The availability of wage labour that could be performed at home reinforced the familial definition of all women's work, and assimilated their paid labour to their unpaid domestic chores. Their only compensation was that their contribution to the welfare of their families was recognized and accorded a secure, if secondary, place.

Labour Substitution in the Factories

While the definition of women's work within the domestic economy remained essentially unchanged in Leicester throughout the middle of the nineteenth century and beyond, the definition of women's work in the political economy did change as the labour process was gradually reorganized. By mid-century, women seamed because they were women, not because they belonged to a family with a particular mix of labour resources. They may have engaged in paid work because of their individual situation, but the job they did was increasingly determined by their sex.

The gender division of labour that existed in the hosiery industry at the middle of the century was extended into the manufacture of boots and shoes when that industry expanded in Leicester after 1850. The wholesale manufacture of footwear, like that of hosiery, was in the middle of a gradual and uneven process of mechanization and centralization; hand and machine labour, in warehouses, workshops, and households, coexisted under the putting-out system. The division of labour established in the boot and shoe trade in Leicester was modelled directly upon that in hosiery. While women stitched uppers in their homes, men performed the other stages of the process in workshops and warehouses. Stitching was a female and domestic employment. The footwear industry could have been organized differently, for power sewing machines for stitching leather were available long before either men's or women's work was drawn into factories. Instead of organizing the labour process on the most economically rational and technically efficient basis, however, capitalists followed the customary division of labour in the town and rented out hand-operated machines for women workers to use at home. The 1871 census exhibits a certain indeterminancy in its description of women's occupations; many women were simply recorded as 'stitcher' with no indication of whether they stitched knitted garments or leather footwear. Within families, too, there was little correlation between the industries in which husbands and wives worked; in 1871, it was only slightly more likely that the wife of a framework knitter would sew stockings than that she would stitch shoes. The social category of women's work seemed to predominate over a more specific industrial work definition in Leicester.

The development of a social category of women's work was accompanied by the emergence of a socially-defined women's wage. Under the putting-out system, workers were paid at a set rate for each unit they completed, regardless of their sex. This custom continued when the employer rather than the male head of the household began allocating tasks to individual men and women. As the gender division of labour became more rigid, however, customary wage-rates for women and men were gradually established. Women seamers earned about half of what male knitters did when both had full employment. Once the gender division of labour had become a division between two whole sectors of the manufacture, the segregation of jobs carried with it a differential in the wages paid to women and men.

It was then only a matter of time before employers tried to substitute lower-paid female labour for higher-paid male labour in other stages of the work process. Between 1850 and 1870, men maintained a monopoly on knitting, even when new, steam-powered automatic knitting machines were set up in factories. While a few young women were hired to tend circular frames, the larger automatic fashioning frames remained a male preserve. The few attempts to introduce women as knitters on these machines were met by staunch and effective resistance. After 1870, however, the invention of a powered linking machine which could sew a permanent seam in knitted fabric meant that women's customary jobs of seaming and finishing were drawn into the factories. Women followed their work out of the home, but were employed on the same terms that had developed when they performed these tasks by hand. As factory workers, even though mechanization had multiplied their productivity, they were paid wage-rates that would yield the earnings that had become customary for women in the industry and the town.

Once traditional women's jobs involved running power machinery in centralized factories, why should women not be employed on knitting machines as well? The definition of women's work that had developed during the previous half-century was an essential intermediate step, but once it had provided the basis for a customary women's wage and for the acceptance of women's factory employment, the content of that work was susceptible to change. The process of labour substitution was carried out during the last quarter of the nineteenth century. Conflict between the male knitters who had defended their jobs from female competition and the women who were being introduced into knitting was avoided by employing women upon new types of automatic knitting machinery; rather than taking over traditional men's jobs, they were employed in an entirely different labour process. Male knitters resisted the de-skilling of their jobs and the erosion of their wage-rates, but they could not prevent the expansion of a female labour force in new branches of the manufacture. Women knitters were paid at the same rates as women seamers and finishers, and earned about half of what male knitters did.

A second factor which made for a relatively smooth transition to a predominantly female labour force in the hosiery industry was the development of the boot and shoe industry in the town. By the time women were finding work in hosiery factories as seamers and knitters, the footwear manufacture had expanded to the point that it was able to provide employment for the young men who would formerly have expected to find jobs in knitting. The boot and shoe industry employed as many workers as hosiery in Leicester by 1871, and continued to increase its relative size through to the end of the century. The gender division of labour within that industry (itself modelled upon that in hosiery at mid-century) meant that hosiery could become a women's industry without the displacement of male workers. Men and women continued to find work at the customary wages, although at different jobs and in different industries than before. Nor was the domestic economy of working-class families significantly affected. Men who would once have worked knitting frames while their wives seamed stockings now made shoes while their wives tended knitting machines. During the course of a century, both the nature and the location of men's and women's jobs had changed, but each continued to contribute to the family income at the necessary times and in the customary proportions.

Conclusion

The gender division of labour that was customary within the working family in the hosiery industry at the beginning of the nineteenth century was embodied in the social division of labour as the work process was reorganized over the next 50 years. The gradual and uneven development of mechanization and centralization in hosiery, and later in boot and shoe, manufacturing meant that while the context of women's work shifted, its content did not, at least until 1870. The persistence of the familial definition of women's work neutralized the potentially liberating effects of the shift from working as part of the family unit to working for an employer. The familial purpose and timing of women's work remained constant, as did its location within the household. When women's work finally moved into the factory, even that change did not transform the domestic economy of working-class families.

On the other hand, the way in which the gender division of labour was amplified, sharpened, and generalized during the nineteenth century by becoming a socio-economic rather than domestic arrangement did have powerfully transformative effects upon women's labour. First it created a new social category of gender-defined work. This provided the basis for the emergence of a customary women's wage, which embodied the inferior value of women's labour power relative to that of men. Finally, once the reorganization of the production process had brought women into the factories, it led to the radical transformation of the work itself, as women became power machine knitters. But the industry remained segregated along gender lines, and women continued to earn wages that were lower than those of men.

The history of Leicester's working-class families and staple industries during the nineteenth century reveals the development of the modern gender system. While family and work diverged over the course of the century, they defined and reinforced one another. Women were secondary wage-earners within their families. Both the nature of their labour and the timing of their employment were determined by their families' needs; paid labour was subsumed by their domestic role, rather than being independent of it. Both at home and in the workplace, women were subordinated to men. Their employment in gender-segregated industries and gender-typed jobs divided them from working men. It allowed the development of wage differentials, and guaranteed that those would be maintained even when the nature and location of women's work was changing. The relatively low wages women earned, in turn, reinforced their status as supplementary rather than primary breadwinners, for their incomes were insufficient to ensure their own security, let alone to enable them to support dependents. In spite of their high rates of labour force participation and their essential contribution to their families' income, women in Leicester were enmeshed in a set of gender relations that relegated them to secondary status both at home and at work. The interaction of family relations and capitalism over the course of industrialization led to the development of a gender system that simultaneously relied upon and restricted women's labour.

Bibliographical Note

The major sources for this study include the reports of the various Royal Commissions and Parliamentary Committees that investigated the hosiery industry at frequent intervals throughout the nineteenth century; the decadal censuses of Leicester, especially the manuscript enumerators' books for 1851 and 1871; the pamphlet collections of the Leicester City Reference

Library and the Leicester County Record Office; the printed histories of the hosiery industry and of the city and county of Leicester.

The reports included in the British Parliamentary Papers that are most useful for examining the gender division of labour are: Report from the Select Committee appointed to take into Consideration the several Petitions presented to this House . . . by the persons employed in the Framework-Knitting Trade. (PP 1812, Cmd. 247, II. 203); Report from the Select Committee appointed to inquire into the grievances complained of in the Petition of the Hosiers and Framework-Knitters in the Woollen Manufactory of the town and county of Leicester, which was presented to the House . . . (PP 1819, Cmd. 193, V. 401); Report from the Commissioner Appointed to Inquire into the Condition of the Frame Work Knitters (PP 1845, Cmd. 618, XV. 151); Report from the Select Committee on the Stoppage of Wages in the Hosiery Manufacture (PP 1854–5, Cmd. 421, XIV. 1); First Report of the Royal Commissioners on the Employment of Children and Young persons in Trades and Manufactures not already regulated by Law (PP 1863, Cmd. 3170, XVIII. 1); Report of the Commissioners Appointed to inquire into the working of the Factory and Workshop Acts (PP 1876, Cmd. 1442, XXIX–XXX).

Nineteenth-century accounts of the hosiery industry and the working people of Leicester include, Thomas Cooper, *The Life of Thomas Cooper, by Himself* (Hodder and Stoughton, 1872; reprinted Leicester University Press, Leicester, 1971).

The standard histories of the hosiery and knitwear industries are: William Felkin, *History of the Machine Wrought Hosiery and Lace Manufactures* (1867; reprinted David and Charles, Newton Abbot, 1967); F.A. Wells, *The British Hosiery and Knitwear Industry: Its History and Organisation* (1935; reprinted David and Charles, Newton Abbot, 1972). J. D. Chapman, 'The Genesis of the British Hosiery Industry, 1600–1750, *Textile History*, (December 1972), pp.7–50; J. D. Chapman, 'Enterprise and Innovation in the British Hosiery Industry, 1750–1850', *Textile History* (October 1974), pp.14–37; Peter Head, 'Industrial Organization in Leicester, 1844–1914', unpublished PhD thesis (University of Leicester), 1960; Peter Head, 'Putting Out in the Leicester Hosiery Industry in the Middle of the Nineteenth Century', *Transactions of the Leicestershire Archaeological and Historical Society*, (1961–2), pp.44–59; J. Walton, 'A History of Trade Unionism in Leicester to the end of the Nineteenth Century', unpublished MA thesis (University of Sheffield), 1952.

Histories of the town and county of Leicester include: A. Temple Patterson, *Radical Leicester: A History of Leicester, 1780–1850* (Leicester University Press, Leicester, 1975); Jack Simmons, *Leicester Past and Present*, vol. i. *Ancient Borough;* vol. ii. *Modern City* (Eyre Methuen, 1974); Norman Pye (ed.), *Leicester and Its Region* (Leicester University Press, Leicester, 1972); W.G. Hoskins, *The Midland Peasant: The Economic and Social History of a Leicestershire Village* (Macmillan, 1965); David Levine, *Family Formation in an Age of Nascent Capitalism* (Academic Press/Harcourt Brace Jovanovich, New York, 1977); Dinah Freer, 'Business Families in Victorian Leicester: A Study in Historical Sociology', unpublished MPhil thesis (University of Leicester), 1975.

Notes

The research for this essay was done on a Fulbright-Hays Fellowship at the Victorian Studies Centre of the University of Leicester in 1976–7, under the supervision of J. A. Banks and the late H. J. Dyos. The argument developed here was worked out with the help of long discussions with Leonore Davidoff, Anna Davin, Catherine Hall, Judy Lown, Barbara Taylor, and other members of the London Feminist History Group in England, and with Susan Amussen, Joan Scott, and Judith Walkowitz in the United States.

1 Felkin, *History of the Machine-Wrought Hosiery*, p. 48.
2 Sir Henry Halford, MP, 'A Plea for the Framework Knitters' (Leicester County Record Office, 1847) p. 19.
3 Raphael Samuel, 'Workshop of the World: Steam Power and Hand Technology in Mid-Victorian Britain', *History Workshop Journal*, 3 (Spring 1977) pp. 6–72, discusses the uneven development that led to a reliance upon manual as well as machine labour in a number of industries. See the exchange of letters between the author and Raphael Samuel in *History Workshop Journal*, 4 (Autumn 1977) pp. 242–3.
4 *Report from the Select Committee on the Stoppage of Wages in the Hosiery Manufacture*, PP 1854–5, Cmd. 421, XIV. 1, Minutes of Evidence, 2724.
5 *Report of the Commissioner Appointed to Inquire into the Condition of Frame Work Knitters*, PP 1845, Cmd. 618, XV. 151, Minutes of Evidence, 1173.
6 *Report from the Select Committee on the Stoppage of Wages in the Hosiery Manufacture*, PP 1854–5, Cmd. 421, XIV. 1, Minutes of Evidence, 5088.
7 Ibid. 4907–17.
8 *Report of the Commissioner Appointed to Inquire into the Condition of the Frame Work Knitters*, PP 1845, Cmd 518. XV. 515, Minutes of Evidence, 194.
9 Sally Alexander, *Women's Work in Nineteenth-Century London* (Journeyman Press edn, 1983). I have transposed the terms of Alexander's argument here. She states that 'Manufacture provided the economic basis for the hierarchy of labour powers', but it was the gender division of labour within the family which ensured that it was women who were given subordinate positions within the capitalist division of labour. I agree with Alexander, but wish to emphasize the importance of the transfer of production from the household work unit to the non-domestic workplace here. Both Alexander and I describe the interaction betwen the gender division of labour in working-class families and in capitalist industry.
10 Data reported in this essay have been computed from massive samples of the censuses of Leicester for 1851 and 1871.

11 For a discussion of the relationship between women's employment and family patterns in the nineteenth century, see Louise A. Tilly and Joan W. Scott, *Women, Work, and Family* (Holt, Rinehart and Winston, 1978) pp. 123–136. Tilly and Scott conclude that 'married women tended to be found in largest numbers in the least industrialized sectors of the labour force, in those areas where the least separation existed between home and workplace . . . ' (p. 124) 'and that wives whose children were very young were often employed, while children replaced wives as earners in situtations where only non-domestic employment was available to women'. (p. 134).

Woman working at a sewing press, 1843

2

Opportunities Lost and Gained: Mechanization and Women's Work in the London Bookbinding and Printing Trades

Felicity Hunt

The advent of the 'machine age' brought the always uneasy relationship between man and machine into sharp focus. Yet the cruder responses of Luddism were by no means the only reaction which the new engines of the industrial revolution evoked. Much more subtle were the attempts which were made to resist and then control the introduction of machinery, especially when new technology was replacing long established craft skills. The resistance to mechanization was never simply the reaction to loss of work, it was also a sometimes desperate response to the prospect of losing control, and thus power, at work. Mechanization had a different impact on different parts of the workforce. For skilled craftsmen it could herald loss of jobs, diminished status and less pay. This in turn created work for a semi-skilled and unskilled workforce of women, men and children so that in some respects mechanization increased women's chances of work. Machines worked by semi-skilled and unskilled labour not only undercut wages but also men's status and value in the workplace and their patriarchal role in the home.[1]

For these reasons we see in certain trades a fierce resistance to mechanization, of which none was perhaps more trenchant nor more successful than in the London printing trade. Both the pressmen and the compositors consistently opposed the introduction of machinery which threatened their work processes and undercut their skilled status. In the closely allied trade of bookbinding similar tussles took place. Originally the trades were restricted to London. The customs and traditions legitimized by the Stationers' Company encouraged the workforce to unionize; the first craft societies appeared at the end of the eighteenth century. London therefore provides an appropriate case study because it was through the trade unions that men sought to restrict the de-skilling impact of machines and to retain their traditional status and wages. The London compositors managed to keep not only their skill and status, but high rates of pay, even after the manual process of composing had been almost entirely mechanized.

But what of the skilled craftswoman? Did mechanization bring similar problems of dilution and de-skilling to her, and how did she react to these? In the two trades considered here, women played the parts of both skilled workers and semi-skilled machine operators. In bookbinding skilled craftswomen faced loss of skill and status as mechanization spread. In printing women joined a growing pool of semi-skilled workers in a craft process which was gradually mechanized but which lost few of its worker-controlled protective and restrictive trade practices.

Before considering the experiences of women workers we should first examine the state of the trades in the early nineteenth century. By 1800 the trades engaged in the production of books and newspapers had divided out into the printing trade on the one hand and the bookbinding trade (often organized by the publisher) on the other. In the printing trade the book and newspaper sectors had also separated, although the skills required in the actual printing process were identical in each.

Within the printing trade the compositors, who set up the type, proof-read and ultimately distributed (or dismantled) it were highly skilled, earning wages of 30/– a week, even in the 1800s.[2] The compositors were 'labour aristocrats'. Their very ability not only to read and write, but to read the type upside down and backwards, set them apart from the ordinary run of working men and their technical skills were jealously guarded. The printing trade had been strictly regulated since the sixteenth century by the powerful Stationers' Company (incorporated in 1555) which limited the number of presses and master printers in London. In 1678 the Company had ruled that 'no Master Printer or any other Printer or Workman . . . shall teach, direct or instruct any person or persons whatsoever, than his or their own Legitimate Son or Sons in this Art or Mystery of Printing'.[3] By 1785 the journeymen printers were sufficiently organized to be able to make a trade agreement with the master printers and, in spite of the Combination Acts of 1799 and 1800, by 1801 they had formed the 'Union Society'. It lasted only ten years but by 1832 two rival societies, the London Trade Society of Compositors (founded in 1816) and the London General Trade Society of Compositors (1826), had formed a combined Union Committee which became in 1834 the powerful London Union of Compositors.

This early unionization was important because the London Union wielded considerable control over the workmen in the metropolitan trade and it was a control which included the historical exclusion of women from printing. While there are numerous examples of women who ran printing businesses and employed apprentices and journeymen in the seventeenth and eighteenth centuries, they did so because they were the widows or daughters of printers.[4] The strict regulation of the size of the trade made it seem vital to limit the numbers of entrants. The exclusion of one sex was an obvious strategy in this control while, as Cynthia Cockburn points out, the custom of the workshop and apprenticeship initiation excluded girls and women just as firmly as any written rules.[5] There had been women compositors since the fifteenth century but, by the beginning of the nineteenth century, there were none in the London printing trade. It was a skill which men had appropriated as peculiarly suitable for themselves. As for operating the presses, the heavy dirty work seemed unthinkable for women and the pressmen, separately from the compositors, also jealously guarded their trade.

Bookbinding was also a family affair regulated by the Stationers' Company. But in the bookbinder's family workshop the women did have a part to play. By 1800 women had strictly demarcated areas of skill for they worked in the 'forwarding' or early stages of the binding process. After the compositor had set up the pages of type they were printed in sequence on to sheets. The sheets were then folded so that, when the bound pages of type were cut, the pages would be in correct chronological order. It was accepted trade practice that folding was always done by women. Every book or journal consisted of a number of folded sheets placed, or collated, in numerical order. This work was also often performed by women. After folding and collating, the sheets were sewn, again exclusively by women, on to strings or bands. The illustration for this essay shows a sewer using a sewing press which acted as a supporting frame for both the sheets and the strings.

Like the compositors, male bookbinders were labour aristocrats. Their apprentice system was strictly regulated and they too formed early and successful trade unions. By 1810 the Bookbinders' Trade Society had a total of 283 members in four London lodges.[6] But although the women binders had an acknowledged place in the trade and were encouraged to share in trade disputes (the earliest example was in a strike of 1786 over a reduction in the working day) they were strictly excluded from the union.

Women bookbinders were female labour aristocrats in an 'honourable trade', and their work carried into the nineteenth century a reputation for high status and respectability. Yet at the turn of the century the sewers and folders earned 10/6d a week compared to the men who earned 17/– to 18/–. Until the 1780s women workers as well as men had a well-established seven year apprenticeship system. Then the women's apprenticeship system began to break down and it was gradually replaced by a 'learner system'.[7] The Children's Employment Commission of 1842–3 shows that learners were very common in the trade and that in the less creditable sectors the business almost wholly relied on them though they were only taught 'the more common part of the work'. One woman, Sarah Sweetman, who worked at a reputable bindery in St Martin's Lane, believed that 'a girl who pays a premium for six months and has no wages, and who is thoroughly taught the business, is better off than one who is not taught the whole of the branches. Those who have been thoroughly instructed, can generally command profitable employment, which the latter cannot'.[8] Thus even before mechanization played any real part in the trade, the women bookbinders were unable to resist the dilution of their skill through the misuse of trainee labour.

By 1820 timework had generally been replaced by piecework for binders of both sexes. This was not a popular move but it did mean that workers could earn 'overtime' wages. This was important as there could be unusually busy times, especially in periodical publication, as well as seasonal fluctuations, such as before Christmas. The serious disadvantage for the women was that much of their work demanded considerable care and exactitude and it was often impossible to work very fast.

In spite of their 'honourable' status, therefore, they not only suffered the disadvantages of piecework and a much abused learner system, but their rates of pay, compared with the men's, were very poor. Both sexes worked an 11 or 12 hour day, with breaks for dinner and tea. By the 1840s the men were earning wages of 30/– a week and more.[9] In contrast, wages for women sewers and folders ranged from 10/– to 18/– but only the most skilled could work fast and accurately enough to earn the highest rates.[10] To make matters worse many binding shops had a 'fines' system so that wages were further diminished when the workers were fined for faults found in the binding. In the 1840s at one bible binding shop where the women's wages averaged less than 10/– a week a woman collator would be fined 1/– for leaving out a folded sheet. A sewer who failed to point out this mistake would also be fined 1/–. It took the women 60 to 65 hours a week to earn these paltry wages.[11]

By the 1840s the London Society of Bookbinders had been involved in several disputes over piece-rates and the numbers of apprentices flooding the trade. By this time the Society was obviously a force to be reckoned with, for the members successfully resisted the worst onslaughts on skill and pay. The employers fought back and by 1839 the master bookbinders had formed an Association and attempted to break the London Society. They failed and it emerged as a stronger single entity whose Secretary, Thomas Dunning, proved to be an able and resilient unionist.

Although the women faced exactly the same problems as the men over pay and apprenticeships, they were consistently excluded from the union. In 1833 Benjamin Teasdale of Manchester, a friend of Dunning, had suggested the formation of a women's society.[12] That year the trade union newspaper *The Pioneer* was encouraging women to join the new union movement.[13] But the bookbinders failed to adopt the idea. As 'An Initiated Weaver's Wife' pointed out the next year 'there is a great number of men that cannot bear the idea of a woman's union, and yet they are unionists themselves'.[14]

The union never took up the women's grievances over learners and only involved them peripherally in the disputes over piece-rates. Dunning did finally take up the case of some women sewers and folders in the bible trade when their piece-rates were cut, along with those of the men, in 1849. The women's decision to strike went against the advice of the Society but once they were committed Dunning worked hard to help them. A Women's Committee was set up and collected a £650 strike fund.[15] This so incensed one section of the Bookbinders' Society that they tried to unseat Dunning. A power struggle was won when the dissenting faction, the 'finishers', were expelled and set up their own separate union. Yet even after this there was no suggestion that the women should be included in the union (though they were allowed to belong to its Pension and Asylum Society).[16]

To be a woman worker in an honourable trade therefore meant enjoying highly respectable status but receiving low wages and being excluded from the single most important source of power for the worker, the craft society or trade union. The significance of this exclusion is clear when we look at pay and conditions. The women bookbinders were quite unable to resist the impact of 'market forces' which forced pay cuts upon them, or to control entry into their sectors of the trade. Their lack of organization, and the refusal of the union to include them, were to prove crucial factors in the way that the women's work developed when new technology mechanized their skills.

Unlike unions, the arrival of mechanization in the printing trades was somewhat delayed. Printing was divided between the hand process of the composing and the machine process of printing and technical innovation proceeded at very different speeds in each sector. In 1800 the printing press, a screw-operated machine worked by hand, enjoyed its first major changes since its invention when the Stanhope Press was constructed of iron rather than wood. As a further refinement this press was operated with a compound lever system rather than a screw. In 1811 the first English patent for a power-driven printing machine was taken out and in 1814 *The Times* was printed for the first time on a steam-driven printing press. In fact *The Times* was in the forefront of technical innovation throughout the nineteenth century. In 1848 the paper was printed for the first time on an Applegarth vertical cylinder press, in 1869 the proprietors introduced the first complete rotary newspaper press and in 1872, entering the realms of the compositor's closed world, they introduced Kastenbein's mechanical composing machine.[17] The print workers' reaction to this enthusiasm for new technology is clear for *The Times* was blacked by the trade societies as an 'unfair' shop from 1816 until 1914.[18]

Before looking in more detail at mechanization throughout the trades we need to consider another influential development, that of a huge increase in the volume of business during the first half of the nineteenth century. The simultaneous increase of both literacy and a consequent and reinforcing demand for reading matter of all kinds had a profound impact on the size of the trade.[19] In the book trade the number of master bookbinders more than doubled between 1794 and 1813 and new publishing firms were appearing as fiction of all kinds became more popular. The newspaper trade was also expanding, although still hampered by stamp duties which did not finally disappear until 1855. The radical press which emerged in the 1790s provided another facet to the collection of daily and weekly newspapers which enjoyed increasing circulations. These in turn were joined by the relatively new field of periodical publication. This was also an enormously expanding market which catered for all classes and all tastes. The 'improving' *Penny Cyclopaedia*, *Penny Magazine* and *Chambers' Edinburgh Journal*, all founded in the early 1830s, were aimed at the working class. There was a similar genre for the middle-class reader of which *Household Words* is probably the best known, while the reviews, like the *Quarterly*, and the *Edinburgh* and the monthlies, such as *Blackwood's* and the *London Magazine*, also fed the growing reading habit. In complete contrast the sensational 'penny dreadfuls' had a huge working-class following.

It was because the volume of trade was increasing at a time when mechanization was making a relatively small impact on the trades that it was much easier for both the bookbinders and compositors to retain control of their skill and maintain their work practices. The new machines helped to cope with the increases demanded in production but did nothing to replace labour.

These improvements in production methods were various and generally small scale. In printing, the general introduction of steam-driven presses was very important but did no more than soak up the extra volume of trade and increase the numbers of jobs for pressmen. Otherwise the major technical innovation in printing came during the 1830s with the invention of stereotyping. Here a section of type which had been set up was moulded in plaster of Paris or papier mâché and the resulting stereotype plates permanently preserved the typeface for large-scale production. Like the steam-driven presses, stereotyping did not replace labour but simply accommodated the need for increased production. In bookbinding the mechanized processes were equally restricted in both number and application. The new rounding and backing machines, rolling and arming presses absorbed the extra work available and caused no demarcation disputes.[20]

The compositors, who formed the most exclusive and highly skilled sector of the printing workforce, watched with glee in the 1840s as various attempts to mechanize typesetting got off to a slow start and then proved to be impracticable. The first automatic composing machine, the Young-Delcambre, appeared early in the 1840s and in 1842 the *Weekly Dispatch* displayed an advertisement offering 'genteel' employment to young women at 12/– a week. Both machine and wages were attacked by the *Compositors' Chronicle* and by 1846 the machine was discarded because it 'cannot be worked profitably'.[21] In the 1850s, however, the composing machine became a practical reality. The Hattersley was the most efficient and most common and by 1857 it was in use in many provincial newspaper offices. Distributing machines were also developed so that the compositor's work was indeed mechanized but in a process involving more than one machine. Even when hand composing ruled supreme the compositors had always refused to allow 'dissing', unskilled as it was, to pass out of their control.[22] Their attitude to the new machines reflected this determination. In the provinces newspaper proprietors employed juveniles and women on these machines. The provincial union, the Typographical Association, tried to reserve the operation of composing machines for men and to 'black' the offices employing women and young people. In London the reorganized London Society of Compositors made it practically impossible for any of these machines to be introduced at all. There was particularly strong resistance by the compositors to the machines which broke composing down into its components, for they knew that this would mean losing control over the work and their claim to both status and high pay.

Their strategies were necessarily contradictory because they both resisted the introduction of the new machines and tried to gain control of their operation where they did appear. For these reasons they found women machine operators a useful target for attack because they could be criticized as women, rather than as workers. This response by the compositors to women at work took two forms. One focused on the suitability of women working at all, the other upon their capacity to do so. The first response was exemplified in a comment in the *Printers' Journal and Typographical Magazine* of 1867. It reported that 'The sensational weekly the *World We Live In* is composited almost entirely by girls . . . I fear the contents of this paper will not improve their minds or render them more fit for matrimonial responsibilities.' Their other argument, that women were incapable of the work, emerged in numerous deprecatory comments in this and other journals on the 'utter failure' of women to learn the art.[23]

The contempt the compositors held for women's skill in the trade was at least partly a defence of their increasingly beleaguered position. The London Union was holding out against the new composing machines but in spite of this there were employers who took on women for both hand composing and as machine operators from about 1860, taking advantage of the universally accepted practice of paying women lower rates than men. The male compositors made no attempt to unionize the women, whether they were machine operators or hand compositors. How successful such an attempt would have been can only be surmised, but their purpose in using exclusive tactics for controlling entry into the trade was not simply protection of wage-rates but protection of skill and status too. This is obvious from the reaction of the compositors to two ventures which took care to pay 'the rate for the job' to the women they employed.

In 1859 the newly formed Society for Promoting the Employment of Women decided that composing might be a suitable new field of work. In March 1860 one of the members, Emily Faithfull, opened the Victoria Press.[24] The Press employed and trained women compositors who worked an eight-hour day and received wages of £1 a week.[25] By 1869 the Press was arousing a good deal of critical comment. The *Publishers' Circular* speaks for them all for it reported that:

> It is very well known in the trade that the employment of women as compositors and printers is in effect a failure . . . that they never really composed any books . . . without the most efficient help of men . . . there is no office . . . open to them, simply because their work won't pay; that 'diseases dire' peculiar to women afflict female compositors if they do work hard . . . Finally . . . there are always in London alone at least five hundred compositors out of work, any one of whom could work cheaper, better and cleanlier than any female compositor.[26]

A second feminist venture appeared under the aegis of the Women's Protective and Provident League (WPPL). The WPPL had been set up in 1874 by Emma Paterson, a former bookbinder's apprentice and the assistant secretary to the Workmen's Club and Institute Union. Her intention was to provide an umbrella organization for women's trade societies and the WPPL played a part in organizing women bookbinders. In 1876 the WPPL founded the Women's Printing Society (WPS), a printing business in which it was intended to provide 'technical training for girls . . . good work . . . should be paid for at the ordinary trade rate, since it is not at all intended to introduce women into an unfair competition as regards wages, such as that to which workmen have hitherto naturally objected'.[27] At the WPS the women compositors set up the type and proof-read their work. Later they carried out every stage of the compositor's work, including imposition (i.e. dividing the galleys of type into 'pages' in a wooden frame or chase and arranging them in a 'forme' so that the pages are printed in the correct order for folding the sheets of printed material) and distributing the type.

The WPS succeeded in a viable and independent existence. The Victoria Press, however, aroused direct antagonism from the London Society of Compositors. In 1879 the Press asked the Society to send them an extra hand to cope with unexpected pressure of business. The Secretary replied that there would have to be assurances that the compositor would not have to work with the women. A resolution was passed in the Society to the effect 'that no man belonging to it should touch work in any way handled by the women' nor work in an office which employed women as typesetters.[28] The same year a London firm, Messrs Smyth and Yerworth, which employed women compositors, found that their male employees suddenly refused to 'make-up, finish or do anything to work that was set up by females' because of a 'by-law of their Society'.[29] The men were sacked but the employers' action was criticized by Edith Simcox of the LondonWomen's Trade Council. She argued that because the women were paid less than union rates the men were right to object because wages were being artificially depressed.

The real problem for the increasing number of women compositors, whether they were engaged in hand composition or as machine operators, was that they could only get work at below union rates. For Edith Simcox the solution was to ensure that women received the union rate but this was not a strategy the men recognized. The London Society, though it deplored the undercutting, refused to unionize the women. By 1879 the members were seriously considering the whole question of women's labour but their attitude was paradoxical. The Society believed that there were disadvantages attached to employing women because they were apparently fast but inaccurate and could not undertake heavy work. This meant that the numbers of women workers would automatically find their own (low) level.[30] As mechanization proceeded apace and women proved to be perfectly competent machine operators, this belief was rapidly shown to be wishful thinking. The trade unionists, however, persisted in their attitude.

A few years later, in 1886, the General Secretary of the London Society proposed at an international conference of Typographical Associations: 'that, while strongly of the opinion that women are not physically capable of performing the duties of compositors, this conference recommends their admission to membership of the various Typographical Unions upon the same conditions as journeymen, provided always the females are paid strictly in accordance with scale'.[31]

The inference clearly was that women would never be able to attain full trade union rates and would therefore never be eligible for membership. At no point did the Society attempt to organize the women. They appeared to prefer to leave them as an unorganized labour force, undercutting union rates. In London the WPS continued to provide secure, well-paid work for women printers (the Victoria Press had closed down in 1882). Elsewhere women's presence in the trade was also increasing, especially in Scotland and the provinces.[32] Women were always paid less than men: 5d–6d an hour compared with 7½–8½d for men for timework and 5d–6d per 1000 ens for piece rates, where men averaged 8½d.[33] However, wages for women compositors could reach £1 a week and this was, for women, a very good rate which made work in the trade especially attractive. They worked both as hand compositors and machine operators and antagonized the male worker in both guises – either because they were co-operating in breaking up skilled work processes by working machines, or because they were undercutting the trade rates as hand compositors. In 1892 the Society's representatives told the Royal Commission on Labour that women were *not* admitted to the Society 'although it had no objection to their working with the men, providing they received the same wages' – an observation hardly consistent with the rule that they would be allowed membership providing they were paid the agreed trade rate.[34]

The increasingly equivocal stance of the London Society coincided with the advent of the most significant technical innovations to occur in the composing room during the entire period. In 1886 Mergenthaler's linotype mechanical typesetter made its first appearance. The linotype first cast the type and then set it mechanically. After printing the type was automatically melted down and used again. The distribution of type was therefore no longer a tedious, unskilled part of the process and the linotype needed one skilled operator to carry out the whole of the compositor's work.

By 1894 the linotype had arrived in London newspaper offices and was followed in 1897 by the monotype which was used in book work.[35] The irony was that this major technical advance placed the advantage of power into the hands of the workman, which was one reason why the machines did not arouse the antipathy of the unions. The London Society of Compositors in particular was very successful in appropriating control over labour practice and rates of pay. Ultimately the compositors, though shorn of many of their original skills, were left in a powerful position in the composing room, able to dictate conditions in the labour market.[36] For once, mechanization had played into the hands of the craftsman and the compositors capitalized on their existing strong position. They were now firmly in control of the skilled process in a mechanized trade which was once more enjoying huge volume expansion.

Yet their response was not to include existing machine operators in their labour organization. On the contrary, once technology had combined machine operation and the need for a single skilled operator, it was much easier for the men to exclude the women from the workshop and one effect of the compositors' victory over labour practices was to reinforce their exclusive attitude to women workers.[37] It is already clear that they had effectively been excluded from the London Society of Compositors – with the exception of Mrs Jane Pyne of William Morris's Kelmscott Press in Hammersmith who joined in 1892. This single instance made no difference to the general attitude of the London Society. Since unions in the printing trades were organized along craft lines and there were so few women compositors it was left to the new 'mass unions' of the 1880s and 1890s to encourage the women print workers into labour organization.

The very real success of the compositors in maintaining their craft pre-eminence helped to ensure a very limited role for women in printing, in spite of the feminist intervention of the 1870s and 1880s. For women engaged in the bookbinding sectors of the trades there was no necessity to force an entry since they had their own well-established and skilled sectors. We have seen that to be a highly skilled women worker conferred a reputation for respectability but not high wages, and that the London Society of Bookbinders, though far less antagonistic than the compositors, especially under the direction of Thomas Dunning, did not feel responsible for unionizing the women bookbinders. As a result, the advance of mechanization in the second half of the century found the women's skill and their status being undercut.

They had no real defence against this encroachment, despite the fact that in 1874 a union was set up for the women bookbinders. The need for some sort of organization became increasingly clear, though it was not a dispute over mechanization which brought this fact home but a general problem of trade regulation. During 1870–1 there was a further upset in the bible trade when there was a prolonged delay in passing a new Lectionary Bill. Sales of prayer books were suspended in 1870 while parliament approved a new text. All printing and binding was suspended and workers in the trade suffered considerable hardship. In October of 1870 2,500 women in the London bookbinding trade petitioned the Queen in an attempt to speed up proceedings. Their plight was far worse than that of the men because the Bookbinder's Society was giving its members assistance. By the time the Bill was passed in July 1871 members had received over £7,000 in benefits. The women received nothing.[38]

The resentment which carried over from this event was one reason why the WPPL decided to make the women bookbinders a particular object of attention and in 1874 Emma Paterson founded the Society of Women Employed in Bookbinding. Besides the delay over the Lectionary Bill there were other factors which brought the bookbinders to her notice. For one thing she had been apprenticed as a bookbinder herself for a short while. Another more influential reason was one which shows clearly the attitude of the vast majority of male unionists towards organizing women workers. Early members of the WPPL were Henry R. King, who had replaced Dunning as secretary of the Bookbinders' Society in 1871, and George Shipton, another prominent London trade unionist. It had been Emma Paterson's intention to work through the WPPL to encourage women to join existing male craft unions. King and Shipton dissuaded her from this plan on the grounds that the entry of women might depress male wages.[39] Once this principle was established King 'promised to give the women in the trade every possible assistance'.[40]

The Society of Women Employed in Bookbinding, for this and other reasons, was to remain something of a dead letter. Like all the WPPL societies it paid sickness and unemployment benefits but none that related specifically to women's special circumstances. There were no maternity benefits, no refund of dues on retirement from work through marriage and no provision made to re-enter the union once the childbearing years were over and paid work resumed.[41] The reason for this was that Mrs Paterson and the members of the WPPL wished to present women unionists on equal terms with men, although this principle was of course completely undermined by the exclusion of the women from the male unions. In addition WPPL affiliated unions had no strike funds or strike procedure and discouraged industrial action. This was undoubtedly a disadvantage since women's unions prepared to use such strategies did succeed in gaining wage rises for their members. Both the

Leicester Society of Seamers and Stitchers and the Dewsbury and Distict Heavy Woollen Weavers were cases in point.[42]

Meanwhile mechanization proceeded apace. In the 1880s the major technological innovation was the introduction of 'casing', a cheap substitute for true binding in which cases were made for the sewn books and glued on to them. By 1890 there were machines for folding, sewing, gathering, cutting, rounding and backing. Work for women bookbinders was increasing and their activities were no longer restricted to folding and sewing. They operated machinery, including the casing machines, took on more collating and also began placing illustrations, laying gold on covers, head-banding and covering magazines. The Society of London Bookbinders received many complaints from its members about women workers encroaching upon male preserves. Like the compositors the binders attacked women's competence and one favourite but unproven argument against the women was that their standards were lower than men's.

Yet the real difficulty was that, in the context of an increasingly mechanized trade, female labour was being directed into jobs which seemed appropriate for women workers and which, *pari passu*, lacked both status and skill.[43] Ramsay MacDonald's investigators argued in *Women in the Printing Trades* (1904) that new machinery made it 'possible for less skilled and lower paid women to do work formerly done by men' but that it was also true that the machines had displaced women and created new openings for men. The machines for folding, for example, were operated by men. The male operators displaced the women workers but ironically only at night. Disparities in wages meant that it was cheaper to use women's hand labour by day and restrict use of the machines to night shifts when the Factories' Acts prevented women from working.[44] The machines were encroaching fast, however, and it was the opinion of one trade union official than ten machines could do the work of 100 women.[45] Sewing machines, though, were operated by women 'the only explanation apparently being that convention determines that in these trades sewing machines and women go together. Sewing machines are domestic implements in men's eyes'.[46] The loss of such craft processes had clearly broken down some traditional gender based demarcations in binding. Yet it seemed that although the traffic in jobs was two-way, women consistently ended up in less-favoured work.

In the 1890s there was another boom in business which compensated for the displacement of all labour in the printing trades. New technology (rotary presses and the linotype) joined forces with Lord Northcliffe's imagination and gave birth to the 1/2d *Daily Mail* in 1896. By 1898 its daily sales were nearly one million. The periodical press, which retained something of its 'improving' tone, also enjoyed a boom. The book world was changing too. The late 1840s had seen the introduction of reprints priced at one-fifth of the original publications. In the 1850s this market was cornered by the shilling Railway Library of George Routledge. Reprint book prices generally declined in the next 30 years and midway through the 1890s the expensive library editions of new books finally disappeared. New publications were now priced at 5/– to 6/– and good quality reprints at 2/6d to 3/6d. These were rapidly followed by series of reprints of the classics (from firms such as Dents, Nelsons and William Collins) at 6d and 7d and the era of the cheap book was firmly established.

The effect of this expansion upon the printing trades was very similar to that in the 1820s and 1830s. The increased volume of business was met by the use of machinery which displaced labour in itself but required large numbers of new operators. The difficulty for the workforce lay not in loss of jobs but in loss of skill and status, both of which could imply depression of wages.

In fact, as we have seen, the compositors succeeded in retaining skill, status and wage levels in a process virtually unmatched in any other industry while women remained very much a despised minority in the trade. A printing census taken in 1888 found only four women printers to every 100 men.[48] Work done by women was consistently abused as below the standard of men's. However, since the evidence for this view comes very largely from union sources any real assessment of its validity is hard to make. Certainly the Scottish printing trade appears to have operated entirely successfully with the help of a large contingent of women compositors.

Whatever the avowed reasons for the attempts to exclude women from printing, the attitude of the unions towards them remained ambivalent. In 1894 the London Society of Compositors drew up a new agreement with the metropolitan newspaper proprietors which included the condition that 'All skilled operators – i.e. compositors, justifers and distributors – shall be members of the London Society of Compositors'.[49] This effectively excluded women who could not be members unless they wre paid agreed union rates which the union took care not to achieve on behalf of the non-unionised women print workers. Women key-board operators were, however, quite common in the provinces, including the provincial branch establishments of London printing houses. The Typographical

Association, umbrella body for the provincial print unions and keen supporter of the London Society's policy on women, objected strongly to this practice. When in 1894 it recognized an office which employed women key-board operators, the Association did succeed in persuading the employers to pay the women at trade rates. It was the height of irony that the Association then refused to admit these women as members.[50]

In bookbinding no single group of workers retained control over any part of the binding process in a way analagous to the success of the compositors. But the strongly unionized male workforce enjoyed minimum wage rates of some 32/– to 39/– for a 54 hour week, for by 1890 they had achieved a nine hour day.[51] They remained amongst the highest paid of skilled working-class men and the degrees of de-skilling which accompanied mechanization in the trade had not meant a drop in wages. In this trade women were in a majority in the workforce and the 1888 census revealed 111 women to every 100 men.[52] The women's wage-rates remained very similar too and they were consistently at one-third to one-half of the men's. MacDonald's very detailed data show averages of 10/– to 15/– with wages falling as low 6/– and rising as high as £1 in all areas of binding (and indeed printing) work for women.[53]

Whatever craft skill remained in demand, the unionized male workers retained control and their monopoly. By 1893 the London Society of Bookbinders and the Society of Day-Working Bookbinders (the breakaway union of 1850) had been joined by a third organization, the Bookbinders' and Machine Rulers' Consolidated Union. That year the three unions drew up an agreement with the London Chamber of Commerce which ensured 'the delimitation of work to be paid for at recognised rates'. It was settled that virtually all the processes of binding after sewing (done by the women) would be reserved for 'bookbinders or apprentices'. The agreement was made on the understanding that 'female or unskilled labour' could carry out certain other processes (largely the less complex ones) if it seemed necessary.[54] The agreement was drawn up because of fears of encroachment by female labour. The women workers were not consulted or represented at the discussion and none of the unions admitted women as members so that they could not be, in union terms, 'bookbinders or apprentices'.

The women workers were now firmly located in the semi-skilled and unskilled sectors of the trade. They had retained sewing as their special responsibility even after mechanization, but were de-skilled and largely ousted by folding machines. They had enjoyed hugely increased opportunities of work but not an increased earning capacity. As in printing women were now mainly machine operators amongst whom there was a clear hierarchy of skill and status. In the words of one manager in a periodicals firm: 'If the machine is large and complicated, men will replace women, if it is small and simple, women will replace men'.[55]

The idea reflected all the premises upon which the concept of 'women's work' was constructed. Even when they had enjoyed skilled status as folders and sewers their work had been components in the binding process and had come in the early manufacturing or 'forwarding' stages; it had been treated as preparatory to the main binding process. Furthermore it had not attracted high pay though it did have the advantages of being a genteel occupation amongst working-class women.

This gentility was the one thing which at least some of the women workers in binding still retained. Barbara Hutchins noted in 1902 that binding was considered to be respectable work and remarked that in the Birmingham trade, the girls at work called the older women 'the ladies who do the binding'.[56] In 1909 Clementina Black made a similar observation, writing that 'Bookfolding is for some not very definable reason, a trade looked up to as especially respectable, and women who practice it are nearly always of a comparatively high social grade'.[57] The wages paid must have made it difficult for the women to maintain their respectability for there was quite a discrepancy between the 11/− or so average wage paid and the minimum of 14/6− to 15/− a week that it was calculated was needed for an independent women to live on away from home.[58] Indeed 17/− to 19/− a week was really required for a woman 'to maintain herself in decency and with a meagre degree of comfort'.[59]

Throughout these years of technological innovation and changing work practices the Society of Women Employed in Bookbinding continued to act as a benefit society for its membership of 300 or so (about 10 per cent of the female workforce). The Society organized co-operative purchase schemes and social events but little in the way of improved working conditions or pay. The WPPL was by the late 1880s facing its real failure to organize the female metropolitan workforce and the leadership felt that larger-scale organization and closer co-operation with male unions was the answer. Emma Paterson died in 1886 and the WPPL split over tactics. Clementina Black argued for a 15/− minimum weekly wage and entry into men's unions. Others, including the Women Bookbinders' secretary, resisted these ideas and the dissent meant that the WPPL failed to capitalize on the 1888–9 boom in trade unionism in London.[60]

Under the leadership of Lady Emilia Dilke the WPPL (which re-organized as the Women's Trade Union League in 1891) did adopt these strategies – but only for its provincial unions. Meanwhile the bulk of women workers in the printing and bookbinding trades needed non-craft-based unions for they fell into the category of semi-skilled and unskilled labour which was denied entry to the craft unions but was ripe for the mass movement for the 1890s.

In 1892 a United Women Bookfolders' Union was formed which enjoyed the support of the new Printers' and Stationers' Warehousemen, Cutters' and Assistants' Union. This union organized semi-skilled and unskilled labour in the printing and paper trades and its formation in 1889 was a major step in unionizing this sector. The Women Bookfolders' survived for ten years, then became a separate branch of the Printers' and Stationers' Warehousemen's Union.[61] But this and subsequent women's sections organized in the expanding print unions of the 1900s came too late to salvage anything of the women's original status and segregated occupations.

Status based upon skill and craft-based labour organization proved to be the key factors for the male workforce. The existence of the two trade societies of London compositors and bookbinders, together with accidents of technological advance, proved crucial. Large-scale mechanization came very late to both trades and by the time it arrived the unions were firmly established. Although mechanization inevitably brought job displacement, ultimately both groups but especially the compositors, were able to consolidate a powerful labour position. In contrast the experiences of women workers in the bookbinding and printing trades are very revealing in an assessment of the impact of mechanization on the workforce, upon work practices and the development of a separate category of women's work. The status of women in each sector and their foothold in the trades were quite different at the beginning of the period. The attitudes of male workers towards them were similar though there were distinct differences in the two sectors. But by the end of the century the women held very similar positions throughout the trades as they were restricted to well-defined categories of 'women's work', which lacked both skilled status and adequate wages. The early union initiatives had been along gender and craft lines and were relatively unsuccessful. Effective unionization only came with the mass movement of the 1890s after the loss of real skilled status. The Victoria Press, the WPS and the Society of Women Bookbinders had aimed at ensuring skilled status and craft-based unions, but the efforts of this feminist intervention went largely unrewarded.

Generally mechanization brought increased employment opportunities for women in the Victorian period. They were brought in as semi-skilled and unskilled machine operators, almost always at rates which undercut those of hand craftsmen. Mechanization was therefore a mixed blessing because while it increased the range of work open to women it reinforced the characteristic nature of women's work as subsidiary and cheap. In these trades especially there was a particularly extreme form of rivalry between the male and female workforces because of the strength of the workmen's position and their jealous regard for their rights and skills – a regard which was manifested in printing even before composing was mechanized.

The craftsmen were therefore able to protect their position because of their highly organized state and their past success in restrictive trade practices. For craftswomen the position was quite different. For the sewers and folders of the early nineteenth century mechanization spelt loss of skill and status for they lacked power in the workplace. Since part of the men's success in retaining their position lay in excluding the women from their unions the women were doubly disadvantaged; threatened by both machines and nearly total non-co-operation from their male co-workers. Union officials in bookbinding certainly tolerated the women workers in their trade, but right up until the 1890s they would brook no encroachment upon their traditional fields of skill – although in this trade the breakdown of occupational segregation found the men encroaching upon the women's preserves.

Mechanization in any trade could lead to the dilution and de-skilling of jobs. It also increased job opportunities, often in semi-skilled and unskilled sectors. The numbers of women in the trades rose dramatically over the period from just over 2,000 in 1840 to nearly 30,000 in 1901. But while the highly organized compositors and bookbinders retained skill, status and control over their work processes, the small, skilled women's sector in bookbinding proved to have a fragile hold upon their privileges and no power at all to achieve, let alone maintain, wages which matched their expertise and the respectable status they held in the skilled working class. Ultimately all that was left to a fraction of the women in the trades of their former 'honourable status' was a reputation for gentility and respectability.

Bibliographical Note

There are numerous accounts of printers and the printing trades available but few of them consider the role of women in any detail. However, a good foundation for further study can be found in Ellic Howe and John Child, *The Society of London Bookbinders 1780–1951* (Sylvan Press, 1952) and Ellic Howe and Harold E. Waite, *The London Society of Compositors (re-established 1848). A Centenary History* (Cassell, 1948). For the experience of women in the trades see Felicity Hunt, 'Women in the Nineteenth Century Bookbinding and Printing Trades (1790-1914), With Special Reference to London', MA thesis (University of Essex, 1979) and 'The London Trade in the Printing and Binding of Books: An Experience in Exclusion, Dilution and De-skilling for Women Workers', *Women's Studies International Forum*, 6 (1983), pp.517–24. For an excellent account of women in printing from the Victorian period to the 1980s see Cynthia Cockburn, *Brothers: Male Dominance and Technological Change* (Pluto Press, 1983).

Unpublished sources are the Jaffray Papers at the British Museum; T.J. Dunning, 'Appeal of the Journeymen Bookbinders of London and Westminster to the Committee, Members, Donors and Subscribers, of the British and Foreign Bible Society, and the Religious Public in General on the Subject of Cheap Bibles' (17 August 1849), at St. Bride Institute, London; Coll. Misc. 486, 2/6 at the London School of Economics.

Notes

1 Catherine Hall, 'The home turned upside down? The working class family in cotton textiles 1780–1850', in *The Changing Experience of Women*, eds. Elizabeth Whitelegg et al. (Martin Robertson, Oxford, 1982), pp.21–4.

2 J.W. Crompton, 'Account of Printers' Strikes and Trades' Unions Since January 1845' in the *Report of the Committee on Trades' Societies, appointed by the National Association for the Promotion of Social Science, presented at the fourth annual meeting of the Association, at Glasgow, September, 1860* (1861), p.85.

3 Edward Arber (ed.), *A Transcript of the Registers of the Company of Stationers of London 1554–1640*, vol. i (London, 1875), p.16.

4 Hunt, 'Women in the Nineteenth Century Bookbinding and Printing Trades', ch. 2 *passim*.

5 Cockburn, *Brothers*, pp.16–19.

6 British Museum, Jaffray Papers. vol. vi, Minute Books, 1807–11.

7 Sally Alexander, 'Women's Work in Nineteenth Century London: A Study of the Years 1820–50', in *The Rights and Wrongs of Women*, eds Juliet Mitchell and Ann Oakley (Penguin, Harmondsworth, 1977 edn), pp.88–91.

8 *Children's Employment Commission*, PP 1843, XII, 716–18, quoted by Alexander, 'Women's Work'.

9 Crompton, 'Account of Printers' Strikes and Trades' Unions', p. 85.

10 George Dodd, *Days at the Factories* (Charles Knight, 1843), p. 371.

11 St Bride Institute. T. J. Dunning, 'Appeal of the Journeymen Bookbinders of London and Westminster to the Committee, Members, Donors and Subscribers, of the British and Foreign Bible Society, and the Religious Public in General on the Subject of Cheap Bibles' (17 August 1849).

12 J. Ramsay MacDonald (ed.), *Women in the Printing Trades: A Sociological Study* (P. S. King and Son, 1904), p. 35.

13 *The Pioneer, or Trades Union Magazine*, No. 8 (26 October 1833). For a detailed analysis of women's part in this movement see Barbara Taylor, '"The Men Are as Bad as Their Masters . . .": Socialism, Feminism and Sexual Antagonism in the London Tailoring Trade in the 1830s', in *Sex and Class in Women's History*, ed. Judith L. Newton et al. (Routledge and Kegan Paul, 1983).

14 *The Pioneer*, no. 28 (15 March, 1834).

15 For a full account see Hunt, 'Women in the Nineteenth Century Bookbinding and Printing Trades', pp. 42–8.

16 In 1866 an unmarried woman member of the Pension and Asylum Society pointed out that although women workers paid the same subscriptions as men they only had rights to benefits for themselves, whereas male workers' widows also received benefit. In 1869 some changes were made for single women members. *Bookbinders' Trade Circular*, vol. iv, no. 11 (21 May 1866); vol. v (2 April 1869).

17 Colin Clair, *A Chronology of Printing* (Cassell, 1969), pp. 133, 134, 148, 156.

18 Ellic Howe, *The London Compositor. Documents relating to wages, working conditions and customs of the London printing trade 1785–1900* (The Bibliographical Society and Oxford University Press, 1947), p. 61.

19 R. D. Altick, *The English Common Reader* (University of Chicago Press, Chicago, 1957), p. 195.

20 Ellic Howe, *The London Bookbinders 1780–1806* (Dropmore Press, 1950), pp. 135–6.

21 *Compositors' Chronicle*, 1 February 1842; *Typographical Gazette*, April 1846.

22 Cockburn, *Brothers*, p. 25.

23 Hunt, 'Women in the Nineteenth Century Bookbinding and Printing Trades', pp. 51, 55–6.

24 For a full account of the Victoria Press see William E. Fredeman, 'Emily Faithfull and the Victoria Press: An Experiment in Sociological Bibliography', *The Library*, xxix (June 1974).

25 Ibid., p. 149.

26 Quoted by W. Wilfred Head in *The Victoria Press* (Victoria Press, 1869), p. 9.

27 *Englishwoman's Review*, xxv (15 March 1876), p. 133. For further discussion of the WPPL see essay 9.

28 From Emily Faithfull, *Three Visits to America* (1844), quoted by Fredeman, *The Library*, xxix (June 1974), p. 152.
29 *Women's Union Journal*, iv (1 September 1879), p. 109.
30 *British and Colonial Printer*, ii (1 September 1879), p. 287.
31 Quoted by MacDonald, *Women in the Printing Trades*, p. 28.
32 The position of women in the Scottish trade was a special one, see Hunt, 'Women in the Nineteenth Century Bookbinding and Printing Trades', pp. 65, 80; and Cockburn, *Brothers*, pp. 153–9.
33 In piecework, payment for the compositor was 'per 1,000 ens', i.e. he was paid for every letter set while 'n' was a standard mid-length letter.
34 *Royal Commission on Labour*, PP 1893, III, p. 56
35 Colin Clair, *A History of Printing in Britain* (Cassell, 1965), pp. 222, 226, 286.
36 For a full discussion of this see Cockburn, *Brothers*, pp. 27–31.
37 Cockburn, 'Material of Male Power', *Feminist Review*, 9 (1981), p. 47.
38 *Printers' Register*, 89 (November 1870), p. 242; Howe and Child, *The Society of London Bookbinders 1780–1951*, p. 188.
39 Teresa Olcott, 'Dead Centre: The Women's Trade Union Movement in London 1874–1914', *The London Journal*, 2 (1976), p. 35.
40 *Bookbinders' Trade Circular*, vi (27 October 1874), p. 76.
41 Olcott, *The London Journal*, p. 35.
42 Ibid., pp. 36, 39.
43 This phenomenon is discussed by Ann Phillips and Barbara Taylor in 'Sex and Skill: Notes Towards a Feminist Economics', *Feminist Review*, 6 (1980), pp. 79–88.
44 MacDonald, *Women in the Printing Trades*, pp. 48, 98.
45 Ibid., pp. 94–5.
46 Ibid., p. 96.
47 Altick, *The English Common Reader*, pp. 312–17.
48 *The Bookbinder*, vol. iii (1887–8), p. 171.
49 Sidney and Beatrice Webb, *Industrial Democracy* (Longman, Green, 1897, 1911 edn) p. 407.
50 A. E. Musson, *The Typographical Association, Origins and History up to 1949* (Oxford University Press, Oxford, 1954), p. 120.
51 Howe and Child, *The Society of London Bookbinders*, p. 201.
52 *The Bookbinder*, vol. iii (1887–8), p. 171.
53 MacDonald, *Women in the Printing Trades*, pp. 113–37.
54 MacDonald quotes the terms of the agreement in *Women in the Printing Trades*, pp. 7–9.
55 Ibid., pp. 95–6.
56 London School of Economics, Coll. Misc. 486, 2/6, 1902, Miss Hutchins in Birmingham.
57 Clementina Black (ed.), *Married Women's Work (Being the Report of an Enquiry Undertaken by the Women's Industrial Council)* (1915; Virago, 1983), p. 56.
58 The 1906 wage census put the average wage in all the paper and printing trades at 12/2d. Barbara L. Hutchins, *Women in Modern Industry* (G. Bell and Sons, 1915), p. 225.

59 Ibid., p.227.
60 Olcott, *The London Journal*, p.40.
61 Clement J. Bundock, *The National Union of Printing, Bookbinding and Paper Workers* (Oxford University Press, Oxford, 1959), p.69.

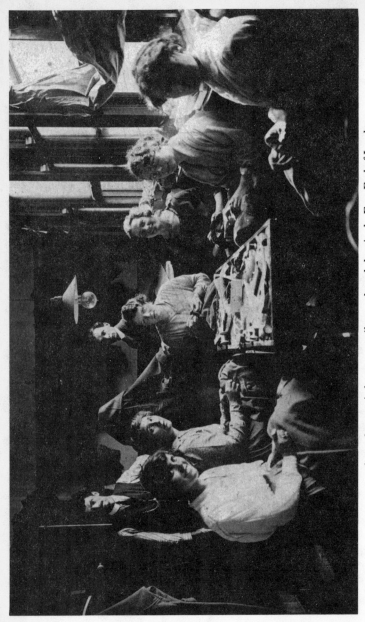

An early twentieth-century tailoresses' workshop in the East End of London

3

The Characteristics of Sweating: The Late Nineteenth-Century London and Leeds Tailoring Trade

Jenny Morris

During the late nineteenth century a great deal of attention was focused on the sweated trades, in particular on the very low wages and appalling working conditions suffered by women workers in such trades. The tailoring trade, where increasing numbers of women were employed, first attracted attention to the problem. Sweating was thought to be a feature of the backward sections of the trade which were dominated by small production units and the giving out of work to be done in the home.

Recently, a reinterpretation of the sweated trades has been put forward by James Schmiechen.[1] He argues that sweating in the clothing trades was a result of industrial growth rather than stagnation. In particular, he contends that the way in which the factory and workshop legislation was implemented forced employers to give work out to unregulated labour, and that it was in these, mainly domestic workplaces, that sweating was found.[2]

Whilst confirming Schmiechen's thesis that outwork and sweating were features of the growth of the clothing trades, this essay argues that the characteristics of sweating were not confined to unregulated workplaces but were a feature of both larger and smaller production units.[3] Analysis of the sexual division of labour is crucial to an understanding of why tailoring was a sweated trade. The characteristics of sweating were associated with the dilution of skills and the development of a sexual division of labour which went hand in hand with the advancement of the trade.

In common with most research on the clothing trades,

Schmiechen's work concentrates solely on London. This essay, however, compares the London tailoring trade with that of Leeds, the most important centre of the modern tailoring trade, and in doing so seeks to show that not only were the characteristics of sweating associated with the growth of the trade, but that they were part of the way in which capital uses female labour.[4]

First, however, a note on terminology. 'Sweating' is a rather unsatisfactory analytical term. The word was used in the nineteenth century to condemn the conditions under which some people worked. It is not a very precise tool for the historian and it is therefore important to specify the characteristics to which the term refers, that is, very low wages, long hours and insanitary working conditions. The House of Lords Select Committee on Sweating[5], which reported in 1890 did not confine itself to that most exploited section of sweated labour, the homeworkers, but was also concerned with the incidence of sweating in workshops and in factories. Witnesses to the Select Committee complained most frequently of low wages and, in their conclusions, the Lords gave greatest weight to this particular characteristic.[6]

The terms homework and outwork are often confused. The crucial point is that not all outworkers were homeworkers, nor were they necessarily to be found in unregulated workshops. As we shall see, outworking, that is the contracting out of work, was a feature of the rapid growth of the tailoring trade. The work contracted out was done either in factories, regulated workshops, unregulated workshops or in the home and was central to the structure of both the London and the Leeds clothing trades. The way in which outworking has often been assumed to be synonymous with homeworking has aided the identification of the characteristics of sweating with backward sections of the clothing trades and it is therefore important to be clear as to the exact meaning of the term before we commence a description of the London and Leeds tailoring trades.

Low wages were the most important characteristic of sweating. How common were low wages in the tailoring trade at the beginning of this century? In order to measure this, we will take the subsistence wage set by Cadbury and Shann in their research published in 1908, that is, 25/– per week for men and 14/– to 16/– for women.[7] The level for women reflects Cadbury and Shann's view that a woman's wage is supplementary to her husband's and that it is only necessary for her to contribute the money for her own needs to the 'family income'. It is of course questionable whether many men's wages were sufficient to support a family and women's wages were often a vital part of the family income. Furthermore, Cadbury and Shann do not take account of women whose husbands were out of work, sick, dead or just not there. Bearing these considerations in mind it does not seem unreasonable to take the upper limit mentioned, namely 16/– per week, as a measurement of a subsistence wage for women.

Workers in the tailoring trade suffered from irregularity of work, and figures provided by the 1906 Earnings and Hours Enquiry, the major source of information on wages in this period, must be qualified in this respect.[8] The London bespoke trade was directly affected by seasonal demand, the busiest times of the year being March to August, and October to December. In between workers were often locked out for many weeks.[9] The ready-made trade also experienced fluctuations. Beatrice Potter estimated that 'indoor' workers for large contractors and the most skilled tailors throughout the trade averaged four and a half days in work per week throughout the year.[10] The secretary of the Jewish Master Tailors' Federation was more pessimistic. He estimated that his members, skilled tailors taking contract work from wholesalers or retailers, averaged three and a quarter days to the week.[9] These two examples refer to the better paid branches of the trade. Potter estimated that two and a half days and under was the average employment throughout the year for those workers at the cheaper end of the London tailoring trade.

The workers in the factories of the Leeds ready-made trade experienced greater regularity of work. Amongst some subcontractors, however, the volume of work fluctuated as in London, according to season, export orders and government orders. The eight subcontractors whom Beatrice Potter and John Burnett met in 1888 experienced irregularity of work from three and a half to five days a week.[12]

Returns made to the Earnings and Hours Enquiry on average weekly wages bills for indoor workers throughout the year show considerable variations. The fluctuations in work were greatest in the London bespoke trade but even the Leeds ready-made trade showed a 19 per cent variation. From the evidence it seems reasonable to assume that some idea can be obtained of wage levels if we calculate what workers in the London and Leeds tailoring trade would have been earning if they worked for four days and five days a week respectively.

Tables 3.1 and 3.2 show that, taking account of the fluctuations in the trade, the average wage for both men and women in the London

TABLE 3.1 LONDON BESPOKE TAILORING: WAGES OF WORKERS IF THEY AVERAGED FOUR
DAYS PER WEEK

			Average				Average
MEN:	Foremen	Time	35/7	WOMEN:	Machinists	Time	11/1
	Cutters	Time	57/5			Piece	9/–
	Journeymen	Time	26/6		Other women	Time	11/7
	Tailors	Piece	28/–			Piece	9/–
	Machinists	Time	22/5		All women		10/7
		Piece	23/–				
	Other men	Time	20/4				
		Piece	23/5				
	All men		28/5				

TABLE 3.2 LONDON READY-MADE TAILORING: WAGES OF WORKERS IF THEY AVERAGED FOUR DAYS PER WEEK

MEN:

Worker	Basis	Average
Foremen	Time	36/8
Cutters (hand)	Time	23/7
	Piece	26/3
Cutters (machine)	Time	22/2
Basters	Piece	17/8
Machinists	Piece	19/8
Pressers	Piece	23/2
Warehousemen and packers	Time	20/7
Other Men	Time	22/7
	Piece	24/6
All men		24/1

WOMEN:

Worker	Basis	Average
Forewoman		41/1
Basters		8/1
Machine sewers (hand or foot)	Time	
	Piece	8/2
Machine sewers	Piece	8/9
Hand sewers and finishers	Piece	8/2
Pressers		6/3
		7/6
Other women	Time	8/1
	Piece	8/–
All women		7/9

bespoke and ready-made sections of the trade was below the subsistence level set by Cadbury. The average wage for women in the Leeds ready-made trade was also below subsistence, whereas for a man in the Leeds ready-made trade (table 3.3) it was 1/5d above subsistence. This was only due to the relatively high wages of the foreman, cutters and piecework pressers who pulled the average wage up, however; all other types of male worker earned below the subsistence wage thought necessary to support a family. So much for the male 'family wage'.

A significant number of women workers in the clothing trades were sole breadwinners for their families. Of the 82,000 people engaged in the clothing trades in 1891 returned as heads of households, 30,000 were women.[13] Yet the average wages for women in all sections of the tailoring trade were too low to meet the subsistence wage set by Cadbury and Shann as necessary to support a family.

It is impossible to assess accurately an average wage for homeworkers.[14] However, the Select Committee on Homework (1908) provides some illumination. A Police Court Missionary gave evidence of a mother and daughter making women's costumes at home, who, working together for two days from 9am to 12.30am, could make seven costumes. If they worked, say, an average of four days per week throughout the year their average weekly wage could be 7/6½d each. The costumes sold in the shops for about 29/– to 39/–.[15]

This particular witness had connections with the Homeworkers' Aid Association which had about 1,000 members. He maintained that the homeworkers with whom he had contact were working for their own living and not supplementing the wage of a husband or father.[16] On the other hand, E.G. Howarth found that of 600 homeworkers in West Ham, 53 per cent were supplementing the casual or irregular earnings of other members of the family.[17] In both cases, however, the earnings of homeworkers would not be mere 'pin money' but were essential to the individual's or the family's survival. Miss Vines, a Factory Inspector, had visited a family of three adults and two children who were entirely dependent on the earnings of the mother who worked at home on 'trouser finishing'. 'Finishing' meant putting the pockets and linings in, sewing on 11 buttons, making five buttonholes, soaping and pressing the seams and felling the legs of the trousers. She could do one pair at 2½d in two hours and one pair at 3½d in three hours. 'She had to find her own trimmings, thread, cotton and also soap and heat for irons, and lost from about half an hour to an hour daily in fetching and returning the work'.[18]

TABLE 3.3 LEEDS READY-MADE TAILORING: WAGES OF WORKERS IF THEY AVERAGED FIVE DAYS PER WEEK

		Average
MEN:		
Foremen	Time	39/3
Cutters (hand)	Time	25/5
Cutters (machine)	Time	27/–
Basters	Time	23/–
Fitters	Time	22/10
Pressers	Time	21/9
	Piece	27/4
Warehousemen and packers		24/9
Enginemen and stokers		25/6
Other men	Time	22/6
	Piece	23/9
All men		26/5
WOMEN:		
Forewomen	Time	18/1
Basters	Piece	11/3
Machines (Power)	Time	12/10
Hand sewers and finishers	Piece	11/9
Pressers	Time	9/7
	Piece	13/4
Other women	Time	11/3
	Piece	9/11
All women		11/5

Source: UK Board of Trade, *Report of an Enquiry into Earnings and Hours of the Workpeople of the United Kingdom*, vol. ii. *Clothing Trades*, PP 1909, LXXX, Cmd. 4844.

Cadbury and Shan compiled a table of hours of work and earnings of homeworkers from their own investigation and from the *Daily News* exhibition on the Sweated Trades held in 1906.[19] Table 3.4 shows the items relating to the tailoring trade.

TABLE 3.4   HOMEWORKERS IN THE TAILORING TRADE, 1906

	Average working day (hours)	*Average earnings per week*
Men's clothing:		
Trousers	16	5/–
Waistcoats	14–15	9/– to 10/–
Women's clothing:		
Skirts	14	6/9
Holland skirts	14	6/–
Melton cloth skirts	10	5/– to 6/–
Voile skirts	10–13	10/– to 18/4
Bolero and Chesterfield costumes	14	21/– (between 2)

Source: R. Mudie-Smith (ed.), *Sweated Industries: Being a Handbook of the 'Daily News' Exhibition* (1906).

It would appear that below-subsistence wages were a feature of the more advanced sections of the tailoring trade as well as what is usually considered to be the residual sector of homeworking and domestic workshops. The payment of below subsistence wages to women was especially prevalent. In order to shed further light on the phenomenon of low wages, we will now look in more detail at the development of the tailoring trade generally and then move on to compare the trade in London and Leeds at the turn of the century. In doing this, we will be looking for indications of why very low wages were so common.

What is meant by tailoring?[20] A tailor is either employed in the making of men's and boys' suits and coats or in the mantle and costume trade, that is women's and girls' costumes, coats and skirts. Before the development of wage labour in the trade, tailoring was a handicraft occupation carried out by men working on their own, making up cloth which they or their customer had bought and often travelling from house to house or village to village. As early as 1721, however, when 15,000 journeymen tailors in London formed a trade union and struck for better conditions of employment, the nature of the trade was changing. These tailors were waged workers, striking for higher day wages and shorter hours of work against capitalist employers. The late seventeenth and early eighteenth century saw the emergence of master tailors and tailor/shopkeepers who bought cloth and employed workers under them to make up garments for sale. The beginnings of an expanding market also marked the emergence of seasonal fluctuations in the demand for clothing and an expansion in the retail and wholesale distribution of the product. One pattern was now used for many garments instead of being drawn up to suit the measurements of a particular customer. Wholesale warehouses entered into this 'ready-made' section of the trade but so too did retailers who either employed tailors on their premises or gave work out already cut to be made up. The journeymen tailors were still skilled workers, however, and garments were mostly made throughout by one worker. Their union was a strong craft union, insisting on proper apprenticeships and negotiating regional 'logs' (rates of payment).

Handicraft tailors had always tended to give over certain parts of the finishing processes to members of their family. Fairly simple tasks such as buttons and button-holing could be done while the tailor was engaged on another part of the garment. At the beginning of the nineteenth century wage labour expanded and master tailors started to employ women to do this type of task in their workshops. It is of fundamental importance that these women were subordinate to the male workers. They were brought in to fill a position that neither journeymen nor apprentices had filled and as such no one, least of all the journeymen, sought to apply the union wage to them. Where women were employed in the tailoring trade, therefore, it was either as waged workers brought in at low wages by the master tailor or sub-contractor or it was as unpaid assistants to their husband or father. In this context, a sexual division of labour developed where certain tasks were separated out and given to women. The main work on a garment was done by the tailor while women felled the lining, turned cuffs, sewed buttonholes, etc. It is worth emphasizing that women went to work in the tailoring trade before the introduction of machinery. Tailoring is an example of a trade which was dominated by a male workforce until the development of a division of labour (brought about by its transition to a capitalist basis of production) pulled in women to perform tasks subordinate to the work tasks performed by men. Mechanization was later to bring about a situation where women made up a majority of the workforce.

As the market for ready-made clothing expanded, the intensification of competition resulted in a subcontracting system of production which was well established in the larger urban centres by the mid-nineteenth century. Many journeymen now became subcontractors of work to be done for master tailors and tailor/ shopkeepers outside the latter's establishments. The work was executed either in a workshop or a 'sitting' hired by the tailor/ journeyman, or in his own home. The narrow margin of profit on which the subcontractors operated meant that, where the work was done in workshops there was an impetus to a more sophisticated division of labour and where the work was done in the tailor's own home, the assistance given to him by his wife and family became even more important. The subcontracting system was the dominant form of organization of production of outerwear clothing in most of the large towns, particularly in Leeds, Manchester, Glasgow and the East End of London.

In 1851, a viable sewing machine was marketed and was quickly introduced into both workshops and into the homes of individual outworkers. Most of these sewing machines were hand or treadle operated and were inexpensive. In 1865, Singer's 'New Family' machine could be bought for 84/– or paid for by hire purchase, a system developed by Isaac Singer especially for the sale of his sewing machines to homeworkers. In the 20 years from 1865, four million of this particular model alone were sold and at one time, Singers' employed 30 collectors in the East End of London 'who visit the customers every week and spend the remainder of their time touting for custom'.[21]

Power-driven machines were used in the trade by the larger employers such as John Barran of Leeds, the first Leeds tailor to move into what the 1878 Factory Act defined as factory production. As we shall see, however, the decision to introduce power-driven machinery and the development of large units of production by no means inevitably followed the invention of the sewing machine.

The other essential piece of machinery for the tailor in the second half of the nineteenth century was the band-knife, an adaptation of the band-saw used for cutting furniture veneers, which made possible the cutting out of more than one garment at a time. This was also inexpensive enough for the small workshop employer to buy. It was not a bulky piece of equipment and was rapidly introduced into tailoring workshops after 1858. The buttonhole machine, which was patented in 1884 and 1889 and could sew six buttons a minute, was more expensive but could be hired. A series of 'goose' irons were installed in some workshops and factories which were fitted with a small flame inside fed from a common gas supply, the heat being varied on each iron by a foot pedal. These mechanical developments were accompanied by the subdivision of the tasks involved in making the garment into many different operations. A coat, for instance, was divided up into five or six operations, unskilled machinists being employed on most of them.

The tailoring trade underwent further considerable expansion in the second half of the nineteenth century. The new ready-made clothes had at first met a demand from small tradesmen, office workers, etc. and their families but towards the end of the nineteenth century there was an acceleration in demand from skilled and semi-skilled manual workers and their families. This was accompanied by a reduction in prices and the development of a sophisticated division of labour in the workshops.

The splitting up of the production process required the division of the workforce in each workshop into teams, and in some workshops, particularly the ones in Leeds, these teams were very large and the division of labour extremely sophisticated. 'In some cases, where each operative concentrates on some small part of the garment, ceaselessly repeating the same process in a mechanical manner, there is nothing to distinguish the workshop from the factory, except the technical distinction that it contains no power-driven machinery'.[22]

The tailoring industry developed most rapidly in Leeds where the declining linen industry provided workshop and factory space and a pool of female labour in an area where engineering firms were alert to the possibilities of new mechanical developments. Leeds also prospered because of the large number of Jewish immigrants, most of whom had been craft tailors and were quick to take advantage of the new developments. In fact the new division of labour in the tailoring workshops was first associated with Jewish subcontractors who accepted work from the retail tailor at a fixed price per garment. Other areas where there was a steady expansion in the production of ready-made clothes were Colchester, Norwich, Bristol and the East End of London.

Mechanization and the development of the division of labour in workshop production together with the transition to factory production meant that the tailoring industry in the last quarter of the nineteenth century experienced an increase in the number of women and girls employed. This increase was associated not only with the dilution of labour skills in the factories and workshops but also with the increase in contract work in the form of homework. 'The simpler operations such as button sewing and plain machining . . . were within the compass of the elderly, the sick, and the young mother tied to her home by growing children'.[23]

The initial increase in female labour in the tailoring trade took place within the context of some introduction of machinery but very little introduction of power-driven machinery. Much work was still done by hand although subdivided into many separate stages and in all branches of the clothing trade contract workers bore the brunt of seasonal and cyclical fluctuations. It was the transition from craft production where the tailor made the garment almost throughout, to a form of production where the production process was separated out into a complicated division of labour, which was initially responsible for the increase in female labour in the clothing trade. In Sheffield and Newcastle, where craft production still dominated in 1891, women and girls only accounted for 33 per cent and 19 per cent of the workforce respectively. The faster the trade advanced, the more women were employed. Thus, in London in that year, women made up 59 per cent of the workforce while in Leeds, the most advanced section of the trade, women accounted for 70 per cent of tailoring workers.[24]

When historians write of the 'sweated trades' they usually concentrate on the London trades. Yet how common were low wages and poor working conditions elsewhere? What was the relationship between women workers and 'sweating'? A comparison of the Leeds and London tailoring trades and the division of labour within these two centres can help elucidate some of these questions.

The London Tailoring Trade

The London tailoring trade was divided into two sections – the production of ladies' outerwear (dominated by male workers) and the production of men's and boys' outerwear (where women were an increasing proportion of the workforce). This section concentrates on the latter part of the trade as this is more appropriate for a comparison with the Leeds (men's and boys' outerwear) tailoring trade.

Both Jewish and Gentile workers were found in the production of men's outerwear in London. In the bespoke men's trade, traditionally dominated by men and with the minimum amount of subdivision, an increasing amount of work was put out to subcontractors who were mainly Jewish. In these workshops a detailed division of labour was common, one result being an increase in the number of women and girls employed. Even within the bespoke trade, certain operations were often given out yet again by the subcontractor, for example buttonhole-making or the addition of various trimmings. Furthermore, the trousers and waistcoats ordered in a West End shop were frequently given out already cut and basted to women homeworkers in the East End. The West End of London had always been the centre of high-class bespoke tailoring and this continued to be the case (although German immigrants provided a less expensive made-to-measure service in some of the boroughs just outside the West End, for example in Islington and St Pancras). It was from this class of tailoring that the Amalgamated Society of Tailors drew its membership, that is, from journeymen tailors and their apprentices. The dependence even of bespoke tailoring on the subcontracting system is demonstrated as early as 1867 when the strike of two thousand journeymen tailors was supported by outworkers employed by the firms concerned, including about 300 women who were allowed to attend business meetings of the union for the first time and were paid strike pay equal to the men. The strike was against such leading firms in London as Henry Poole's of Saville Row and Robert Lewis's of St James's and most of the work that was given out was completed in workshops rather than in the homes of tailors.

The cheaper end of the market for men's outerwear exhibited a very detailed division of labour. The production of ready-made men's outerwear – jackets, coats and trousers – was very easily broken down into stages in such a way that the tailor's skill was no longer required and he tended to lose control over the production process. Not only was there a sophisticated division of labour within the workshop but there was a multiple 'giving out' of work. An example of the way in which the trade developed is the history of the firm, Moss Bros., who started trading in second hand men's clothing and buying up 'mis-fits' in 1860. In the 1880s, Moses Moses started to buy up the remnants at the end of the season and to make up suits, cut out by his son, George Moses, and put together by the tailors who were experiencing a 'slack time' as the West End season was over. These tailors, who received work from both shops and wholesalers, themselves often gave out parts of the work to be done outside their own workshop or home. Sometimes, most of the work was done by one tailor who gave the subsidiary tasks to be done by a woman. An account is given in the 1890s of a West End tailor

> employed at a shop where all the work is put out, each tailor having to find his own workroom – [he] told me that he pays a

woman 12/– for doing work which at the same quality and for
the same quantity he would have to pay a man at least 18/–.[25]

These women and girls would either be employed in the tailor's
workroom (sometimes they were the wives and daughters of the
tailors) or they took the work into their own homes. Other tailors
took large amounts of work, either directly from shops or from
wholesalers, and employed several people under them.

In these workshops the workers were divided into teams
corresponding with the division of the garment into several stages of
production. The work was divided as follows: the tailor basted the
garment, then it was passed to the machinist (often a woman) to
machine the main seams, then the tailor fixed the shoulder seams
and the collar; a woman would then be employed to fell the linings
and to stitch the buttonholes. In the larger workshops, the work was
further divided according to parts of the garment, for example, one
machinist would do nothing else but stitch sleeves or make pockets.
The tailor-employee retained his status as long as he was only
assisted by, say, a couple of tailoresses, a machinist and a couple of
apprentices but as soon as the work was divided amongst a larger
team – particularly when the pressing and the main tailoring parts of
the work were separated – the majority of tailors became little more
than 'hands' and their working lives were correspondingly
dehumanized. An example of a large team was a foreman-tailor, two
tailors, two machinists, two finishers, one presser and one girl
apprentice. If the tailor did not have a large enough workshop the
garment would be given out to be pressed by an individual worker or
workshop specializing in pressing. Often, even if the jacket or coat
was completed within one workshop, the trousers would be given
out, ready cut out and basted, for machining by a woman machinist.
Waistcoats were, by this time, firmly established as 'women's work'.
In 1834, the Grand Lodge of Operative Tailors had fought the
Lodge of Female Tailors over the entry of women into waistcoat-
making but by the end of the nineteenth century, waistcoat-making
was almost completely in the hands of the cheapest labour offered on
the market and was often done by homeworkers.

The retail distribution of cheap to medium quality men's suits and
coats underwent rapid development at the end of the nineteenth
century. In the 1880s and 1890s large shops were established in the
West End which, like Moss Bros., integrated both manufacturing
and selling functions by contracting work out to tailors, most of
whom lived in the City or East End. By the end of the nineteenth

century there was also a booming export trade in cheap men's outerwear, especially to South Africa and to Australia. The Select Committee on Sweating was told that the export of clothing had doubled in the previous 20 years.[26]

In this ready-made section of the London tailoring trade – where a prospering tailor would employ a number of machinists – power-driven sewing machines were most likely to be introduced. These changed workshops into factories overnight, for new premises were often neither sought nor available. The District Factory Inspector for North London reported in 1905 that the introduction of a small electric motor was common in some of the small workshops and resulted in many small factories being added to the register where only a few people were employed on each premises.[27] The possibility of dividing up the work into many different stages many of which could now be completed by machinery was obviously one incentive to mass production; another was the development of standardized cutting in men's tailoring.

Factory production was most advanced in the manufacture of army, navy, police and railway uniforms where large production runs were needed. Men did all the cutting out and also worked on the better class of work, but women were employed on all other stages of the production process except supervisory and warehouse tasks. Each stage was divided up into corresponding departments – machining, finishing, buttonholing and pressing – and within these divisions there was further subdivision according to the type of garment being made; for example, a woman or girl might be employed specifically as a 'tunic hand', or a 'trouser hand'.

However, the high rents and increasing rates which prevailed not only in central London but also in the East End, were a strong discouragement to the larger premises which were required where more than a very few power-driven machines were installed. Moreover, the seasonal nature of the demand for clothing was also a constraint on investment, particularly as London trade generally was especially prone to seasonal fluctuations owing to its commercial life being dominated by the parliamentary and 'society' season which not only directly influenced the retail bespoke section but indirectly affected the rest of the tailoring trade. The 'quiet season' experienced by almost all London trades meant that working-class demand for clothing also diminished. Fluctuations in demand for the product of the larger production units were therefore also fairly common and to a large extent the smaller factories, the workshops and the homeworkers acted as a buffer against these fluctuations by taking on the extra work in the busy season. Even in the most advanced sections of the tailoring trade, homework was used as a buffer between the factory and seasonal fluctuations. The rush of work at certain times meant that women and girls were often sent home with work at night. Ada Nield Chew, a tailoress and later an active trade unionist, experienced this when working on a government order in a large factory; although this giving out of work to 'indoor workers' was banned under the Factory and Workshops Act, the employers resorted to it as necessary overtime which was less visible to the Factory Inspector's eye than working illegal hours in the factory.[28]

Looking at the London tailoring trade at the turn of the century reinforces the picture of what the Select Committee on Homework called 'the anarchy of competition'. Various factors would seem to have encouraged the predominance of small units of production which frantically competed with each other in undercutting prices. One factor seems to have been the ease of entry into the production of ready-clothing. Workshops and domestic workshops could be set up or homework could be undertaken fairly easily as the essential tool, the sewing machine, was relatively cheap or could be bought on hire purchase. Machines were also lent to tailors by employers and by the Charity Organization Society and the Jewish Board of Guardians. There was often only a thin dividing line between being a worker and becoming an employer. A tailor could take work from a wholesaler and employ his family and neighbours on the various parts of the production process and little or no capital would have been required. In the East End, there was a proliferation of what were ironically called 'garden workshops', that is an extension into the backyard of the home.

At the same time, the high rents in London and the scarce opportunities to build factories discouraged the physical expansion of small workshops or factories even when they prospered. Successful employers tended to move out of London into Essex, and these provincial factories heightened competition amongst the small London employers.

The seasonal nature of the London tailoring trade was also a severe curtailment to its prosperity and further discouraged employers from capital investment in space and machinery which would be underused for perhaps four or five months of the year. A wholesaler was thus better advised to contract his work out in the busy season.

A final factor was the weakness of trade unionism and of

employers' organization at the turn of the century in the London tailoring trade. Both were no doubt a result of the economic vulnerability of the industry. Their lack of organization meant that there was little constraint on the anarchy of competition amongst both employers and workers. Workshops and small factories were set up overnight in the busy season only to disappear in the chaos of price-cutting in the slack season, and the lack of effective organization amongst the workforce or the employers and sub-contractors meant that there was little hope of stabilizing the trade and therefore sparse encouragement for large-scale investment.

Against this background, the clearest correlation with low wages in both factory and workshop production is the employment of women and girls. The breaking down of the production process brought about the employment of women and girls on detailed parts of the garment. The result was that the skill content of the work deteriorated and the workers' control of the work situation diminished. Women were brought in by the skilled tailor to assist them; they were brought in as unskilled unapprenticed labour and it was not in the interest of the tailors' unions to allow them into their organization. Table 3.5 indicates that by the beginning of the twentieth century, there was a clearly defined sexual division of labour in both branches of the London tailoring trade. This sexual division of labour was associated with the clear-cut wage differentials between men and women employed in the trade.

Where the tailor retained control of the work process, as in the bespoke men's tailoring trade, wages for these men remained relatively high. The production of the garment was not broken down into semi-skilled and unskilled tasks and the employment of women and girls was limited. This was the more traditional part of the tailoring trade. By contrast, in the ready-made trade, skilled workers lost a great deal of control, semi-skilled and unskilled work increased, together with the employment of women and girls, and the payment of very low wages was more common. Below subsistence wages could not be said, in this case, to be a feature of an under-developed trade. It is often assumed, however, that there were particular factors operating in London which, in creating a proliferation of small businesses and discouraging the installation of power-driven machinery, were responsible for the London trade being a sweated trade. The high rents and rates in London were obviously a discouragement to the expansion of factory production but is it the case that such an expansion would have diminished the incidence of sweated labour? Leeds, where the tailoring trade was at

TABLE 3.5   THE SEXUAL DIVISION OF LABOUR IN THE
LONDON TAILORING TRADES*

(a) Men and women returned as engaged in the bespoke tailoring trade in
London in 1906 shown according to what percentage of total men and total
women were returned as foremen, cutter, machinist, etc.

	Type of worker	Percentage so returned
Men:	Foremen	1.9
	Cutters	8.3
	Journeymen tailors	51.6
	Machinists	16.3
Boys:	Apprentices	48.1
Women:	Machinists	14.0
Girls:	Machinists	87.6

(b) Men and women returned as engaged in the ready-made tailoring trade
in London in 1906 shown according to what percentage of total men and
total women were returned as foremen, cutter, machinist, etc.

	Type of worker	Percentage so returned
Men:	Foremen	12.0
	Cutters (hand)	28.8
	(machine)	6.2
	Basters	8.8
	Machinists	10.0
	Pressers	13.8
	Warehousemen and packers	11.1
Women:	Forewomen	1.9
	Basters	5.0
	Machinists (hand)	16.0
	(power)	30.0
	Hand sewers and finishers	26.0
	Pressers	5.6
Girls:	Machinists	53.2
	Hand sewers and finishers	4.5

(The number of boys returned are not given according to type of worker)
* The percentages for each category of worker do not add up to 100. The figures are
given here as they appear in the *Report on Earnings and Hours* and we must assume
that those workers not included were employed in a more general capacity. Some of
the younger workers were certainly employed to fetch and carry, clean up, etc. and
some of the women and girls were employed as hand workers on various parts of the
garments.
Source: UK Board of Trade, *Report*, (ii) *Clothing Trades*, PP 1909, LXXX, Cmd.
4844.

its most advanced form at the turn of the century provides a useful basis for examining this question.

The Leeds Tailoring Trade

In the second half of the nineteenth century, Leeds developed as an important centre of the wholesale trade in ready-made men's and boys' outerwear.[29] In the 1850s John Barran was the first wholesale tailor in Leeds to introduce power-driven machines together with the first band-knife and goose irons. Barran had been a cloth dealer but now he went into the business of cutting cloth and bringing in machinists, finishers and pressers to make it up. He also relied heavily on Jewish subcontractors to do the work for which his premises lacked the capacity. The expansion of the trade encouraged a subdivision of labour. Previously, although some of the finishing processes had been undertaken by subsidiary workers, the garment had been 'put together' by the tailor. Now the making up of coats and jackets was divided up into, at first, five or six different operations, and then even more subdivision took place, unskilled and semi-skilled workers being introduced to replace the skilled tailor. When John Burnett carried out his investigation into the Leeds tailoring trade, he found, for instance, that some women were employed solely to sew on buttons.[30] The subdivisional system in Leeds was generally agreed to be more advanced than that in London and this system was developed at its most sophisticated level in the Jewish outworkers' (i.e. contractors') workshops, most of whom were new immigrants, while the small English tailors tried desperately to preserve their skills and status. In the Jewish workshops the workers were split up into teams, each person specializing on one part of the production process. The workshops were larger than those of the London outworkers, indeed some of them should strictly be called factories for small gas engines were installed to drive the machines. Yet it was in some of these more modern workshops/factories that contemporary investigators found sweating to take place. John Burnett reported that 'The largest sweating master in the Leeds trade has 40 machines and the average of machines to each master is somewhere between 20 and 30'.[31] The largest workshops in London, on the other hand, had about eight to ten machines.

As the dilution of skilled labour progressed, so the numbers of women and girls employed increased. This influx of women and girls into the Leeds tailoring trade, accompanied as it was by a division of labour and a dilution of skills, was also associated with the payment of low wages.

The development of the tailoring trade from production dominated by skilled tailors to that dominated by machinists, pressers and other semi-skilled workers was reflected in the changing representation from the clothing trade on the Leeds Trades Council.[32] This also illustrates the influx of Jews and of women into the trade. In the 1850s tailors formed the largest membership represented on the Trades Council, and the delegates were not Jewish, and referred to themselves as master tailors. In 1855, the first tailors' machinists appeared on the Trades Council and these were Jewish men, the forerunners of the fluctuating but steadily growing Union of Jewish Tailors, Tailors' Machinists and Tailors' Pressers. By 1891, the master tailors had lost their dominance of the Trades Council,[33] and the Council was helping the Wholesale Clothers' Operatives Union to increase its membership. In 1889, the tailoresses (that is, machinists) working at Messrs Arthur and Co., wholesale clothiers, came out on strike for the abolition of the 1d charge for steam power. Two male delegates to the Trades Council, together with two middle-class feminists, Isabella Ford and Clementina Black, helped the striking women to form the Leeds Tailoresses Union, and their delegates, Lily Thackray and Maud Storey, were the first women elected on to the Trades Council.[34]

Throughout the second half of the nineteenth century, Leeds employers engaged in the making of men's and juveniles' outerwear went from strength to strength and the 1870s and 1880s saw an expansion of both size of firms and number of firms. This expansion of production also meant an expansion in the work given out to homeworkers, however. Women's wages were higher in Leeds than in London, but they were still below subsistence level (as table 3.3 showed) and although factory production was more common in the Leeds tailoring trade than in London, the Leeds employers were still subject to the accusation of sweating.

In 1888 *The Lancet* published an article which claimed that insanitary conditions and the payment of below subsistence wages existed in Leeds to a far greater extent than was claimed by the large wholesalers.[35] The journal's concern – and that of the people of Leeds – had been aroused by the outbreak of smallpox in an area where tailoring workshops and homeworkers were common. *The Lancet's* investigators visited a neighbourhood which was known for frequent outbreaks of typhus fever and they found work being carried on in unsatisfactory conditions:

> Immediately opposite the door of the common lodging house, from whence nine small pox patients were removed, separated from this door only by the width of a narrow street, is the entrance to an old abandoned mill, where there are no less than five sweaters' workshops. Here, altogether, from 300 to 400 people, for the most part women, are engaged in tailoring.[36]

They also found homeworkers in this district. The sanitary conditions amongst both homeworkers and Jewish workshops were sometimes very bad. *The Lancet* reported that although the workshops in Leeds tended to be bigger than those in the East End of London, they were often just as insanitary. In the 'Jewish Quarter' of the town *The Lancet's* investigators entered a house where there were three different workshops, employing altogether about 160 people and exuding 'a most appalling stench' owing to the lack of sanitary facilities. In the uproar which followed the publication of *The Lancet's* report, the *Leeds Mercury* took up the investigation. They agreed with the findings of *The Lancet* that, while the workshops were large and the middlemen few the amount of contracting out was enormous and much work was done by homeworkers. Very low wages were common. One of the homeworkers visited earned between 5/– and 17/– per week, but 'she has to pay out of this sum for her thread and trimmings, rent, gas, iron – in fact, every incidental expense'.[37] Much was made of the inadequate sanitary facilities:

> The sanitary accommodation is altogether inadequate, and in some cases, the most revolting consequences ensue. In one street, where a great number of tailors live, we found only two closets for seven houses. The houses on this side of the street have no back yards or back windows; and it is therefore no easy matter to supply proper sanitary accommodation . . . . As a result, the whole passage leading to these two closets is one mass of filth. People come here and empty utensils outside the closets, being fearful to approach such foul places. The flagstones are covered with soil, the liquid is seen oozing from under the stones, where it contaminates the subsoil, and passing out into the street, stains the pavement of the causeway till it reaches the gutters. The stench is so great that in the cottage on one side of the passage in question we found the inhabitants could not open their windows. Yet the little room thus deprived of ventilation contained, when we looked in, no less than nine persons huddled together, one of them was a tailor, and there was a child suffering from whooping-cough.[38]

Accusations of sweating, particularly those relating to the payment of very low wages, were not confined to workshop employers. John Barran was frequently accused of sweating his workers[39] and the conditions at his factory prompted many tailoresses employed to attempt to organize into a trade union. A tailoress reported in 1889 that during the previous six years, the prices paid to workers for each garment had been pulled down. This, she said, was a direct result of new machines being introduced, for 'as the manager believed that they would run quicker than the old ones and do the work in less time, the prices were reduced'.[40] Low wages were also reported to be paid in the finishing department of another large Leeds factory where a girl received 4½d for finishing an Eton jacket and vest.

> For this amount she has to fell the neck of the vest, to put the buttons on the coat and waistcoat, then to take the coat and vest to the button-hole machinists and pay 3d for the button-holes on the coat and vest and ½d for the button-holes on the jacket, so that only one penny is left for payment for the rest of the work.[41]

Although the level of wages for women was higher in Leeds than in London bespoke or ready-made trades, the average wage for a woman was still below subsistence. Only forewomen earned a wage adequate for subsistence needs (table 3.3 illustrated the extent of the payment of below subsistence wages in the Leeds ready-made tailoring trade). A man's average wage in the Leeds trade was 1/5d above subsistence level but within six of the 11 different types of work for men in the trade, the average wage was below subsistence. 'Pocket money' wages for girls were universal in the Leeds tailoring trade – as elsewhere in the country. At Barran's, for example, a girl named Mary Ellen Ashton was taken on at 15 years of age for 6/– per week. This was increased by 1/– three months later and then by 1/– per year so that by 1893 she was earning 11/– at the age of 19.[42]

These examples of girls being paid below subsistence wages touch on two fundamental features of the tailoring trade: the competition between indoor and outdoor workers, and the employment of young girls at very low wages. The first girl was competing with homeworkers for the finishing work, for coats and waistcoats were frequently sent out to be finished by homeworkers who accepted the work for lower rates than those paid to 'indoor' workers. Although the number of homeworkers was said to be smaller in Leeds than in East London, they were still estimated to make up between one-fifth and one-eighth of the total workforce engaged in the trade.[43] Wages amongst finishers employed directly by the wholesaler were therefore very vulnerable to being forced down by competition. Both cases demonstrate the way in which girls, who generally lived with their parents, could be paid a below subsistence wage on the grounds that they themselves did not have to meet the full cost of their subsistence.

Investigators such as Charles Booth maintained that the development of factory production in the clothing industry 'with its better sanitary condition and greater regularity of earnings'[44] was diminishing the incidence of sweating in towns such as Leeds. Yet this perception of the nature of factory production is a mistaken one. Bad sanitary conditions may have been less common in factory production but long hours and low wages were encouraged by the system of contracting work out, a system which the ready-made trade evolved in response to the fluctuations in demand for the products of the clothing trades. The Leeds ready-made trade, just as the London trade, was 'essentially a seasonal trade'. This seasonal nature of the trade, together with the ease of entry into tailoring made its employees especially vulnerable to the inevitable outcome of intense competition – the forcing down of wages. Contracting work out was as inherent a part of the Leeds clothing trade as it was of the East London trade. Large wholesalers were more common in Leeds and more work was done on their own premises, but much work was contracted out, not only to workshops and homeworkers but also to smaller factories.

Therefore, the Leeds tailoring trade, like the London trade, was divided into three levels of production, all intimately linked by contracting and subcontracting. The wholesale businesses in Leeds were run by non-Jewish businessmen (who sometimes went into retailing as well), many of whom had been dealers in cloth or clothing. Although some of the wholesalers had attempted to carry out all production under their roof, it was common practice for much of the work to be contracted. The next level was therefore the workshops and smaller factories which took the contracts and the final level was the homeworkers who took work from both wholesaler and contractor.

The fundamental characteristic of sweating – the payment of below subsistence wages – was to be found in Leeds as well as in the London tailoring trade. It becomes clear that the major section of the workforce who received below subsistence wages were the women and girls in both factory and workshop production. It is also clear that, as in the London trade, there was a very definite sexual division of labour which accompanied the large wage differentials between male and female workers (see table 3.6).

TABLE 3.6   THE SEXUAL DIVISION OF LABOUR IN THE LEEDS READY-MADE TAILORING TRADE*

		Percentage so returned
Men:	Foremen	11.7
	Cutters (hand)	26.4
	(machine)	4.8
	Basters	4.7
	Fitters	8.6
	Pressers	12.2
	Warehousemen and packers	15.0
	Enginemen and stokers	2.8
Boys:	Apprentices	11.3
Women:	Forewomen	0.6
	Basters	1.2
	Machinists (power)	58.7
	Hand sewers and finishers	30.0
	Pressers	4.7
Girls:	Basters	1.6
	Machinists (power)	58.1
	Hand sewers and finishers	24.4
	Pressers	2.4

*Men and women returned as engaged in the ready-made tailoring trade in Leeds in 1906 shown according to what percentage of total men and total women were returned as foremen, cutter, machinist, etc.
Source: UK Board of Trade, *Reports*, vol ii *Clothing Trades*, PP 1909, LXXX, Cmd. 4844.

It is evident from this analysis of the London and Leeds tailoring trades that the problem of sweated labour was by no means a problem confined to workshop or domestic production. It is also clear that outworking was as much the basis of the more 'advanced' Leeds trade as it was of the supposedly backward London trade. The main characteristic of sweating – the payment of very low wages – was found in factory as well as workshop production. Furthermore, below subsistence wages were a phenomenon found particularly amongst women workers. This fact was well recognized by contemporary campaigners for minimum wage legislation – particularly by some employers who were concerned about the social consequences of sweated labour.[45]

The causes of low wages in the tailoring trade lie with the sexual division of labour – the ability of employers to split up the work process into many different parts and to employ semi-skilled and unskilled female labour on these new processes at low and very low wages. This is why neither factory and workshop legislation nor, in 1909, the Trade Boards Act (which established minimum wage rates in the industry) made much of an impact on sweating.[46] The Tailoring Trade Board in fact further institutionalized the sexual division of labour by setting different rates for men and women.[47] As long as employers were able to pay women wages which were below subsistence and were justified in doing so because they were supposed to be supplementary to a man's wage, the most important characteristic of sweating – low wages – would continue and does continue today.

Bibliographical Note

Two books recently published on the sweated trades in general are Duncan Bythell's *The Sweated Trades* (Batsford, 1978) and James Schmiechen's *Sweated Industries and Sweated Labor* (Croom Helm, 1984). Earlier secondary sources on the tailoring trade include S.P. Dobbs, *The Clothing Workers of Great Britain* (G. Routledge and Sons, 1926), F. Galton, *The Tailoring Trade* (London School of Economics, 1923), Joan Thomas, *A History of the Leeds Clothing Trade* (Hull Occasional Paper, 1955), and M. Stewart and L. Hunter, *The Needle is Threaded* (Heinemann, Newman and Neame, Southampton, 1964), the latter being the official history of the National Union of Tailor and Garment Workers. In recent years, research by some feminist historians has cast new light on the sexual division of labour in nineteenth-century industries. Of particular interest are Sally Alexander's *Women's Work in Nineteenth Century London: A Study of the years 1820–50*, (Journeyman Press edn 1983), Barbara Taylor 'Sex and Skill' in *Feminist Review*, 6 (1980). For a full bibliography on the subject matter of this chapter the reader is referred to Jenny Morris, 'The Sweated Trades, Women Workers and The Trade Boards Act of 1909: an exercise in social control?', PhD (London School of Economics, 1982).

Notes

1 Schmiechen, *Sweated Industries*.
2 Ibid, ch. 3.

3 Idem, 'State Reform and the Local Economy: An Aspect of Industrialisation in Late Victorian and Edwardian London', *Economic History Review*, 2nd ser., xxviii (1975), pp. 413–28. See also Jenny Morris, 'State Reform and the Local Economy', *Economic History Review*, 2nd ser., xxxv (1982), pp. 292–300, and Schmiechen's reply in the same issue.

4 I have sought to use the sources in a way that promotes an understanding of the intimate details of the work process. The statistics available are unreliable and while they have to be used (for they are all we have), a more comprehensive analysis can be achieved if we use the available sources in a qualitative as well as a quantitative fashion. See Alexander, *Women's Work*, and R. Samuel, 'The Workshop of the World: Steam Power and Hand Technology in mid-Victorian Britain', in *History Workshop*, 3 (1977), which use the resources available.

5 *Fifth Report of the House of Lords Select Committee on the Sweating System*, PP 1890, XVII, Cmd. 169.

6 Ibid, p. xlii.

7 E. Cadbury and G. Shann, *Sweating* (Headley Bros, 1907).

8 UK Board of Trade, *Report of an Enquiry into Earnings and Hours of the Workpeople of the United Kingdom*, vol. ii. *Clothing Trades*, PP 1909 LXXX, Cmd. 4844.

9 C. Booth, *Life and Labour of the People of London* (Macmillan, 1902), vol. 4, p. 53.

10 Ibid, p. 54.

11 *Report of the Committee appointed to consider and advise with regard to the application of the National Insurance Act to Outworkers*, vol. 1, PP 1912–13, XLII, Cmd. 6178.

12 *Report to the Board of Trade on the Sweating System in Leeds*, PP 1888, LXXVI, Cmd. 5513, p. 5.

13 Booth, *Life and Labour*, vol. 7.

14 *Select Committee on Homework*, PP 1908, VIII, Cmd. 246.

15 Ibid, p. 14.

16 Ibid.

17 E. Howarth and M. Wilson, *West Ham: A Study in Social and Industrial Problems* (Dent, 1907).

18 *Select Committee on Homework, Minutes of Evidence*, PP 1908, VIII, Cmd. 246, q. 1133.

19 R. Mudie-Smith (ed.), *Sweated Industries: Being a Handbook of the 'Daily News' Exhibition* (Bradbury, Agnew, 1906).

20 This section on the history of the tailoring trade draws on a long list of primary and secondary sources which can be found in Morris (thesis), 'The Sweated Trades'.

21 Booth, *Life and Labour*, vol. 4, p. 45.

22 Dobbs, *The Clothing Workers*, p. 15.

23 Stewart and Hunter, *The Needle is Threaded*, p. 16.

24 *1891 Census*, PP 1893, CVI, Cmd. 7058.

25 Webb Trade Union Collection, London School of Economics, section A, vol. 47, item 31.

26 *Report of the House of Lords Select Committee on Sweating*, PP 1889, XIV, Cmd. 331, qq 32055, 32060.

27 *Report of the Chief Inspector for Factories and Workshops*, 1905, p. 5.

28 Ada Nield Chew, 'Victims of our Industrial System: I. Tailoresses', *Young Oxford*, vol. ii, no. 18 (March 1901).

29 This section draws on primary and secondary sources given in my thesis and in particular on business records and newspaper cuttings deposited in the Leeds (Chapeltown) Archives Department.

30 *Report to the Board of Trade on the Sweating System in Leeds*, PP 1888, LXXXVI, Cmd. 6513.

31 Ibid., p. 4.

32 Leeds Trades Council, *Annual Reports for the years 1850–1900*.

33 There were now a larger number of delegates from the engineering trades.

34 Leeds Trades Council, *Annual Report for the year 1889*.

35 'Report of Special Sanitary Commission on the Sweating System in Leeds, Part I', *The Lancet*, 9 June 1888, p. 1147.

36 Ibid.

37 *Leeds Mercury*, 16 June 1888.

38 Ibid.

39 *Yorkshire Daily Observer*, 4 May 1905.

40 *Leeds Daily News*, 18 October 1889.

41 Ibid.

42 Barran Collection, Wage Book 1884–1893.

43 *Yorkshire Post*, 23 February 1887 and 12 June 1888.

44 *House of Lords Select Committee on Sweating, 1st Report and Mins. of Evidence*, PP 1888, XX, Cmd. 361, q. 307.

45 *Report of Chief Inspector of Factories and Workshops*, PP 1892, XX, Cmd. 6720, p. 17.

46 See Morris (Thesis), 'The Sweated Trades'. 1982.

47 See this volume, chapters 8 and 9.

Part II

Expansion and Restriction in Employment

The twenty-three domestic servants of Hanham Hall, Suffolk

A maid of all work, 1856

4

Domestic Service
and Household Production
Edward Higgs

The Accepted Image of Nineteenth-Century
Domestic Service

Domestic service is, at first sight, one of the most familiar occupations of the nineteenth century. It may be difficult today to imagine the inside of a Victorian cotton mill or dye works but the image of a small 'alternative community' of paid servants living in the home of a well-to-do family and looking after their personal comforts has been widely disseminated by the media. The world of *Upstairs, Downstairs* is now indelibly printed on the popular historical imagination.

The existing historical literature tends to assume a certain stereotyped image of domestic service.* The 'typical' servant is seen as residing with other servants in an upper or middle-class household and as being part of the ritual of conspicuous consumption for the purposes of status identification. Servant employment is seen as part of the 'paraphernalia of gentility' which defined the middle classes.

This has led to certain assumptions about the effect of domestic service upon servants themselves. Service has been seen by some scholars as a 'bridging occupation' facilitating the movement of rural women into the town, and their acquisition of urban mores and domestic skills. It has been argued that this process, and the ability to save most of their wages, enabled such women to make advantageous marriages and to be upwardly socially mobile.

This assumed link between servant employment and middle-class status has led some scholars to seek the reason for the decline in the

*See bibliographical note for a summary of the existing literature.

relative size of the servant population in the period after 1871 in terms of the assumed financial difficulties of the class at this period. Middle-class parents were supposed to have reduced the size of their families in order to save money and thus needed fewer servants. On the other hand, a 'supply school' exists which sees the decline of domestic service as reflecting the growing availability of alternative employment in transport, retailing and office work. There is, therefore, an apparent contradiction in the literature. On one hand service is seen as an improving and beneficial experience but on the other it is an institution to be avoided if alternatives exist.

In order to to get beyond such stereotypes it is necessary to look at all servants and servant-employing households in order to establish the 'average'. Some servants may have been upwardly mobile, some may have worked for middle-class families, some of the latter may have regarded servant employment as indispensable for the maintenance of their social status, but unless the historian can quantify such phenomena and show them to be numerically significant it is difficult to speak of them as having any social importance. Historians have often failed to do this when examining domestic service in the nineteenth century. Rather than examining a random, and therefore representative, sample of households containing servants, they have tended to study service at the national level through an analysis of manuals of household management such as that of Mrs Beeton, the account books of aristocratic households and the numbers of servants found in the occupational tables of the published census reports. The history of domestic service has tended to be written in terms of what Mrs Beeton said about their duties or what went on in the homes of dukes and duchesses. The use of such sources reflects the difficulty of examining an occupation which was so widely scattered throughout the country in small household units and which was without any collective organization. Most industries and occupational groups in this period are studied through the records produced by capitalist firms and trade unions, or by parliamentary committees reporting on their activities. But domestic servants did not form trade unions, nor were they employed by large organizations, and, as a consequence, nor did they interest parliament.

The sources used to write such histories have serious limitations. The most detailed and comprehensive records showing domestic life in the nineteenth century come from the largest households. Records from lower middle and working-class homes are not as detailed, have not survived or were never produced in the first place. It is to the detailed account books, reminiscences and diaries of the landed classes that the historians of domestic service have turned. In Horn's *The Rise and Fall of the Victorian Servant*, for example, of those employers mentioned whose rank or employment is indicated, over 60 per cent were titled or landed proprietors. In Burnett's *Useful Toil*, a collection of working-class autobiographies, a similar proportion of the employers mentioned by his servants were from this social milieu.[1] Relying on the use of domestic manuals, such as Mrs Beeton's *Book of Household Management*, to write such histories is equivalent to reconstructing the average modern home from the pages of *Vogue*. As Branca has shown, the 'normal' middle-class servant retinue of cook, parlourmaid and nursemaid described in such works would have been totally beyond the means of most middle-class families with an income of between £100 and £300 a year.[2] Such manuals reflected the aspirations and daydreams of middle-class families rather than the realities of their lives. Lastly, although the published results of the nineteenth-century censuses give the number in servant occupations both nationally and by locality, it is difficult to establish what is meant by the term 'servant' in this context. When used in the census it could cover, as we shall see, a wide spectrum of social relationships and tasks performed. Works based on such sources have great difficulty in getting behind the image of Victorian service to its reality.

But given these problems, how can the historian study the individual circumstances of hundreds of thousands of households in order to determine that which was normal? Such a study would also need to examine local and regional differences which might be of fundamental importance. It is unlikely that any single research project will ever have the resources to study every servant in the nineteenth century or enough samples of servants in individual localities to build up a picture of the circumstances of the entire servant population. A way round this problem would be to examine representative samples of servant populations in particular localities. This would enable historians to ask quantitative questions about such servants. If multiplied for differing areas such studies would eventually produce a realistic picture of the national servant and servant-employing populations.

But where is it possible to find a source which provides information on every servant and servant employer in a particular locality? The answer lies in the documentation produced in the course of taking the nineteenth-century censuses of population. From 1841 onwards temporary enumerators were employed every ten years by the General Register Office to leave householders with a census schedule to fill in. In the mid-nineteenth century householders were asked to provide information on the name, relationship to household head, marital status, sex, age, occupation and birthplace of each member of the household resident there on census night. These schedules were collected by the enumerators and copied into printed books which were then forwarded to a Census Office in London. In London the information in the enumerators' books was tabulated and the results published as part of a decennial census report. These give the number of people, their ages, sex, occupations, birthplaces, etc., both for the whole country and broken down by locality.[3] These published figures have been used widely by historians, including those working on domestic service. These tables are, however, one dimensional. They tell the historian that a certain number of people in a locality were servants but they do not indicate where these individuals came from. This information can be found, however, in the original enumerators' books which are currently available for public inspection at the Public Record Office for the years 1841 to 1881.[4]

The local servant population examined below is that of the registration district of Rochdale in Lancashire in the years 1851, 1861 and 1871. This was a rapidly expanding industrial district of about 50 square miles centred on the town of Rochdale. Its population growth in this period was spectacular, rising from 72,515 in 1851 to 109,858 in 1871.[5] The basis of this growth was the employment opportunities offered by the manufacture of cotton and woollen textiles. In 1861 such manufacture employed 40 per cent of the occupied males aged 20 years and over, and 60 per cent of occupied women of the same age. The comparable figures for England and Wales were 7 per cent and 14 per cent respectively.[6] As such, Rochdale was a very different place from the estates of the landed gentry which bulk so large in some histories of nineteenth-century domestic service. In some senses the area might also be said to represent future trends since in the course of the nineteenth and early twentieth centuries much of the population of England and Wales came to live in such large towns as opposed to the countryside. For comparison some material has been collected and analysed for the predominantly rural county of Rutlandshire in 1871.

In order to study the homes in which servants were employed, as well as the servants themselves, it was necessary to sample households containing servants and not just the individuals in servant occupations. A 'servant-employing household' was defined as one containing someone with a servant occupation.[7] This definition of the unit of analysis had very interesting implications for the resulting study since many people with servant occupations were not 'servants' in relationship to the head of the household in which they lived. Many were living with relatives.

Once these households had been identified in the Rochdale district, 25 per cent were selected randomly from each census for further analysis. The resulting samples for the years 1851, 1861 and 1871 contained 530, 726 and 1,021 servants and 433, 677 and 900 households respectively. The information contained in the Census enumerators' books was converted into a machine readable form and analysed by computer to produce various cross-tabulations and statistical measurements.[8] Such an analysis would not reveal whether the characteristics of servants and their employers were in any sense unusual when compared with the rest of Rochdale's population. Thus, the proportion of servants who were born outside Rochdale may have been over 75 per cent. Was this a peculiarity of the servant population or did it merely represent a high rate of in-migration for all people in Rochdale? In order to answer such questions a 'control sample' of 200 randomly chosen households was selected from each census and analysed in the same manner as the households containing servants.

An objection to such an analysis could be that any results based on samples could merely reflect chance. The samples might contain an unusually large number of untypical households. Chance, however, works according to mathematical rules. If a coin is flipped a sufficiently large number of times, about 50 per cent of the results will be heads and about 50 per cent tails. If there are enough households in the sample it is possible to calculate statistically how confident one can be that the sample's characteristics approximate to those of the underlying population. It is possible to be 99 or 95 per cent certain that the figures derived from a sample are the same as those which would have been found in the total population plus or minus a certain amount. Using such statistical techniques it is also possible to be 95 per cent certain that the difference between the characteristics of two samples (one containing, for example, more migrants than the other) reflects a real difference in the populations from which the samples were drawn and is not due to 'sampling errors', i.e. to chance. In these circumstances it is the convention to say that the difference is 'statistically significant at the 95 per cent level'. There is thus a one in 20 chance that the difference between the two samples merely reflects 'bad luck' with respect to the households which were chosen for analysis.[9]

The analysis of this data reveals a rather different picture of domestic service from the usual stereotype.

Service and Kinship in the Nineteenth-Century Census

As was noted above, the criterion used to select households in the censuses for analysis was that they contained individuals who were described as following a servant occupation. When the resulting samples of households were examined, however, it became apparent that many of the servants they contained were not servants in relationship to the head of the household in which they lived. In 1851 such people accounted for only 56 per cent of the 367 'servants' over the age of 19 years in the sample. This proportion had fallen to a mere third in 1871. The vast majority of the rest were related by kinship to the household head.

What was the status of these servant-relatives and what sort of work were they performing? There are several possibilities. They may have been day-servants who returned home at night to sleep.[10] They may have been unemployed and the householder neglected to note this in the household schedule. Lastly, they may have been performing domestic tasks at home for their relatives. Revealingly, the terminology of domestic servitude may have been applied to the work of women in the home. The census itself cannot tell the historian directly which of these possibilites is most important in explaining the phenomena observed. There are patterns in the data, however, which suggest that many of these women may indeed have been working at home for their kin.

About 12 or 13 per cent of the servants over the age of 19 years in the three samples were women whose relationship to the head of the household was that of lodger, or men in occupations such as gardener, coachman or groom. Such people may well have been day-servants who did not sleep in the homes of their employers.

A numerically more important group were those women described as 'housekeeper' or 'servant working at home' whose relationship to the head of the household was one of kinship. These women represented 15 per cent of the servants over the age of 19 years in the 1851 sample, 36 per cent in 1861, and no less than 45 per cent in 1871. The housekeepers made up the largest portion of this group, servants 'working at home' representing only half of one per cent of the total in 1871. Between 36 and 40 per cent of these women in the three samples were heads of households. They were often widows who presumably looked after the home whilst their children were at work. In 1861, for example, Alice Coupe of the High Street, Rochdale, was enumerated as a 'housekeeper'. She was 69 years old and the widowed head of a household which comprised her two daughters, a niece, a son-in-law and a granddaughter. All, apart from Mrs Coupe and her granddaughter, were employed outside the home.

In 1851, 23 per cent of this whole group were wives of household heads and this had risen to 40 per cent in 1871. For some enumerators 'housekeeper' and 'housewife' were synonymous. The rest of the sub-set were the sisters, mothers and other female relatives of single or widowed male heads. In 1851, for example, 85 per cent of all male heads in the Rochdale control sample were married but this proportion was reduced to 57 per cent amongst the males heading households containing servants in this group.[11] The probability is that most of this group were performing domestic tasks at home for their kin.

In 1851, 36 households contained 'nurses' who were relatives of the household heads, and there were 22 and 17 such households in 1861 and 1871 respectively. These households contained significantly large numbers of children. Over half contained three or more in 1871 compared to 15 per cent of the control sample households. Many of these 'nurses' were themselves under the age of ten years; 18 out of 38 in 1851. A considerable proportion of these 'servants' may therefore have been childminders for the family or for neighbours.[12]

The residual group of servants whose relationship to the head of the household was one of kinship numbered 88, 99 and 83 in the three census samples. They lived in households which exhibited aggregate characteristics suggesting that extra domestic help was required there. This is not to say that such 'servants' necessarily worked at home but it is suggestive of the possibility. Such households had a low proportion of married heads. In 1851, for example, 48 per cent of the 79 households contained a married head compared with 72 per cent amongst the Rochdale control sample. In the absence of a housewife, and given the separation of spheres which placed a taboo on men working in the home, such households would require extra domestic help. Despite the absence of married couples such households tended to be large. In 1861, 67 per cent of the 94 households in this group contained five or more people, compared with 45 per cent in the control sample. These households were also, on average, of a fairly high social status. In 1871, 19 per cent of the 80 households were in Social Economic Groups 1 and 2, using the Booth-Armstrong classification.[13] This compares with a figure of only 8 per cent in the control sample.

A few examples will help to indicate the sort of households which could appear in this sub-set. In 1861 the family of John Smith of Moorhouse comprised his wife, two employed sons in their twenties and three daughters, one of whom was described as a 'housemaid'. The Smith household did not contain any servants even though he was a woollen manufacturer employing 68 hands. In the same census James Lord, a calico manufacturer employing 12 hands, lived with his wife, daughter, two adult sons and 76 year old mother-in-law at 175 Broadoath Lane. The latter was described as 'House Cook'. Lord was hardly likely to be sending out his aged relative to cook in the homes of his social equals.

The existence of such usages makes the interpretation of the published census tables somewhat problematical. In 1851, for example, the published census gave the number of servants in Rochdale aged 20 years and over as 1,425. The full servant sample gave an estimated figure of 1,468 for the same age group. Similarly, the sample indicated that there were 264 housekeepers in this age group whilst the published tables gave the number as 262.[14] The census clerks plainly counted everybody described as having a servant occupation as being a domestic servant despite the confusion between domestic service and the work of women in the family home. The distinction made between paid employees and poor relatives might, of course, have been a narrow one.[15] The above analysis suggests, however, that such terms as 'housekeeper', 'general servant' and 'nurse' do not necessarily imply any contractual relationship between employer and employee when used in the census tables.

If it is assumed, for argument's sake, that all those women in servant occupations whose relationship to the household head was one of kinship were working at home for their relatives, and were not domestic servants in the sense of being employed for wages, then the census figures for domestic service in Rochdale in 1851 would have to be reduced by a third. If this was repeated across England and Wales this would reduce the official number of servants by hundreds of thousands. The number of 'classical' servants in the popular sense would thus be greatly reduced. Rochdale may, of course, have been unusual in this respect but some support for this view is given by an analysis of a one in four sample of households containing servants in Rutlandshire in 1871. A quarter of the people in servant occupations here were living with household heads with whom their relationship was not that of 'servant'.

Given this ambiguity, all those in servant occupations whose relationship to the head of the household was not 'servant' were excluded from further analysis. The residual sub-samples for the three censal years contained 228, 233 and 282 households, and 296, 315 and 402 servants respectively. The rest of this study focuses more closely on these servants and the households in which they lived.

Servant Employers
in Mid-Nineteenth Century Rochdale

An analysis of this remaining group of households indicates that a neat identification of servant employment and the middle classes is too simplistic. It is true that in 1871 the 'middle classes' (defined as the professions, proprietors of land and houses, manufacturers employing two or more hands, farmers and retailers) represented 64 per cent of the heads of servant-employing households but only 19 per cent of the heads in the control sample. An analysis of all households with heads in Social Economic Group 1 in Rochdale in the same census revealed, however, that one-third did not contain living-in servants on census night. Many of the heads of such households may have employed day-servants but still others regarded their own children as domestic help. Nelson Brierly of Haugh Heyside, a woollen carder employing 30 hands, described his eldest daughter as a 'Domestic at home'. Similarly, James Meanwood, a master dyer employing 25 hands, described his three eldest daughters, aged 17 to 20 years, as performing 'Home duties'.

At the same date 16 per cent of the heads of households were apparently in artisan or manual occupations. As Prochaska has recently pointed out, the employment of servants by such people need not necessarily represent conspicuous consumption since the work-house provided a ready supply of girls who could be employed without wages in return for their board.[16] Of the people who took girls from the Rochdale Workhouse in the period 1851 to 1870, the occupations of 97 can be identified. Just over half of these were manual workers; factory operatives, joiners, weavers, miners and the like.[17]

If the correlation between status and servant employment was not exact it is necessary to look more closely at servant-employing households to see why they required extra domestic labour. Servant employment also varied according to the life-cycle stage of the families involved.[18] The figures in table 4.1 indicate that, when compared with the control samples, servant-employing households with heads in all Social Economic Groups tended to be concentrated in life-cycle stage 0, that is, where there was no married couple.[19] Servant-employing families with heads in the first three Social Economic Groups were also concentrated in life-cycle stage 3, where there were children at home but none was in employment.[20] This pattern was also found by Ebery and Preston in their study of 10 per cent samples of households in 20 English districts in the 1871 census. Only an average of 61 per cent of servant-employing households in their samples contained a wife, compared with 74 per cent amongst all households.[21] Servant employment can be seen, therefore, as a reaction amongst all social classes to the crises of Victorian family life, such as the death of a wife and mother, or the birth of children. In a society where household work was regarded as the woman's sphere of activity, the loss, incapacity or absence of a wife necessitated the recruitment of extra domestic help. The ability to meet such domestic crises through servant employment reflected the middle-class ability to pay for necessary services, as well as the search for status.

TABLE 4.1   LIFE-CYCLE STAGE OF SERVANT-EMPLOYING
FAMILIES, RESULTS 1851–71 POOLED*

Social-Economic Group	Life-Cycle Stage (%)							Cases
	0	1	2	3	4	5	6	
1 Professional	30.4	7.5	3.5	35.8	5.0	8.0	10.0	201
2 Intermediate	31.5	7.9	3.5	36.0	5.9	10.8	4.4	203
3 Skilled manual	31.8	6.1	1.5	40.2	5.8	9.6	5.0	261
4 Partly skilled	57.9	5.3	0.0	21.1	0.0	5.3	10.5	19
5 Unskilled	46.2	7.7	0.0	23.0	0.0	23.0	0.0	13
6 Unknown	93.8	0.0	0.0	0.0	0.0	0.0	6.3	16
7 Indeterminate	85.7	0.0	0.0	10.7	3.6	0.0	0.0	28
Rochdale households	22.2	9.7	5.5	25.2	6.2	24.5	5.5	598

* Households in *known* life-cycle stages as a percentage of all households; see note 18 for an explanation of life-cycle stages; see note 13 for an explanation of social-economic groups.

Source: Compiled from Rochdale Servant Household Data Base.

The middle-class propensity to employ servants may also have reflected the special economic functions of some of their homes. The largest occupational group amongst the heads of servant-employing households was retailers of one sort or other. Households headed by retailers contained between one-quarter and one-third of all servants in the three censal years. This group of shopkeepers, butchers, grocers, drapers, innkeepers and restaurant owners contained the 'typical' servant employer. Horn confirms this picture in her study of the rural market towns of Wantage, Thame and Fakenham, in which about two-fifths of the servant-employing heads were small tradesmen 'drapers, grocers, plumbers, coal merchants, corn dealers and the like'.[22] In a rural district such as Rutlandshire, a large proportion of the servant employers were farmers. Thus out of the one in four sample of persons in servant occupations in the county, 148 contained servants whose relationship to the head of the household was that of 'servant'. Of these households 37 per cent were headed by farmers and 19 per cent by retailers.

Were these domestic servants rigorously segregated from the productive activities of such households, that is, from agricultural production and retailing? The 'gentrification' of farming households and the rise of chain stores and the lock-up shop noted during the nineteenth century may have dissociated the homes of shopkeepers and farmers from their places of work.[23] In many cases, however, this segregation can hardly have been possible. A recent survey of women who were servants in Edwardian Lincolnshire reveals that they were expected to undertake many agricultural tasks, such as tending animals, milking cows, making butter and cheese, and so on.[24] The evidence from Rochdale points to similar ambiguities in the households of retailers in the mid-nineteenth century. On 9 May 1851, for example, Lazarus Collinge of Market Place, Heywood, a confectioner, appeared before the Workhouse Committee of the Board of Guardians and applied for Elizabeth Holt from the Spotland Workhouse 'to learn his trade and perform domestic duties'. The same source also reveals that on 11 May 1866, 'Robert Whitehead of Hamer Place, Bread Baker, had a girl named Catherine Garner who was sent out to sell late at night'. The girl had been employed by Whitehead 'to be a servant' a fortnight before and was selling bread and cakes in the street.[25] Much the same could be said no doubt about the many 'general servants' who were employed by innkeepers and beer sellers.

The correlation between middle-class status and servant employment might also not be a direct one. Servants might not have been status symbols in their own right but a necessary adjunct to running that supreme focus of conspicuous consumption, the Victorian home. Entertaining, the emphasis placed on privacy and the sheer inefficiency of the heating and cooking facilities of mid-Victorian houses must all have contributed to the demand for domestic labour.

This analysis suggests a shift in the emphasis of the study of nineteenth-century domestic service away from a discussion of middle-class status towards an appreciation of the productive work of women in the home. Servants were employed in the homes of retailers, farmers and members of all social classes to perform productive work; caring for animals, making cheese, tending the shop, cooking, cleaning, making fires, fetching and carrying water, helping out during times of domestic crisis and so on. Although social status was a major determinant of servant employment it was not the only one. The employment of servants may have reflected a greater demand and ability to pay for labour within the middle-class home rather than any simplistic equation of such employment with the maintenance of status.

The history of the home as a place of production is only just beginning to be written despite its importance for an understanding of economic change.[26] The role of the work of domestic servants is an important part of that story.

The 'Typical' Servant in Mid-Victorian Rochdale

Domestic servants in Rochdale during this period were not associated exclusively with well-to-do households with large servant retinues. Indeed the typical servant in Rochdale was the maid-of-all-work who was the only living-in servant in the household. Servants did not usually live in large domestic establishments with other servants and did not have specialized duties. In Rochdale in 1851, 61 per cent of all servants were the only resident domestic in the households in which they were enumerated. The servant-employing household with only one resident domestic was typical of the country as a whole. Thus, in the 20 representative districts in the 1871 census sampled by Ebery and Preston, the average proportion of servant-employing households with only one servant was 63 per cent.[27] Similarly, 68 per cent of the servants in the 1871 sample of Rochdale were general servants, compared with an average of 54 per cent amongst the 20 districts sampled by Ebery and Preston.[28] Such a picture could not be derived from Mrs Beeton's manual, where out of 63 pages devoted to the servant household in her 1863 edition only five were devoted to the maid-of-all-work, whilst seven pages were given over to the footman, eight to the lady's maid and no less than 13 to the upper and under housemaids.[29]

Domestic service was predominantly a life-cycle occupation. It was a job for women between leaving home and getting married. Amongst general servants in Rochdale in 1871, 53 per cent were aged between 15 and 24 years whilst 71 per cent of all servants were aged under 30. In England and Wales as a whole in 1871, 59 per cent of all female indoor servants were aged between 15 and 24 years. Of the 270 female general servants in Rochdale in 1871, 88.5 per cent were single, whilst the percentage for other female servants was 87 per cent. Servants were mainly young, unmarried women. There is evidence, however, that some women remained in domestic service as a career in preference to, or default of, marriage. Of the 36 general servants in the 1871 sample aged over 40, half had never been married, compared with 10 per cent of the 103 Rochdale women in the same age group in the 1871 control sample. Amongst the 22 other, more specialized, servants of the same age the proportion of single women was as high as 64 per cent.

Nineteenth-Century Domestic Service and Social Mobility

Service has often been interpreted as an improving and educative process which enabled servants to be upwardly mobile through marriage. It certainly appears to have been a comparatively well-paid occupation in this period. In Table 4.2 some crude wage-rates for general servants and cooks are compared with annual wages paid to women in industry.[30]

These figures are, of course, hopelessly inadequate. The servants' wages do not take into account local variations or differentials due to age and experience. They overlook the role of tips in the income of servants[31] and the possibility that girls from the workhouse could be hired for no wages at all. Above all they ignore the value of board and lodgings provided to servants. According to Anderson the minimum cost of subsistence in Lancashire in the period was 5/6d a week.[32] In table 4.2, 5/– a week has been added to the annual wages of domestic servants to give the final income in brackets. This is undoubtedly an underestimate since even Anderson's figure allows

TABLE 4.2 AVERAGE WAGES (£ PER ANNUM) FOR GENERAL SERVANTS AND COOKS IN ENGLAND, 1823–1907

Date	General Servants	Cooks	Female Workers in Wool	Cotton	General Industrial Average
1823–27	7.7 (19.7)	12.5 (24.5)	—	22.9	19.3
28–32	9.2 (21.2)	12.5 (24.5)	—	—	18.6
33–37	9.5 (21.5)	12.3 (24.3)	20.6	20.8	19.1
38–42	10.4 (22.4)	13.5 (25.5)	19.1	18.8	19.1
43–47	12.5 (24.5)	14.5 (26.5)	19.1	20.6	19.1
48–52	11.4 (23.4)	14.9 (26.9)	20.2	20.6	19.6
53–57	12.6 (24.6)	15.0 (27.0)	—	20.8	20.8
58–62	11.7 (23.7)	16.3 (28.3)	25.8	22.1	22.9
63–67	12.8 (24.8)	20.4 (32.4)	28.8	24.9	24.9
68–72	13.3 (25.3)	18.7 (30.7)	29.9	25.2	27.2
73–77	13.2 (25.2)	29.8 (41.8)	32.0	32.7	30.6
78–82	14.4 (26.4)	22.0 (34.0)	34.0	28.4	31.0
83–87	14.0 (26.0)	29.7 (41.7)	31.9	34.7	29.2
88–92	16.1 (28.1)	29.1 (41.1)	30.3	35.7	33.8
93–97	18.8 (30.8)	24.0 (36.0)	30.3	37.1	31.2
1904	16.7 (28.7)	23.4 (35.4)	—	—	—
1907	18.0 (30.0)	29.1 (41.1)	—	—	—

Source: See note 30, p. 148

nothing for washing or clothing. It was also generally considered that the food and lodgings of servants were superior to those of most other working women.[33] The resulting wage-rates for domestics are not beyond the bounds of possibility. Contemporary advertisements in the *Rochdale Observer* carry wages roughly equivalent to the wage-rates in table 4.2.[34] Similarly, mid-nineteenth-century manuals of domestic economy regarded the cost of a female servant as about £25 per annum all in.[35] It must also be noted that the wages of women in industry assume no stoppages and constant work and therefore represent an upper bound. The latter are also far in excess of what women could earn in the countryside. Given that the figures for domestics are almost certainly too low whilst those for other women are undoubtedly too high, they indicate that servants had a relatively good income.[36]

One might therefore assume that service would have been perceived by Rochdale women as a good job opportunity but this does not appear to have been the case. Comparatively few local women could be found amongst the servant population. Amongst the 196 women aged between ten and 30 years in the 1851 control sample, 70 per cent had been born in the Rochdale district. Amongst the sample of servants at this date the equivalent figure was only 38 per cent. The proportion of Rochdale-born women in the control sample 20 years later had fallen to 61 per cent but the figure for the Rochdale women in the servant sample had declined even further to 21 per cent. In 1871, 60 per cent of all servants were born 30 or more miles from Rochdale, compared with 23 per cent of the women aged ten to 30 years in the control sample.

As can be seen from table 4.3, the tendency was for the servant population to become more migrant over time, with a disproportionate increase in the number of women from English counties south of Lancashire and from Wales. These areas provided 21 per cent of all servants in 1851 but 44 per cent in 1871. There is also an interesting pattern of expansion as the main area of recruitment spread from Lancashire in 1851, to Lancashire and Yorkshire in 1861 and then southwards in 1871 to those counties stretching in a line from Caernarvonshire to Lincolnshire.

This propensity to recruit migrants could be seen as an attempt to employ servants from a rural background. Women from agricultural

TABLE 4.3   THE AREAS WHERE SERVANTS WERE BORN, 1851–71

	1851		1861		1871	
Area of birth %	Servants	Rochdale females (10–30)	Servants	Rochdale females (10–30)	Servants	Rochdale females (10–30)
Rochdale	38.2	70.4	22.2	69.8	20.9	60.7
Lancs.	15.2	13.3	17.2	13.2	14.4	15.8
Yorks.	16.6	11.2	24.1	5.7	11.9	7.7
South England*	14.6	1.4	16.2	2.8	29.6	6.8
North England**	3.4	0.8	1.2	0.0	1.4	1.1
Wales	6.1	0.0	8.5	0.5	14.7	2.5
Scotland	0.3	0.2	3.1	0.0	3.0	1.6
Ireland	5.0	2.7	6.9	8.0	4.1	3.8
Abroad	0.6	0.0	0.6	0.0	0.0	0.0
Cases	296	196	315	212	402	183

*English Counties South of Lancashire and Yorkshire.
**English Counties North of Lancashire and Yorkshire.

Source: compiled from Rochdale Servant Household Data Base and control samples.

areas have commonly been associated with domestic service in such diverse societies as nineteenth-century Lancashire, Germany and France, and modern Peru.[37] Advertisements for servants in the Rochdale press contain clauses such as 'one from the country preferred', which indicate such a preference in the district in the nineteenth century.[38]

Various reasons can be advanced for this phenomenon. Rural women could be seen as cheap labour, whilst some regarded women from urban backgrounds as sexually promiscuous and bereft of domestic accomplishments.[39] Rural women may have been perceived as a cheap source of labour given the lack of employment opportunities for women in the countryside,[40] and the inability of such women to find employment in urban industries where family links appear to have been of paramount importance in recruitment.[41] According to Ernest Gittins, who was a plainclothes policeman in Rochdale in the 1920s and who was charged with the supervision of local employment agencies, many country girls who came to the town, 'did not get work in factories or shops in town as this would mean finding accommodation and having to pay their way, and then probably most of these girls had never been in a factory or large town'.[42]

These explanations, however, do not stand up to serious examination. If rural women were a cheap source of labour, why did the incomes of servants approximate to those of women industrial workers? If it were the case one would expect rural women to be distributed evenly throughout the servant employing population. In fact rural-born servants were most heavily concentrated in the households of the highest social classes. Thus in 1851, 24 per cent of servants in Social Economic Group 1 households came from settlements with fewer than 5,000 inhabitants, compared with 9 per cent employed by household heads in Social Economic Group 3. The rural districts of nineteenth-century England also had the highest levels of illegitimate births and some of the lowest standards of living.[43] Rural-born women were, therefore, neither particularly chaste nor used to elaborate cooking and other skilled domestic tasks.

Similarly, there is little statistical evidence that servants made, in general, particularly 'good' marriages. Despite the anecdotal evidence of well-to-do ladies who liked to see their employment of servants as an act of improving charity, a servant in nineteenth-century Lancashire does not appear to have been regarded as a 'good catch' for an aspiring working-class man.

In the absence of suitable marriage records from Rochdale, a study was made of the parish registers of St John the Evangelist in Preston, another Lancashire textile town, for the years 1851 to 1856.[44] These records give the ages of servants and other women at first marriage and the occupations of their fathers and husbands. It is possible to calculate the average age of servants at first marriage, to establish a rough measurement of the social status of their fathers and husbands and to compare these with similar figures for other women.[45]

The results of this exercise are striking. Servants do *not* appear to have been upwardly socially mobile. In table 4.4 the women analysed have been divided into categories according to the Social Economic Group of their fathers. Within these sub-groups the average social economic status of the husbands of servants and other women at first marriage has been compared. Since husbands in Social Economic Groups 6 and 7 were of indefinite social status they were removed from the calculations. By summing the social economic value for each woman's husband an average value was obtained. Since value 1 stood for the highest Social Economic Group and 5 for the lowest, the larger the value of the resulting average the lower the average social status of the husbands. As can be seen, servants within each of the Social Economic Groups tended to marry husbands of a *lower* social economic status than their peers.

TABLE 4.4 SERVANTS AND OTHER WOMEN AT FIRST MARRIAGE IN PRESTON. THE AVERAGE SOCIAL ECONOMIC CLASS OF HUSBANDS OF FEMALES IN DIFFERENT SOCIAL CLASSES*

Social economic group of father	*Average social economic class of husbands*			
	Servants	Cases	Other Women	Cases
Group 1	3.0	1	2.3	11
Group 2	3.5	47	3.1	109
Group 3	3.4	90	3.2	876
Group 4	3.7	22	3.2	117
Group 5	3.6	67	3.5	267
Group 6	3.8	8	3.3	89
Group 7	3.0	1	2.4	9

* See note 13, p. 147 for an explanation of social economic groups.

Source: Manchester Central Library, MFPR 242–259.

This pattern was not confined to mid-nineteenth-century Lancashire. Wilcox has come to similar conclusions after pursuing a more rigorous examination of marriage patterns in Victorian Cambridge.[46] Given the nature of the evidence and the blunt methodological tools used, these results are not particularly robust but they point consistently in the same direction and that is towards service as a channel of *downward* social mobility.

A more likely explanation of the preference for employing rural women, and perhaps for the propensity of servants to be downwardly socially mobile on marriage, may be the social stigma attached to such employment amongst the urban population. According to the Women's Industrial Council in 1916,

> It is very difficult to analyse the cause of the 'social stigma' [attached to domestic service]. Clearly it does exist, but by no means universally. In the country, as many mistresses point out when describing their former maids' marriages, the servants often represent the 'aristocracy of the village'. In many towns, especially small towns, the girl who goes into service does not lose caste, partly because there are so few alternative occupations for her. It is chiefly in the suburbs of the large towns and the industrial districts that the caste difficulty crops up.[47]

Flora Thompson tells us that in Oxfordshire villages servants home on holiday were regarded as objects of admiration and encouraged to walk out in their town clothes 'in order to impress the neighbours'. On the other hand, a cook in Preston in 1916 could complain that, 'in this part of the country servants are treated very badly. They think that because we are in service, we spent our early days in prison'.[48]

This difference in attitude might well be attributed to differences in employment opportunities for young women. Compared with the countryside such opportunities were far greater in the towns especially in the textile districts of the industrial North. As was noted above, even if rural women moved to the towns, they had little chance of obtaining such employment. Access to wages gave young urban women greater independence. As one contemporary noted,

> Children frequently leave their parents at a very early age in the manufacturing districts. Girls of sixteen, and lads of seventeen, find that they can enjoy greater liberty, and if not greater comforts, that at least they can have their way more completely in a separate house, and these partings cause little surprise or disturbance.[49]

For such women service was an unacceptable occupation given the inherent limitations to personal freedom consequent upon being at the constant beck and call of employers. They also objected to the institutionalized marks of servitude, such as the distinctive uniform and being called by one's christian name unbidden. Again, according to the Women's Industrial Council in 1916,

> In the face of the persuasion of teachers and mothers and outside 'social superiors' the most promising girls are apt to prefer lower wages, less material comfort and much less security of employment in shop or office or factory work, to the oft quoted advantages of domestic service.[50]

Faced with such attitudes, 'unspoilt' country women must have seemed much more suitable for domestic employment.[51]

It may be too simplistic, therefore, to view domestic service as a 'bridging occupation' between the rural and the urban world. It may have been a physical but not a cultural bridge. Indeed the institution may have served to maintain rural deference in the urban milieu and thus to insulate part of the ex-rural population from the dominant ideology of the urban working classes.

The Decline of Domestic Service

A similar process of historical revision may need to be undertaken with regard to the causes of the decline in domestic service in the late nineteenth century. The arguments of the 'demand school' do not appear to fit the facts. If the middle-class demand for servants was falling one would not expect the wage-rates for servants to be rising (see table 4.2). Nor would one expect the difficulty of getting servants and keeping them to be a proverbial complaint in the late Victorian and Edwardian periods. The middle classes were not facing an economic crisis in these years. The rate of increase in their real incomes was slowing down but was still increasing at a higher rate throughout the period 1871 to 1901 than it was in the 1850s, when servant numbers were rising.[52] Banks's argument is also circular since servants were part of that 'paraphernalia of gentility' which he argues the middle classes wished to maintain by reducing their expenditure on children. In any case the decline in the size of the middle-class family appears to have been under way prior to 1851.[53]

There is evidence that a crisis in the Rochdale servant market was imminent in the early 1870s and there was little indication of a slackening of local demand for domestics at this date. In the *Rochdale Observer* in the period 1856 to 1866 the number of positions advertised by employers never rose above 50 per annum but after this date the figure was consistently higher, reaching 108 per annum in 1871. Similarly, there were never more than 3 servant registries advertising each year in the *Rochdale Observer* before 1869, but there were 7 doing so in that year and 11 in 1870. In the latter year registries advertised themselves 123 times compared with an average of just four times per year in the period 1856 to 1868. In April 1866 the local Poor Law Guardians refused to let out young girls from the workhouse as domestics until the workhouse itself was 'better supplied with servants'.[54] Prior to 1866 annual wages paid to servants in the Rochdale workhouse had never risen above £7 16s 0d but in August of that year a servant was hired at £12 per annum and by 1879 wages as high as £20 were recorded.[55] A supply side crisis appeared imminent with too many would-be employers chasing too few servants.

If there was a supply side crisis what was its root cause? The oft quoted argument that 'alternative' employment opportunities existed for women in catering, retailing, transport and business in the late nineteenth century is superficial. More women may have been working in these economic sectors in 1901 than in 1851 but could the rural women who worked as domestics in the mid-century have found and kept such employment? These industries were predominantly urban phenomena employing urban women. Rural women still went into domestic service, as Flora Thompson testifies.[56] By the end of the century, however, there were far fewer rural women as the population in the countryside diminished. Thus the number of male agricultural labourers and farm servants recorded in the 1851 census of England and Wales was 1,097,800 but this figure had declined to 735,000 by 1891.[57] A similar decline in the number of families headed by such men would have seriously reduced the pool of daughters for recruitment into domestic service. As Burnett puts it, 'Once settled in a town and educated at a town elementary school . . . [women] were more likely to look to factory or shop work than to what was increasingly considered a low status occupation, fit only for country bumpkins and orphan girls from the local Poor Law Institutions'.[58] It was probably this decline which created the supply side crisis in the domestic service labour market in the late nineteenth century.[59]

Urban women, with greater accesss to other work, refused to perform what they regarded as personally restricting, and therefore degrading, labour. In its turn the difficuly of persuading women to do such work may have encouraged the expansion of new forms of catering and retailing. Urban women may have been unwilling to wait upon the middle classes in their homes or to be servants in family shops but were prepared to work in cafes and restaurants, and as the new styled 'shop assistants' in the lock-up and chain stores which proliferated in the period. The new employment pattern for women at the end of the century may therefore be, in part, a result of the decline in domestic service and not its cause.

Such an explanation of the decline of domestic service would also help to remove the apparent contradiction between the occupation as an opportunity and as an institution to be avoided in the current historiography of the period. Service might be seen as an opportunity by rural women but not by their urban counterparts. The nineteenth-century urbanization of the population might thus have radically altered the manner in which the majority of women perceived the occupation.

Conclusion

The results of this local study contradict many popular conceptions regarding domestic service. They also indicate that 'sociological' assumptions about the institution are too simplistic. Sweeping theories of social causation or effect based on shaky empirical evidence seldom prove very robust on closer examination. This study has been mainly confined, however, to an examination of one or two local servant populations, although its results have been corroborated by other local studies and by data from the national level. In order to settle the debate other local studies of contrasting communities will have to be undertaken.

The evidence so far, however, points towards the existence of a tension between domestic service in the home and the emancipation of women. For contemporaries the difference between the terminology, and presumably the reality, of domestic servitude and the work of women in the family home was ambiguous. Urban women with access to factory employment avoided domestic service if they could. Access to an independent wage and to the networks of mutual support found in factory life led to a rejection of the position of subordination inherent in this institution. The rejection of domestic service was a partial rejection of domesticity by working-class women.

Bibliographical Note

The main studies of Victorian domestic service are P. Horn's *The Rise and Fall of the Victorian Servant* (Gill and MacMillan, Dublin, 1975), T. McBride's *The Domestic Revolution* (Croom Helm, 1976) and M. Ebery and B. Preston's *Domestic Service in Late Victorian and Edwardian England, 1871–1914* (University of Reading, Reading, 1976). A book which has had a great effect on the way in which domestic service has been studied is J.A. Banks's *Prosperity and Parenthood* (Routledge and Kegan Paul, 1954). Banks argues that servant employment was part of a 'paraphernalia of gentility' required to establish middle-class status. The decline of service in the late nineteenth century reflects, therefore, the financial difficulties of the class at this time. He argues that they reduced the size of their families to save money and so needed fewer sevants. McBride follows him in this whilst Ebery, Preston and Horn favour an explanation in terms of the rise of alternative work for women. Another sociological work of importance is L. Broom and J. H. Smith, 'Bridging occupations', *British Journal of Sociology*, 14 (1963), pp. 321–34. For the present author's other works on this subject see 'Domestic Servants and Households in Rochdale, 1851–1871', (unpublished University of Oxford DPhil thesis, 1979); 'The tabulation of occupations in the nineteenth century census with special reference to domestic servants', *Local Population Studies*, 28 (1982), pp. 58–66; and 'Domestic servants and households in Victorian England; *Social History*, 8, no. 2 (1983), pp. 201–10.

Notes

1   Horn, *Victorian Servant*: J. Burnett (ed.), *Useful Toil* (Allen Lane, 1974).
2   P. Branca, *Silent Sisterhood: Middle Class Women in the Victorian Home* (Croom Helm, 1975), pp. 38–57.
3   For a history of nineteenth-century census taking see M. Drake, 'The Census, 1801–1891', in *Nineteenth Century Society*, ed. E. A. Wrigley (Cambridge University Press, Cambridge, 1972), pp. 7–33. For a list of the published parliamentary papers relating to the census see R. Lawton (ed.), *The Census and Social Structure* (Frank Cass, 1978), pp. 289–319.
4   HO107, RG9–11, Census Returns, Public Record Office. Census records are closed to public inspection for 100 years in order to preserve confidentiality. When research for the present paper was undertaken the 1881 material was not available. On the other hand, the 1841 returns were not as fulsome as those produced later. The study was confined, therefore, to the years 1851, 1861 and 1871.
5   PP 1852–3, LXXXVI, Census of Gt Britain 1851, Population Tables I, vol. II, div. VIII, p. 44; PP 1872, LXVI, Census of England and Wales, 1871, Population Tables, pt II, pp. 403–4.

6 PP 1863, LIII, Census of England and Wales, 1861, pt II, pp. 635–47.

7 A general servant, man servant, butler, coachman, gardener, housekeeper, cook, housemaid, nurse, governess, ladies maid, kitchen maid, laundry maid, footman or companion.

8 SPSS, a ready made package of computer software, was used to manipulate the data.

9 For an explanation of the principles involved see R. Floud, *Introduction to Quantitative Methods for Historians* (Methuen, 1973); R. S. Schofield, 'Sampling in historical research', in *Nineteenth Century Society*, ed. E. A. Wrigley (Cambridge University Press, Cambridge, 1972), pp. 146–90.

10 Examples of such servants have been noted in M. P. Reeves, *Round About a Pound a Week* (Virago edn, 1979), p. 141; M. Brayshay, 'Depopulation and changing household structure in the mining communities of West Cornwall, 1851–1871', *Local Population Studies*, 25 (1980), pp. 38–9.

11 All differences in this paper are statistically significant at the 95 per cent level unless otherwise stated.

12 For another example of this phenomenon see Brayshay, 'Depopulation and changing household structure', pp. 32–3.

13 The construction of social economic groupings depends upon the assumption that social status can be correlated with occupation, usually that of the household head. Although such classifications have obvious drawbacks they can be used as a very rough and ready means of reconstructing status groups from census data. Using this classification the households of all the members of the professions, all proprietors, and all manufacturers employing more than 24 hands were placed in Social Economic Group 1. Farmers, manufacturers employing between two and 24 hands and retailers employing more than one assistant formed Social Economic Group 2. Other retailers, skilled industrial workers and clerks formed Social Economic Group 3. Social Economic Group 4 contained all servants and those in occupations defined as partly skilled. Labourers were placed in Social Economic Group 5. People without occupations or with an indeterminate occupation (e.g. 'a lady') formed Social Economic Groups 6 and 7 respectively. For a detailed discussion of these groupings see W. A. Armstrong, 'The use of Information about Occupation', in *Nineteenth Century Society*, ed. E. A. Wrigley (Cambridge University Press, Cambridge, 1972), pp. 198–225.

14 PP 1852–3, LXXXVIII, pt. II, Census of Gt Britain, 1851, Population Tables II, p. 645.

15 For various discussions of this problem see N. M. Howlett, 'Family and household in a nineteenth century Devon village', *Local Population Studies*, 30 (1983), pp. 46–7; M. Chaytor, 'Household and kinship: Ryton in the late sixteenth and early seventeenth centuries', *History Workshop Journal*, 10 (1980), pp. 47–8; O. Harris, 'Households and their boundaries', *History Workshop Journal*, 13 (1982), pp. 148–51.

16 F. K. Prochaska, 'Female philanthropy and domestic service in Victorian England', *Bulletin of the Institute of Historical Research*, liv (1981), pp. 82–3.

17 PUR 7. Rochdale Board of Guardians: Workhouse Committee Minute Books, 1851–1870, Lancashire Record Office.
18 Life-cycle stages relate to the changing size and structure of the family. The stages distinguished for married couples were the following:

> (1) Wife under 45, no children at home.
> (2) Wife under 45, one child under one year at home.
> (3) Children at home, but none in employment.
> (4) Children at home, and some, but under half, in employment.
> (5) Children at home, and half or over half, in employment.
> (6) Wife 45 and over, no children, or one only aged over 20, at home.

A residual stage 0, where there was no married couple, was included in the present analysis. For a broader discussion of this classification see Michael Anderson, *Family Structure in Nineteenth Century Lancashire* (Cambridge University Press, Cambridge, 1971), pp. 31–2, 202 n.
19 Difference between Social Economic Group 5 and control sample significant at the 90 per cent level.
20 Difference for Social Economic Groups 4 and 5 not significant at the 80 per cent level.
21 Ebery and Preston, *Domestic Service*, p. 68.
22 Horn, *Victorian Servant*, p. 18.
23 I. Pinchbeck, *Women Workers and the Industrial Revolution, 1750–1850* (Virago edn, 1981), pp. 33–7; J. B. Jeffreys, *Retail Trading in Britain, 1850–1950* (Cambridge University Press, Cambridge, 1954), p. 36.
24 J. A. S. Green, 'A survey of domestic service', *Lincolnshire History and Archaeology*, 17 (1982), pp. 65–9.
25 PUR 7, 11 May 1866, Lancashire Record Office.
26 E. Roberts, *A Woman's Place. An Oral History of Working Class Women, 1890–1940* (Basil Blackwell, Oxford, 1984). See D. Gittins's essay in J. Lewis, *Women's Experience*, (companion volume).
27 Ebery and Preston, *Domestic Service*, p. 70.
28 Ibid, p. 73.
29 I. Beeton, *Mrs Beeton's Book of Household Management* (2nd edn, S. O. Beeton, 1863), pp. 961–1024.
30 The servants' wages (figures outside brackets) are averages for particular dates of wage rates recorded by W. T. Layton in 'Changes in the wages of domestic servants during 50 years'. *Journal of the Royal Statistical Society* 71 (1908), pp. 515–24 and by Horn, *Victorian Servant*. The sources used include newspaper advertisements, account books of institutions and households, manuals of household management and so on. The figures for the textile industry are average weekly wages multiplied by 52 weeks found in G. H. Wood, 'The course of women's wages during the nineteenth century', in *A History of Factory Legislation*, eds B. L. Hutchins and A. Harrison (London School of Economics and Political Science, 1903), Appendix A, pp. 257–316.
31 According to William Tyler, a footman in London in 1837, his average annual takings from tips were between £10 and £15 on top of an annual wage of £40, cited in Horn, *Victorian Servant*, p. 117.

32 Anderson, *Family Structure*, p. 128.
33 See, for example, C. Booth, *The Life and Labour of the People in London*, vol. 8 (Macmillan, 1903), p. 219; C. V. Butler, *Domestic Service. An Enquiry by the Women's Industrial Council* (Women's Industrial Council, 1916), p. 44.
34 *Rochdale Observer*, Rochdale Public Library Newspaper Collection.
35 J. A. Banks, *Prosperity and Parenthood* (Routledge and Kegan Paul, 1954) pp. 71–2.
36 Studies of domestic service in societies as diverse as nineteenth-century Paris and modern Peru have come to the same conclusion. See McBride, *The Domestic Revolution*, pp. 62–3; M. L. Smith, 'Institutionalised servitude: the female domestic servant in Lima', PhD dissertation, 1971 (British Library Reference 72–10007), p. 197.
37 Horn, *Victorian Servant*, p. 28; McBride, *The Domestic Revolution*, p. 94; E. Sagarra, *A Social History of Germany, 1648–1914* (Methuen, 1977), p. 383; Smith, 'Institutionalised servitude', p. 166.
38 *Rochdale Observer*, op. cit.
39 P. Gaskell, *The Manufacturing Population of England* (Arno Press, New York, 1972), p. 147; *Hansard*, 1844, lxxxviii, cols 1,093–4.
40 *Report of His Majesty's Commissioners for Inquiry into the Administration and Practical Operation of the Poor Laws, Appendix B(i), Answers to Rural Queries*, pt 1, PP 1834, XXX.
41 Anderson, *Family Structure*, pp. 118–19; B. Preston, *Occupations of Father and Son in Mid-Victorian England* (University of Reading, Reading, 1977), p. 31.
42 Personal correspondence with Mr E. Gittins in possession of author.
43 M. Hewitt, *Wives and Mothers in Victorian Industry* (Virago, 1969), pp. 51–2; Pinchbeck, *Women Workers*, p. 310.
44 MFPR 242–59, Parish Records of the Parish Church of St John the Evangelist, Preston, 1851–1856, Manchester Central Library.
45 There are problems with using the social economic groups outlined in note 13 since they depend on knowing the number of people employed to differentiate between large and small manufacturers and retailers, and between employers and employees. In the absence of such information Social Economic Group 3 is greatly inflated. But since this would apply to both servants and other women the results are still of some use for comparative purposes.
46 P. Wilcox, 'Marriage, mobility and domestic service in Victorian Cambridge', *Local Population Studies*, 29 (1982), p. 32.
47 Butler, *Domestic Service*, pp. 39–40.
48 F. Thompson, *Lark Rise to Candleford* (Penguin, Harmondsworth, 1973), p. 155; Butler, *Domestic Service*, p. 89.
49 R. A. Arnold, *The History of the Cotton Famine* . . . (Saunders, Otley, 1864), p. 62.
50 Butler, *Domestic Service*, p. 11.
51 See Sagarra, *Social History of Germany*, p. 383 and Smith, 'Institutional servitude', p. 166, for similar examples of a preference for rural-born servants in nineteenth-century Germany and modern Peru. Such

arguments do not explain, however, why servants should be downwardly socially mobile on marriage in nineteenth-century Cambridge.

52 Banks, *Prosperity and Parenthood*, p. 132.

53 J. W. Innes, *Class Fertility Trends in England and Wales, 1876–1934* (Princeton University Press, Princeton, 1938), p. 43.

54 PUR 7, 13th April 1866, Lancashire Record Office.

55 DB 154, List of Guardians and Paid Officers of the Rochdale Poor Law Union, 1859–1879, Rochdale Public Library; PUR 7, 31 August 1866, Lancashire Record Office.

56 Thompson, *Lark Rise*, p. 155.

57 Armstrong, 'The use of information', p. 255.

58 Burnett, *Useful Toil*, pp. 139–40. In this he is supported by Prochaska, 'Female philanthropy', p. 85.

59 One should note, for example, the data in table 4.4 which could be interpreted as evidence of a need on the part of servant employers to go further afield in search of suitable servants. Does this indicate the exhaustion of local rural sources as urbanization spread?

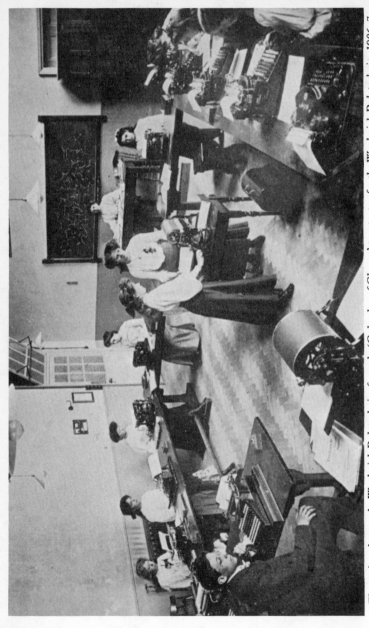

The typing class at the Woolwich Polytechnic, from the 'Calendar of Classes' prospectus for the Woolwich Polytechnic, 1906–7

5

Jobs for the Girls: the Expansion of Clerical Work for Women, 1850–1914

Meta Zimmeck

In the last decade there has been an important redirection of interest, both scholarly and activist, towards women's work. A veritable mountain of new data has been generated; various kinds of women's work and work-related activities, hitherto unsung, have found champions; and a comprehensive reformulation of subject areas, concepts, methodology, and tactics is now in train. At the root of all this is feminists' realization that what women do has been seen as either unimportant or in some way deviating from the 'normal' (i.e., what men do). Woman are, according to Ann Oakley, 'conspicuous for their absence'.[1] What feminists seek, then, is to redress the balance, to make women conspicuous for their presence. As Elizabeth Garnsey has suggested: 'All that is necessary is to recognize that the participation of women in the labour market affects the nature of labour markets for both men and women; changes in the occupational and industrial distribution of male and female workers are complementary and interdependent'.[2]

The subject of this essay is the development of clerical work[3] in the late nineteenth century and in particular the process (or at any rate the beginning of the process) by which clerical work was transformed from 'men's work' to 'women's work'. It has two aims. The first and simplest is to make women clerical workers' presence felt, to see them as significant subjects in their own right. The second is to examine the 'complementary and interdependent' relationship between men's and women's work, to investigate how the boundary between the two was established and from time to time renegotiated.

Clerical work was transformed in the years 1850 to 1914. From 1851 to 1911 the number of clerks increased from 95,000 to 843,000 ($\times$ 9) and the proportion of clerks to all occupied persons from 1.2 per cent to 4.6 per cent ($\times$ 4). In the second place the gender mix of clerical workers changed, as women made even more spectacular gains than men. While the number of men rose from 93,000 to 677,000 ($\times$ 7), that of women rocketed from a mere 2,000 to 166,000 ($\times$ 83); or from 2 per cent to 20 per cent of the total.[4] Finally, the nature of clerical work altered fundamentally. Improved communications via telegraphy, telephony, and a multi-delivery postal service; inventions for word-processing and number-processing such as shorthand, typewriters, dictating machines, carbon paper, adding machines and stencil duplicators; new ways of storing and retrieving data such as card indexes, vertical files, and loose-leaf ledgers – all facilitated an enormous increase in the volume, complexity and intensity of clerical work. The various work processes were subdivided, simplified, and isolated, and office organization in consequence was streamlined. Units became larger and more specialized and were sited and linked in such a way as to ensure the smooth flow of work. Thus the Dickensian counting house gave way to the recognizably modern office – Bob Cratchit's high stool, quill pen, and correspondence spike to Roberta Cratchit's desk, typewriter, and filing cabinet. Only his muffler survived, like the smile of the Cheshire cat, since some things in British life (the weather and appallingly bad heating) remained the same.[5]

There have been surprisingly few studies of the historical development of clerical work, and these have concentrated on the factor of class rather than gender. Thus they have addressed primarily the issue of 'proletarianization', the worsening of the position of clerical workers *vis à vis* manual workers. F. D. Klingender uses wage level data to describe the 'process whereby the clerical worker has been downgraded from lower-middle-class to proletarian levels'. What he sees as the most significant and pressing aspect of proletarianization, however, is clerical workers' 'false consciousness', which inhibits their realization of 'the identity of their basic interests' with the working class and the necessity of their joining with the working class in an alliance against capitalism and fascism. In the historical introduction to what is basically a sociological study, David Lockwood examines the 'factors affecting his sense of identification with, or alienation from, the working class', and concentrates on the absence of trade union militancy, although without sharing Klingender's sense of impending doom.

Lee Holcombe provides a synthesis of available printed and secondary material, and, in so far as she has any theoretical framework at all, accepts that of proletarianization. Geoffrey Crossick explores the position of the lower middle class, of which white collar workers comprised a moiety, in a European context and focuses on the 'central points of intersection between the lower middle class and the social structure as a whole' – its role in social mobility, its contribution to conservative politics, and its impact on the aristocracy of labour and the rest of the working class. Finally, Gregory Anderson embarks on an exploration of 'the work and market situations of Victorian and Edwardian clerks' and fleshes out his thesis of proletarianization with descriptions of how and why it took place and the way in which clerks fought a rearguard action against it.[6]

Where then are the women in these studies? When Klingender was writing, women constituted 46 per cent of all clerical workers (1931 census); Lockwood, 60 per cent (1951 census); Holcombe, Anderson, and Crossick, 72 per cent (1971 census).[7] Klingender posits a direct relationship between the employment of women and proletarianization: the greater the one, the greater the other. He also implies a causal relationship as well: women are not only the yardstick of proletarianization but its active, if unwitting, agents (and thus are guilty of a double dose of false consciousness with regard to their male colleagues and the working class generally). Lockwood sees women as one of the barriers to proper trade union organization and writes off 'the white bloused worker' as a sort of clerical anticlimax:

> It is a far cry from the blackcoated male careerist of the counting house, whose aspirations and successes helped to confer the substance of prestige on the occupation, to the routine girl clerk or typist of the modern office, whose future status depends less on her own career than on that of the man she ultimately marries.

Holcombe assumes uncritically that, notwithstanding some 'real grievances', women's position was similar to that of men but they let down the side by being bad trade unionists. She also swallows whole certain gender stereotypes: 'women were probably much more easily reconciled than men to the lack of opportunity for advancement which was becoming characteristic of many clerical positions'. Crossick, in what is probably the most interesting and ambitious study, excludes women from consideration – though at least with protestations of regret – on the grounds that stratification theory, which underpins his analysis, does not apply to women: 'the focus of this essay is upon the process of lower middle class stratification at a time when it was male occupations that defined status'. Finally, Anderson, after analysing the objective factors in the worsening position of clerks relative to manual workers – the difficulty of professionalization without defensible skills, organization, and a code of practice – concludes that male clerks' paranoia about the depredations of German clerks, youths, and women was valid and, moreover, justified. Blaming women was 'reasonable. After all female clerks, like other female workers, did accept lower wages than men'.[8]

Thus women in the occupation which they have come to dominate (and were in fact dominating when these studies were made) have been written off as tools of capitalist exploitation, oppressors of male breadwinners or persons to all intents and purposes indistinguishable from men. This traditional treatment of clerical labour is illustrative of Garnsey's point that an unbalanced analysis produces unbalanced conclusions. From this marginalization of women's participation in clerical work it is almost impossible to draw the obvious conclusion. If clerical work was passing out of the men's sphere, it was passing into the women's. If men were losing, women were gaining. If there were fewer jobs for the boys, there were more for the girls. Although the overall shape of the feminization of clerical work is clear, the details are not. Investigations along these lines have been pioneered by women sociologists and journalists, who actually have asked women about their work experiences or have done the work themselves.[9] Nineteenth-century women clerks are, unfortunately, beyond the reach of the questionnaire and the gimlet eye of the participant observer, and it is the task of this essay to fill in, as much as the somewhat unyielding sources allow,[10] the gaps in our knowledge.

Although middle-class women reputedly found their 'El Dorado'[11] in clerical work, they were not free to mine its riches but were, in fact, subject to the constraints imposed by the patriarchal ideology of Victorian society. This ideology dictated that the natural role for middle-class women was that of the angel in the house and not the angel in the office. However, there existed an anomalous group of middle-class women, the 'surplus' or 'odd' women[12] who, because of uneven mortality rates, patterns of emigration, the tendency of middle-class men to delay marriage (or forego it altogether), lack of marketable 'charms', would not be able to find husbands[13] and who, because of insufficient means, could not be supported by their families. Despite the dictates of ideology Victorian society found it difficult to countenance the spectacle of 'distressed gentlewomen' suffering gross physical hardship, loss of class or a fall into prostitution, which would otherwise have been their fate. Rather it resolved to find something for these poor things to do, some 'suitable' work by which they might decently exist. But providing work suitable for surplus women was not the same thing as opening the door to all forms of work to all women – that is to say, equal opportunity. Rather, Victorian society applied the test of less eligibility to work for middle-class women in the same way as it applied the test to relief of the poor. While it was the duty of society to help the deserving to help themselves, it was not its duty to assist them to be better off than they would have been had they married or remained at home. It was not society's goal to create work which was more attractive than the home – offered more interest and satisfaction, gave financial independence, fostered 'strong-mindedness' – lest this work become more than a *pis aller*: lest it become an inducement for women to violate 'nature', shirk their 'home duties', and wallow in 'selfishness'.

The search for 'fresh modes of activity'[14] for surplus middle-class women became a sort of occupational hunt the thimble. Assisted emigration to the overmanned colonies of European settlement, the most seductive proposal, 'solved' the problem by packing it off elsewhere, but such schemes were awkward to manage and difficult to sell in quantity (since it was all too obvious that 'exercising a civilizing influence' meant marrying the uncivilized).[15] Some occupations, especially those suggested by philanthropic ladies – for example, art needlework, table decoration, breaking-in of new boots, shopping for country folk, specialist cleaning of delicate furniture and china, and dog-walking (for those of 'bashful shrinking dispositions')[16] – were essentially frivolous. They did not generate many jobs and verged perilously close to domestic service and the concomitant loss of middle-class status. Nursing and teaching (especially after the introduction of a national system of primary education in 1870), though able to accommodate relatively large numbers, took place in insalubrious locations and required prolonged (and in the case of nursing, intimate) contact with social inferiors and persons of the opposite sex. Shop work, also an expanding field, was tainted by the moral dangers of the living-in system and exposure to the attentions of male staff and customers and was considered respectable – just. Likely occupations such as printing and law writing, in which the Society for Promoting the

Employment of Women had actually provided training and established all-women firms, foundered on intractable opposition by male workers.[17]

The one occupation which avoided all the pitfalls of the occupations available to or proposed for middle-class women, the ideal occupation by general agreement, was clerical work. It was able to provide employment on a large scale and to achieve this at no immediate cost to incumbent males (who were, in fact, insufficiently organized, powerful, and anyway motivated to oppose employers' initiatives). It did not cause the loss 'of those feminine graces, of dignity, of delicacy, of reserve, which are the essential characteristics of an English gentlewoman'.[18] It was clean. It was dainty. It allowed women to dress nicely. It could be organized so as to limit contact with social inferiors and with men. It did not disqualify those poor women who otherwise possessed the full complement of allurements from making a decent match.[19] Most importantly, it could be made to conform to the workhouse test. In short, so neatly does clerical work satisfy all these requirements that one suspects that had it not existed, it would have been necessary to invent it.

Underpinning the organization of clerical labour by means of the workhouse test was the attribution, fundamental to patriarchal ideology, of different inherent characteristics to each sex which fitted each for different types of work. The distinction between masculine and feminine was rather more forced in the case of clerical work than other occupations since there was little, if any, work taking place under dangerous conditions or requiring brute strength – since no one was 'expected to lift cwts. or knock people down.'[20] Indeed male clerks felt this ambiguity very keenly and were already suffering from a crisis of machismo summed up by the oft quoted phrase, 'Born a man; died a clerk', even before women came on to the scene. In clerical work the line was drawn roughly between the intellectual, which was the province of men, and the mechanical, which was the province of women. According to this view, men's intelligence was wide-ranging, bold, and penetrating, whereas women's was narrow, timid, and receptive. Women were quick, dextrous, neat, painstaking, keen to find fault and had 'natural resisting power to the dulling effect of monotony on the sharpness of attention',[21] but they were also delicate and unable to withstand the pressure of sustained work and had neither the desire nor the capacity for responsibility. Thus while men were capable of incisive analysis, conceptualization, and command, women were only good for tying up the loose ends of execution. On the one hand women were useful as instruments of a higher intelligence: '[The women clerk] is at the service of the mind, the wits, of her employer. Her training and her efforts are centred upon the swiftest and most accurate voicing of his ideas, in whatever direction those ideas may run'.[22] On the other hand they were useful as drudges: 'I suppose that it may fairly be said that women do as well or better than men [on] routine work requiring care and patience but that many of them are less adapted than are the majority of men to work of a complex nature requiring judgment and initiative'.[23] These assumptions, which owed more to men's fantasies, self-interest, and *amour propre* than to any real understanding of what women could or wanted to do, nevertheless were the foundation on which the occupational structure of clerical work was erected.

Clerical work was divided into two clear-cut spheres of activity for men and women. Although the boundary between the two spheres moved from time to time, the separation between them remained constant and absolute. Women were not employed at random and were not evenly distributed throughout the field of clerical work. Rather women worked with women, under women, and in women's jobs, processes or parts of processes. Most women clerks were employed by commercial firms, the Civil Service or local government, with a disproportionately small number by law firms, banks, insurance or railway companies.[24] Women were heavily concentrated in those work processes seen as corresponding to their abilities – for example, typing, sorting, telephony, telegraphy, checking accounts and so forth.[25] Even when men and women were engaged on the same processes, women were put in separate compartments (however imaginary):

> The Male Telegraphist has a better power of 'management' and . . . his style of manipulation (like male handwriting as compared with that of females) is so much firmer as to be suitable for long distances, and indeed in practice it is found that a Male Signaller secures better results than a female over busy Circuits. This more particularly applies to duplex and quadriplex 'key' circuits, and to busy Wheatstone Circuits.[26]

Changes in the distribution of work between men and women took place not by the aggregate permeation or integration of individuals but in chunks through the renegotiation of the boundary between the spheres. Women acquired work which was new, without a tradition of male occupancy. They also acquired work which was transferred ('downgraded') to them from the men's sphere, generally work which was no longer perceived as masculine or the more 'mechanical' parts of 'intellectual' work.[27] For example, women clerks in the Savings Bank Department of the Post Office, which was organized into ledger divisions, started off 'experimentally' in a few divisions where the work was thought least taxing and proceeded over several decades to take over one division after another from the men, until in the end they made a clean sweep and ledger work became 'women's work'. The goal of the process was fairly straightforward: 'The women to gain in quantity, the men in quality'.[28]

The separation of these spheres of work was emphasized by separation of accommodation. In all but the smallest offices, women were kept strictly apart from men – on women's floors, in women's rooms, or in women's sections complete with partitions to prevent even eye contact. The ideal women's space was a self-contained suite of rooms, complete with private staircase and a matron of the dragon class at the door. The office of the Electric and International Telegraph Company was typical: 'The male and female telegraphists have separate stair-cases . . . that for the men leads from the principal staircase. The female clerks have a private staircase, leading . . . to the street door of the premises . . . [and] . . . to a dining-hall and cloak-room, which are provided exclusively for them'.[29] Less well-endowed offices had to shift as best they could. Typists at the Treasury were kept in a room 'at the top of the House' (i.e., the attic), and their entrances and exits were made through the main hallways in convoy under the supervision of the head of the Registry.[30] In pursuit of a low profile for women many employers did not permit women to leave the premises at lunchtime. Women at the Post Office only secured liberty and fresh air in 1911 after a strenuous campaign and personal appeals to the Postmaster General.[31] At times separate accommodation took on an almost surreal importance as a justification for opposing the employment of women. Various employers or, in the case of the Civil Service, government departments, staved off the evil day by standing, literally, on their WCs (or rather, the structural impossibility or ruinous expense of providing them).

If there were rigid boundaries between the spheres of men's and women's work, there were equally rigid boundaries between the grades or types of work within those spheres. Clerical hierarchies, which mirrored the class hierarchies of Victorian society, were held as a principle to be absolute. They did not reflect clerks' current (i.e., temporary) position in the office game of snakes and ladders but rather the exact position for which he or she was fitted by sex, class, education and manner. Employers regarded too much mobility within the system as suspect, an implied criticism of the natural order, and made few transfers between parts of the same firm and even fewer promotions between grades or types of work. As Sir Robert Chalmers, speaking for the Treasury, the Civil Service, and possibly all employers, noted, 'the divisions should be maintained, and promotion from one to the other should be exceptional'.[32] Office organization was in this sense all snakes and no ladders. It was obviously necessary and expedient for employers to reward good performance and avoid the build-up of frustration by some means, and they did so by creating numerous divisions or steps or efficiency bars within grades and by having very long age-related salary scales, which gave the impression of progression without the substance. This system of compartments and hierarchies caused enormous frustration. Robert Thorne, hero of a novel of the same name, agonizes about 'the Line' between the lower and higher grades at the 'Tax Office' where he works (the Inland Revenue):

> It's what's below *them* and above us, and it's what we can't pass. We're not good enough. We aren't good enough . . . Do you see how we're labelled, each man with his little *Mister* and his little salary? That's official etiquette. Above the Line you're an Esquire, below it you're plain Mister and be damned to you![33]

Nevertheless, whatever male clerks' darkest thoughts, they still cherished expectations of rising to the top or at least close to the top.

Women had no hopes or even fantasies of such a success (marrying the boss was not quite the same thing). The women's hierarchy, even when it paralleled the men's, terminated well below the managerial level, so that the most women could achieve was the supervision of other women. Women seldom, if ever, exercised power over men or even boys and were always, ultimately, under the control of men. Also, because women tended to work in large units doing the most routinized work, the ratio of supervisory to subordinate posts was low and movement from the bottom to the top of a grade was either blocked or very slow, much more so than that for men, who had higher levels of supervision or access to the higher posts from which women were excluded. For example, in small offices women worked directly for the employer. In larger offices there was, it seems, probably one supervisor for 15 or so women staff, and mobility depended on 'dead women's shoes' – the marriage, resignation, retirement, or death of the supervisor. Thus if Robert Thorne had one worry, his fiancée, Nell, had two:

> Rob: It's a shame. It's a shame. You work harder than I do,
> Nell, and better too, and your hours are longer. Yet you only
> get half what I get. Why is it, Nell?
> Nell: Because I happened to be born a girl, . . . I suppose.[34]

Below 'the Line' was another line under which everyone was labelled 'plain Miss'.

The marriage bar was a fairly unsubtle part of the system of less eligibility. Most employers of clerical labour hired only single women or, in rare cases, widows. Some gave marriage gratuities or 'dowries', a grant of money calculated on length of service, *pour encourager les autres*. The marriage bar policed the notion that women's primary duty was to marry and have children by removing the possibility of their doing otherwise once they had taken the fatal step to the altar. It also removed an incentive for women to 'take precautions and . . . outrage nature' by practising birth control:[35] 'It may be urged that this is a matter for Husband and Wife to arrange between themselves, and that the Post Office has no further concern than to see that its work is done. To this view we venture to demur'.[36] Moreover, the marriage bar contained a veiled threat. Paradoxically, though Victorian society glorified wifehood and motherhood, it only glorified them in their place, and for middle-class women that place was the home. Any middle-class woman who exposed herself to the 'public' view at work after marriage or, heaven forfend, when pregnant lost the character of a lady[37] and laid herself open to insults:

> The females cannot be so isolated that they will not be seen and recognised, at all events, as they enter and leave the office, by male employees entering and leaving about the same time, and if any become observably *enceinte* they will, I fear, be subjected to rude remarks or behaviour which cannot be for their good.[38]

In addition to promoting these worthy social goals the marriage bar reinforced the gender and grade compartmentalizations of clerical work. It was meant to facilitate a high turnover of women staff and thus to lower costs, since women would tend to bunch up at the bottom of salary scales and few would remain in service long enough to rise to the top of the scale or to earn a pension: 'It must be remembered that it is cheaper for us to get rid of the ladies in this way than to keep them on until pensioned.'[39] It would also render uneconomical the provision of greater opportunities or lengthy training for women. Since the majority of women were only marking the time until the 'Deliverer' appeared, any investment by employers in their skills would be wasted. For the few confirmed spinsters the supervisory posts extant would suffice. Indeed for these relicts, it was said, the opportunities were excellent.

Deriving from the segregation of the spheres and the marriage bar and indeed reinforcing their effect was the employers' practice of paying women wages just sufficient to maintain them in decency though not in comfort. These wages were low both absolutely and relatively (25–50 per cent less than men's wages on comparable work). Of course all employers endeavoured to cut their costs of production, but they explained low wages not in terms of the wages bill alone but by reference to the necessity of paying men a 'family' wage and women a 'single' wage:

> If you pay women who are unmarried the same wage as you pay to the men the majority of whom are married and have to maintain a family, you will really be paying the woman what is an individual wage at the same rate as you are paying the man what is a family wage . . . The right phrase I think in this connexion is 'Equal standard of Comfort for People doing equal Work.' If you pay a single woman the same wage as you pay a family man, you are giving her a much higher standard of comfort than you are giving them.[40]

There were exquisite elaborations of this argument: a woman was paid enough to be 'independent of marriage from mercenary motives, and to marry more happily from the fact that she offers no pecuniary attraction to a man'[41] – in other words, low pay also provided a social service by making sure that a beau's intentions were honourable!

The argument for the single wage was circular and ran thus. Since women clerks were single, they lived at home with their families (and indeed some employers demanded signed statements from families and friends with whom provincials were allowed to live that this was the case). Since they lived at home with their families, they were not self-supporting. Since they were not self-supporting they worked for pin money. Alternatively if they were self-supporting they had only themselves and no dependants to support. Alternatively, if they ('not the average of the type') had dependants to support, these responsibilities were 'far less than those falling upon . . . men who have to maintain a household and a family'.[42] Employers had little if any evidence on which to base these sweeping contentions and, moreover, even when challenged, did not stoop to shore up their 'common sense' argument with elaborate statistical proofs. They also eschewed linking wages to family responsibilities by accurate and gender-neutral means (say, income tax), which would have eliminated anomalies and silenced some of their critics. Employers were, in making this distinction between the single and the family wage, thus arguing in effect that wages should be determined not by any quantifiable measure of output or productivity but by the social value of the producer, and women's social value was, of course, inferior to that of men's.

This career structure in clerical work was indeed unappetising in and of itself. The workhouse test – the consignment of women to what was by general consensus the 'worst' kind of work with only the acquisition of the 'worst of the best' to look forward to, the lack of scope for demonstrating their abilities to full tilt and the near hopelessness of altering in this way the patriarchal view of these abilities, the imposed dichotomy between work and marriage which blighted the hopes of even those who chose a career, low pay, the artificial isolation from and resultant alienation from their male colleagues – should have made (and was designed to make) all but the most deserving women quail at the office door. It did not do so however, and one of the most remarkable aspects of the feminization of clerical labour is the alacrity with which women sought employment. The ratio of applicants to posts was high, as much as several hundred to one. The Post Office was regularly mobbed by prospective employees. In 1874 there were 700 candidates for just five posts of women clerk and in 1901, when there were greater alternative opportunities, there were still 329 candidates for 25 posts.[43] This was, as all employers were well aware, a buyer's market: they need only beckon and flocks of eager women would appear, and if they disappeared there would always be others to take their place.

In this pioneer era women clerks were motivated by an enormous zest for life and adventure. Even their indignation, when roused by the absurdities of their position and the pettiness of the restraints imposed upon them, was good-natured. This sense of embarking on a voyage of discovery is captured by two picaresque novels. In Tom Gallon's *The Girl behind the Keys* (1903) the heroine gushes breathlessly but confidently, 'I was down to the last sixpence – and I was a woman', immediately lands a post at a dodgy typing agency run by (as it transpires) a good-looking crook, and plays a role in thwarting his endeavours quite different from that of the 'mere machine' she was supposed to be.[44] In Olive P. Rayner's *The Type-writer Girl* (1897), the heroine is 'a Girton girl' of good family but limited means, who wanders from a firm of shyster lawyers to an anarchists' commune (on her bicycle and in rational dress), to a publishing company run by a handsome Cambridge graduate (whose love she nobly eschews because of his prior engagement to 'a wax doll': 'John Stuart Mill, stand by me!'). She sees her life in classical terms: 'I mean to sail away on my Odyssey, unabashed, touching at such shores as may chance to beckon, yet hopeful of reaching at last the lands of Alcinuous'.[45] Many women were 'odd' not only because they were unmarriageable or from poor families but also because they were dissatisfied with the choice between 'a very early marriage, philanthropy, or nothing particular to do'.[46] They felt keenly the waste and meaninglessness of a life devoted to needlework, social calls, and 'accomplishments':

> Aunt Ina came to lunch – conversation languished so much we were thankful to untwist tangles of gimp . . .

> We were to have gone to a garden party but it rained . . . so Aunt Minnie . . . said it was too wet to go, and we sat on campstools instead and looked at a holly being transplanted in the rain. It is so *fearfully* pottery.[47]

They felt in themselves the power to do something productive and meaningful and real – to plunge into the hurly-burly of the world hitherto monopolized by men, to become, in the words of Gissing's Miss Barfoot, proprietor of a typewriting school and agency, *'rational and responsible human beings'*,[48] to work. For these women the typewriter, the ledger, and the shorthandwriter's pad were instruments not of oppression but of liberation.

If women clerks were enthusiastic, they were not, however, naive. They understood quite clearly that their work, and indeed, their lives, so long as they worked, were governed by constraints not applied to men and that their overall position was one of inferiority. Whatever their theoretical orientation most women clerks keenly felt at one time or another in their working lives the injustice and inconvenience of the system of less eligibility – pay so low that skilled and experienced workers earned less than boys or seniors in charge of women's departments earned less than humble male foot soldiers; the interference of busybody employers with their intimate affairs; the assignment to dull work when they felt bursting with energy and ideas; the general insulting imputation of second-class status to their sex. Many did something about it. In the first instance many played the existing system for all it was worth. In the second some attempted to reform the system by demonstrating its inconsistencies and contradictions in order to secure 'logical' revisions in their favour. Finally, some sought to explode the system by interposing a new, democratic and feminist, ideology based on equal opportunity and the right to work. These three levels of response were not mutually exclusive, and in fact women clerks tended to use them separately or in combination in a fairly *ad hoc* way. During the course of the period 1850–1914, in response to the growing influence of the women's suffrage and trade union movements, there was an overall shift from the individual to the collective, from the personal to the political – from constructive acceptance to rebellion.

Within the boundaries of the women's sphere most women clerks attempted to make the best of a bad deal. Although crimes of omission such as concealed marriage were possible, their chief tool in this regard was mobility. They were knowledgeable about the pay and conditions on offer through the secretarial colleges where they trained, the agencies from which they got work, the professional associations to which they belonged, the social clubs where they met their friends, the newspapers and journals which they read. They were willing to change jobs in pursuit of the 'ideal'. Individual decisions had aggregate effects. Around the turn of the century the Civil Service, for 30 years the leading employer, began to suffer from a mass exodus of the best-qualified clerical workers and the drying-up of sources of re-supply. In 1907 its complacency shaken, the Treasury commissioned Clara Collet, then an investigator for the Board of Trade, to study the problem. This she did and in a survey of 167 business firms and four local government or quasi-government bodies illuminated women's responsiveness to the labour market. The business firms, while offering adequate but not outstanding conditions of service, paid good wages: 23 per cent of ordinary typists and 50 per cent of shorthand typists earned more than the Civil Service maximum of 25/– per week; 5 per cent of ordinary, 9 per cent of shorthand typists, and 46 per cent of supervisory staff earned more than the Civil Service maximum for chief superintendents of 35/–. The Bank of England, the Metropolitan Water Board, the Metropolitan Asylums Board, and the London County Council (which now replaced the Civil Service as the top employer) paid equally well and offered conditions of service more generous than the Civil Service. But most importantly these outside employers tempted women with greater opportunities. The Civil Service, in Collet's estimation, scored points for safety – protection from sexual harassment ('annoyance of a kind which refined girls greatly dread'), permanency, liberal sick leave, superannuation – and appealed to 'the unenterprising', 'the delicate', and 'the younger women who expect to marry and are only aiming at earning enough money to be able to dress and board themselves without their relatives being out of pocket'. But outside employers enticed the ambitious, the robust, and the clever by offering rewards for increased efficiency, straightforward recognition of special skills such as fluency in foreign languages, and greater scope for advancement: 'The outside market offers more valuable prizes to older women in the shape of positions of confidence and well-paid posts for highly skilled Shorthand Writers'.[49]

While women clerks clearly had a healthy respect for money, they also, it seems, sought intangibles such as respectability, interest, and long-term advantage for which they were willing if necessary to make financial sacrifices. A. J. Munby employed a law stationer's clerk, 'a young woman of 23 or so, respectable and decently drest; a Cockney girl however with something of the pertness and sham gentility of the species', who preferred her independence and her own standards of conduct to those of the firm where she had been employed, even if it cost her something: 'Said she liked copying very much; had worked for Kerr the law stationer, who keeps 29 female hands, and earned 20/– a week; more than she gets now, but Kerr's girls were low and "larky", she did not like them'.[50] Jessie Mary Fausset, an assistant at a sub-post office, preferred present interest to future security when she decided not to seek establishment as a counter clerk and telegraphist in the Post Office but to remain where she was, though she was under the direct control (like a shop assistant) of the sub-postmaster, had no pension rights, and received lower pay. Her reasons for this seemingly irrational choice were the greater enjoyment, freedom, and responsibility of the work (i.e. frequently being left in charge): 'It is not so monotonous as ordinary clerical work, as a constant succession of people require attention, most of whom are kindly and many of whom have something of interest to say before passing along'.[51] L. M. Andrews, 'probably the senior Typist in the service of the Crown, having served for upwards of 14 years' at the Principal Probate Registry, requested that her post be put on a permanent footing even if it meant going off piece-rates and taking a cut in pay of 2/– to 3/– per week: 'With respect to the [Treasury's] inference that a pecuniary loss would be sustained should the appointment be acceded to I may remark that I am not unwilling to submit to a small loss as I wish to obtain the benefit of a permanent situation with prospective pension'.[52] Women clerks thus exercised a good deal of autonomy in their choice of work. They decided what they wanted and then went after it, even if this meant changing jobs many times over.

In addition to, as it were, voting with their feet, some women clerks attempted to use the system of less eligibility against itself in order to secure concessions. Without demanding the general abolition of the marriage bar, about which they had mixed feelings (a lump sum was useful in setting up house), they nevertheless pressed for fair and humane treatment of 'the exceptions' – widows, divorcees, abandoned wives, heads of households by virtue of the husbands' incapacity. Their argument was that if single women were permitted to work because of their need, then logically work should not be denied to those whose need was equally great, if not greater. Some may have hoped that a series of exceptions and increased familiarity with the presence of married women might be the thin end of the wedge, but at any rate, spinsters with expectations of marriage could not but hope that rescue would be at hand if they embarked upon the 'Gulph' of Matrimony only to have their ship strike a rock. Without demanding equal pay, women clerks agitated for better pay on the ground that it was necessary for a decent existence. If pay was pushed too low, the workhouse test would not operate, since it would so demoralize those whom it was trying to help that they would (metaphorically but in some cases actually) die in the ditch outside the bastille door:

> I have struggled on hoping my efforts would receive consideration and I much regret being obliged to make this appeal, but it is a case of necessity. I find it impossible to pay rent etc., make a respectable appearance and provide the common necessaries of life on 30/– a week, and any provision for the future is quite out of the question.[53]

Moreover, women clerks demanded respect for the work they were doing:

> As to the alleged mechanical nature of the work we perform, we would respectfully point out that so far as our actual experience has gone, the work is not more mechanical than other work . . . which is more highly paid. But though the operation of typing may appear mechanical to an observer [male], every person of experience [female] knows that the efficient performance of the duty is impossible without the possession of average judgment and skill.[54]

Women clerks understood less eligibility rather in the light of a bond or contract, by which they exchanged humble service for a competency, and if it was not fulfilled punctiliously, they were prepared to take a stand on the fine print.

Finally, some women clerks rejected completely patriarchal ideology and the paraphernalia of suitabilities, structured inferiority, and social control based on it, and in its place they espoused the principle of equality between the sexes. With one fell swoop they abandoned the endowment of the sexes with different and mutually exclusive characteristics and the necessity of allocating work on that basis and instead declared that if all artificial barriers were removed, individuals, men and women, would find the work which they liked and rise to the limits of their capabilities:

> The time has gone by when women were considered inferior in mental capacity, and their ability to perform any kind of clerical work which has been made over to them has been fully demonstrated and testified to . . . The experimental stage is now over, and we contend that the time has now arrived when they should be treated with fairness . . .

> We consider that the manner in which [the employer] endeavours to maintain a line of demarcation between men's and women's work is both trivial and vexatious, and the so-called 'scientific frontier' proves to be no frontier at all by the ease with which the landmarks are moved to different positions to suit the special end in view.[55]

They thus abandoned making do and doing deals, on the whole a complicated and messy business, and opted for simplicity and freedom.

In practical terms these women clerks demanded the rigorous adoption of an equal opportunity programme – equality of recruitment, service, prospects and pay. This meant that men and women should be regarded for the purpose of work as being interchangeable and that 'aggregation' and not segregation should govern their distribution. There should no longer be separate spheres or watertight compartments but a *carriere ouverte aux talents* and one in which the ladders went all the way to the top. Men and women should be recruited via the same procedures (preferably some form of examination by which an objective assessment of the various candidates could be made) for service in the same grades and types of work under the same conditions of service (which excluded egregious interference with women's private lives) with the same opportunities for promotion by merit and the same financial rewards: 'I think that all women should have their chance to do what they choose to do, and if they cannot obtain a post they must give way; but they should have the right to go in for everything. That is what we feel very strongly'.[56] This new regime, women argued, would not only benefit themselves but by abolishing 'the Lines' would benefit men, the frustrated Robert Thornes of the clerical world, as well.

Women clerks can be, as this preliminary investigation has shown, coaxed from the shadows, and when this has been done they turn out to have been rather prepossessing creatures, not simpletons or tools of employers or oppressors of men. They were quite simply human beings with all the hopes, talents, foibles and failings of the species. They leaped at the opportunity to work outside the home. They struggled under conditions which were often difficult, exhausting and demoralizing. They worked hard and gave satisfaction, and indeed the quality of their work is visible to all who rummage through the archives – faultless and beautifully set-out typing done at speeds comparable with today's on machines of almost surreal primitiveness without benefit of tipp-ex. They enjoyed their work as much as they could and were proud of their skills. They searched for the best jobs and the best employers. If necessary they stood up for their rights with tact, dignity and energy. They certainly did not plot the doom of male clerks. If the transformation of clerical work is viewed through women's eyes, the issue of proleterianization, which has hitherto dominated historical debate, seems somewhat ephemeral. Proletarianization is downward movement, and for middle-class women there was nowhere to go but up. What happened to clerks in the period 1850–1914 was not so much a decline into the working class (which still has not happened) as the achievement of a new equilibrium in the wake of the removal of restrictive practices. Some male clerks went to the wall because the prop on which they depended for their superiority, the exclusion of a large number of competent persons (women) from eligibility for clerical posts, was removed. Some women benefited from the opportunities afforded. Was this proletarianization or was it simply the cost of social justice?

Bibliographical Note

As indicated above, works providing detailed information about the feminization of clerical work are rather thin on the ground. Gregory Anderson's *Victorian Clerks* (Manchester University Press, Manchester, 1976) and Geoffrey Crossick (ed.), *The Lower Middle Class in Britain, 1870–1914* (Croom Helm, 1977) are useful starting points from the men's point of view. Lee Holcombe's *Victorian Ladies at Work: Middle-Class Working Women in England and Wales, 1850–1914* (David and Charles, Newton Abbot, 1973) and Rosalie Silverstone's 'Office Work for Women: An Historical Review', *Business History*, 18 (1976), pp. 98–110, are useful starting points from the women's perspectives. Flora Mayor's novel, *The Third Miss Symons* (Virago, 1980 [1913]), describes in painful detail the wasted life of a spinster who never found her metier. George Gissing's novel, *The Odd Women* (Virago, 1980 [1893]) imaginatively recreates the joys and pains of the process of liberation through typing. Hilda Martindale's *Women Servants of the State, 1870–1938: A History of Women in the Civil Service* (George Allen and Unwin, 1938) is both a dispassionate survey and an eye-witness account of women's penetration of the Civil Service. Fiona McNally's *Women for Hire: A Study of the Female Office Worker* (Macmillan, 1979), although sociological rather than historical, explores in an exciting way women's attitudes to work and the way in which they attempt to maximize job satisfaction through mobility.

Notes

An earlier version of this paper was presented at the Social History Society's Conference on Gender, Reading, January 1985. The author would like to thank Dr Angela John and Dr Suzanne Dohrn, who read this preliminary version, for their useful comments and criticisms.

1 In *The Sociology of Housework* (Martin Robinson, Oxford, 1974), p. 19. She goes on to pinpoint areas of greatest 'absence': 'There is a notable paucity of studies analysing . . . the occupations in which women workers have traditionally been concentrated – food and clothing manufacture, retail sales work, clerical work, teaching, nursing, and domestic work'. These observations are, of course, applicable to disciplines other than sociology.
2 Elizabeth Garnsey, 'Women's Work and Theories of Class Stratification', *Sociology*, 12 (1978), p. 234.
3 For the purposes of this paper clerical work is roughly defined as work below the level of management which is carried on in offices. The *OED* defines a clerk as 'an officer who has charge of the records, correspondence, etc., and conducts the business of, any department, court, corporation, or society'.
4 There are difficulties in arriving at absolutely impeccable statistics from census data, due to inconsistencies in classification. There are two sets of data, the one for commercial clerks and the other for government employees. The two are conflated only for 1851. Until 1881 commercial clerks were not grouped together but were subsumed under the various industries in which they were employed. In addition, within the category of government employees it is not always possible to disaggregate administrative, clerical and manipulative workers. The author has used the statistics provided by F. D. Klingender in *The Condition of Clerical*

Labour in Britain (Martin Lawrence, 1935). These are consistent over the period under consideration and, as Klingender has massaged the government service data in order to isolate the clerical element, they give the best available approximation of the combined total. The author has calculated the various proportions of increase herself.

5 Clerks' memoirs generally mention how cold and miserable some offices were and how they had various ploys to keep warm: 'No heating and we were advised to take hot water bottles to work in winter' (Alfred Marks Bureau, *Suffragette Secretaries: A Report on Office Life 60 Years Ago* [Alfred Marks Bureau, 1979], p. 23). Some of these devices proved dangerous: 'It has just come to my knowledge that certain members of the Staff have been bringing into the Office muff-warmers filled with charcoal and that already two cases have occurred in which a fire has been the result and serious damage only averted by prompt action. It must be distinctly understood that such a practice is prohibited' (P[ublic] R[ecord] O[ffice], NSC35/2, f. 29, Post Office Savings Bank General Order Book, 9 January 1895).

6 Klingender, *The Condition of Clerical Labour* pp. vii and 103; David Lockwood, *The Blackcoated Worker: A Study in Class Consciousness* (George Allen and Unwin, 1969 [1958], p. 13ff. Holcombe, *Victorian Ladies at Work* chs 5 and 6, pp. 141–62 and 163–93, respectively; Geoffrey Crossick, 'The Emergence of the Lower Middle Class in Britain: A Discussion', in Crossick (ed.), *The Lower Middle Class in Britain*, and Gregory Anderson, *Victorian Clerks* and 'The Social Economy of Late-Victorian Clerks' in Crossick, pp. 113–33.

7 McNally, *Women for Hire*, table 3.1 'The Proportion of Female Workers in White Collar Occupations, 1911–71', p. 43. These are the percentages for 'clerks'.

8 Lockwood, *The Blackcoated Worker*, p. 125; Holcombe, *Victorian Ladies at Work*, pp. 179, 146; Crossick, *The Lower Middle Class*, p. 18; Anderson, *Victorian Clerks*, p. 132. See also Rosalie Silverstone, 'Office Work for Women: An Historical Review', *Business History*, 18 (1976), pp. 98–110.

9 See, for example, McNally, *Women for Hire*; Rosemary Crompton, Gareth Jones and Stuart Reid, 'Contemporary Clerical Work: A Case Study of Local Government' and Jackie West, 'New Technology and Women's Office Work' in J. West (ed)., *Work, Women, and the Labour Market* (Routledge and Kegan Paul, 1982), pp. 44–60 and 61–79, respectively; Jenny Beale, *Getting it Together: Women as Trade Unionists* (Pluto Press, 1982); Cynthia Cockburn, *Brothers: Male Dominance and Technological Change* (Pluto Press, 1983); and Ann Game and Rosemary Pringle, *Gender at Work* (Pluto Press, 1984 [1983]).

10 Data of the sort needed to provide detailed descriptions of the process of feminization are difficult to locate, except for the Civil Service. The author's research concentrates on the Civil Service. See 'Strategies and Stratagems for the Employment of Women in the British Civil Service, 1919–1939', *Historical Journal*, 27 (1984), pp. 901–24, and she has tended to illustrate her general points about clerical work with examples from

the Civil Service. She has discussed her findings with Suzanne Dohrn of the University of Hamburg, who is currently engaged on a study of women clerical workers in commercial employment, and they are in agreement as to the representativeness of the Civil Service data. For the Civil Service see also the classic study by Hilda Martindale, *Women Servants of the State*, and a regrettably brief report of a seminal conference paper by Anna Davin, 'Telegraphists and Clerks', *Bulletin of the Society for the Study of Labour History*, 26 (1973), pp. 7–9.

11 Agnes Amy Bulley and Margaret Whitley, *Women's Work* (Methuen, 1894), p. 41.

12 George Gissing gave this title to a novel which dealt with the struggles of such women. Its main characters were the daughters of a doctor who, despite their embarrassed urging ('I don't think girls ought to be troubled about this kind of thing'), failed to insure his life and so left them penniless. The occupations of the five sisters who survived to adulthood summarize the opportunities open to women of no great education or drive: companion to an old lady, two shop assistants (of whom one died from consumption and the other contracted a loveless marriage to a wealthy older man in order to escape), nursery governess, board school teacher. The other two protagonists, feminists both, ran a typing agency which catered for 'the great reserve': 'When one woman vanishes in matrimony, the reserve offers a substitute for the world's work. True, they are not all trained yet – far from it. I want to help in that – to train the reserve'. (*The Odd Women*, pp. 1, 37)

13 For a discussion of the causes of the surplus see J. A. and Olive Banks, *Feminism and Family Planning in Victorian England* (Schocken Books, New York, 1972 [1964]), pp. 27–8. In 1851 there were 231,200 more women than men aged 20–44 in Great Britain; and in 1911 636,100. In 1851 there were seven per thousand more single women than men aged 45–54 in England and Wales and in 1861 66 in Scotland; and in 1911 37 and 48, respectively. (B. R. Mitchell and Phyllis Deane, *Abstract of British Historical Statistics* [Cambridge University Press, Cambridge, 1962] ch. 1, 'Population and Vital Statistics', table 4, 'Population by Sex and Age Groups (Quinary), England and Wales, Scotland and Ireland, 1841–1951', p. 12, and table 5, 'Proportions of Each Age Group [by Sex] according to Marital Condition, England and Wales, 1851–1951, and Scotland, 1861–1951', pp. 15–18 [calculations by the author].) It is arguable that this disparity was even greater for the middle class. Clara Collet showed that the ratio of unmarried women to unmarried men aged 35–45 was very favourable to women in working-class areas like Poplar and St George's-in-the-East (50 women: 100 men), but it was decidedly the reverse in such haunts of the middle class as Hampstead and Kensington (366 and 378:100, respectively) (*Educated Working Women: Essays on the Economic Position of Women Workers in the Middle Classes* [P. S. King and Son, 1902], pp. 38–40).

14 Margaret Harkness, 'Women as Civil Servants', *The Nineteenth Century* X, (1881), p. 369

15 See A. James Hammerton, *Emigrant Gentlewomen: Genteel Poverty and*

Female Emigration, 1830–1914 (Croom Helm, 1979).

16 This astonishing list – excluding the old chestnut of art needlework – was compiled by Elizabeth L. Banks in 'New Paid Occupations for Women', *Cassell's Family Magazine* (1893–4), pp. 586–7. She also suggested 'furnishing ideas for other people to use'!

17 For a description of the efforts of unscrupulous male typographers to drive women out of the trade see Cockburn, pp. 152–9. For a case study of the same process in France see Charles Sowerwine, 'Workers and Women in France before 1914: The Coriau Affair', *Journal of Modern History*, 55 (1983), pp. 411–41. See also essay 2.

18 Lady John Manners, *Employment of Women in the Public Service* (William Blackwood and Sons, Edinburgh and London, 1882), pp. 50–1. Her husband was Postmaster General, 1874–80 and 1885–6.

19 As the noble lady noted (ibid., p. 40) bright-eyed and rosy-cheeked women clerks might hope to retire after an honourable career not with a gold watch but with a gold ring.

20 'Report of the 29th Annual Conference of the Postal Telegraph Clerks' Association', *Telegraph Chronicle*, 30 April 1909, motion of Miss Slade.

21 P[ost] O[ffice] A[rchive], POST 30/1815/E4309/1910 [Matthew Nathan?, secretary], memo, 18 February 1910.

22 M. Mostyn Bird, *Women at Work: A Study of the Different Ways of Earning a Living Open to Women* (Chapman and Hall, 1911), p. 126.

23 POST 30/2256/E10244/1912, Matthew Nathan, memo, 'Association of Post Office Women Clerks: Memorial for Better Pay and Prospects', 22 July 1910.

24 Holcombe *Victorian Ladies at Work*, has calculated on the basis of the 1911 census the following distribution of men and women (as a proportion of the total for each sex) among the various categories of work: commerce or business, men 64.2 per cent and women 93.8 per cent; law, 6.1 per cent and 1.8 per cent, respectively; banking, 7.1 per cent and 0.4 per cent, respectively; insurance, 7.5 per cent and 3.2 per cent respectively; railways, 15.1 per cent and 0.8 per cent respectively (table 4C, p. 211).

25 Even though, paradoxically, this had the effect of putting women in charge of machines, usually the prerogative of men. Masculine honour was saved by defining away the 'machineness' of office machines. For example, the skills involved in typing were trivialized: they were not compared to, say, typography, which was a man's 'craft skill', but to piano playing, the universal 'accomplishment' of young ladies.

26 POST 30/364/E171/1880, H.C. Fischer (controller, Central Telegraph Office), memo, 10 December 1878.

27 Logically, then, all 'mechanical' work should have been transferred to women, and by 1914 many employers, including the Civil Service, were prepared to take this route. The only obstacles were the heated opposition of male clerks and residual feelings of male solidarity among employers.

28 PRO T1/11464/18470/12, C. A. King, Post Office, marginal note on a letter from R. Wilkins, Treasury, 14 November 1907.

29 'Electric and International Telegraph Co., Bell Alley', *Illustrated London News*, 31 December 1859, p. 649.
30 T1/8371A/18349/88, R. Welby, confidential memo circulated to principal clerks, Treasury, 12 October 1888. Harkness (p. 371) describes the women's eyrie in the Receiver and Accountant General's Department of the Post Office: 'This apartment is far up above the noise of the streets, and a small balcony allows the clerks to breathe the fresh air from the river. A few withered ferns outside the window struggle to keep life in them, and are carefully tended by their owners, but the smoke and fog do not encourage the growth of young leaves'.
31 Deputation of the Association of Post Office Women Clerks to Sydney Buxton, Postmaster General, 6 November 1911, reported in *Association Notes*, 14 (1911), p. 126. Miss C. S. Howse described the thinking behind this rule: 'The Offices were all in the City, and men were not so much used to see women about, and very likely the places were not there for women to go to'.
32 *Royal Commission on the Civil Service, Appendix to First Report, Minutes of Evidence*, 11 April 1912, PP 1912–1913, Cmd. 6210 q. 921.
33 Shan Bullock, *Robert Thorne: The Story of a London Clerk* (T. Werner Laurie, 1907), p. 42.
34 Bullock, *Robert Thorne*, p. 94
35 POA, POST 33/329/M20612/1921 (Dr A. H.) Wilson (medical officer), memo, 4 March 1892. I am indebted to Dr Martin Daunton for this reference. Employers were very conscious of their eugenic responsibilities: 'After all there is a good deal to be said for not making the employment [of typists] too attractive as a permanent career. We do not want to become dependent, like the USA, on alien immigration for maintenance of our population' (T1/9988B/14659/03, H. W. Primrose, Inland Revenue, to T. L. Heath Treasury, 1 April 1903).
36 POST 33/329/M20612/1921 (Post Office Departmental Committee on the Marriage Bar), Report, 24 March 1892.
37 Ibid. Miss Maria Constance Smith, lady superintendent of women staff in the Savings Bank Department, noted that some women sorters (daughters of artisans and better-off members of the working class) might wish to remain at work after marriage ('though I have never had evidence of such a wish'), but women clerks (pukka middle-class ladies) would find this 'positively distasteful' ('Evidence of Miss Smith . . .', 7 March 1892).
38 Ibid., G. R. Smith, (Controller, Returned Letter Office), memo, 30 March 1875.
39 T1/8905S/19220/94, J. M. K(empe), memo, (October 1894).
40 POST 30/2256/E10244/1912, 'Extract from Report of Deputation of the National Joint Committee [of Post Office unions], October 8th 1916'.
41 POST 33/329/M20162/1912, 'Evidence of Miss Smith'.
42 POST 30/2256/E10244/1912, 'Extract'.
43 POST 30/275/E3613/1875, John Tilly, (Secretary), Post Office, to Treasury, 22 July 1874, and POST 30/2489/E11951/1913, 'Statement showing the number of candidates who competed for Women and Girl

Clerkships during the 5 years 1901–1905', figures for the October 1901 examination. (I am indebted to Dr Martin Daunton for these references.)

44 Tom Gallon, *The Girl behind the Keys* (Hutchinson, 1903), pp. 5, 11 ff.

45 Olive P. Rayner, *The Type-writer Girl* (C. Arthur Pearson, 1897), pp. 17, 247, 255 ff.

46 'Colleges for Girls', *The English Woman's Journal* II (12 February 1859), p. 373.

47 Quoted from entries in Flora Mayor's diary for 1899 and 1897, respectively, by Sybil Oldfield in *Spinsters of this Parish: The Life and Times of F. M. Mayor and Mary Sheepshanks* (Virago, 1984), pp. 54–5.

48 Gissing, *The Odd Women*, p. 135. Miss Barfoot argues specifically for clerical work as a career. 'Because I myself have had an education in clerkship, and have most capacity for such employment, I look about for girls of like mind, and do my best to prepare them for work in offices. And . . . I am *glad* that I can show girls the way to a career which my opponents call unwomanly . . . A womanly occupation means, practically, an occupation that a man disdains . . . I want to do away [with this defininition] . . . and I see very clearly that this can only be effected by an armed movement, an invasion by women of the spheres which have always been forbidden us to enter'.

49 T1/10614B/5925/07, C. E. C[ollet], 'Salaries and Conditions of Employment of Women of 18 years and Upwards Employed as Typists in April 1907' [calculations by the author]. The last quotation is from a memo on the report by G. C. U(pcott) of the Treasury, 21 June 1907. A similar, though not so detailed, report by B. L. Hutchins, 'An Inquiry into the Salaries and Hours of Work of Typists and Shorthand Writers', *Economic Journal*, 16 (1906), pp. 445–9, gives similar wage data: 79 per cent of typists and shorthand writers in business firms were earning 25/– or more and 38 per cent 35/– or more per week (calculations by the author).

50 Derek Hudson, *Munby: Man of Two Worlds: The Life and Diaries of Arthur J. Munby, 1828–1910* (Abacus, 1974 [1972]), diary entry for 15 July 1865, p. 209.

51 'Women's Work in a Sub-Post Office', *The Englishwoman*, X 28 (April 1911), p. 47.

52 T1/8840A/10974/94, L. M. Andrews to Sir Francis Jeune, president, Probate, Divorce, and Admiralty Division, Supreme Court, 18 June 1894.

53 T1/9796B/4628/02, petition of S. I. Fulcher, (superintendent of typists), 12 March 1902, enclosed in T. H. Sanderson, Foreign Office, to secretary, Treasury, 15 March 1902.

54 T1/9988B/14659/03, petition of Agnes Healey, Clara Mills, Carrie Sayer, typists, to secretary, Treasury, 2 April 1902. Women were equally capable of playing 'poor me' if it suited them. When the Post Office attempted to ban needlework and reading during slack time, one telephonist pulled out all the stops: 'Before we read your rule, we wore aprons with *large* pockets and were allowed to knit with the understanding that nothing had to rest on the sections and the floor had

not to be littered. I am not a young girl, and I have had a lot of experience, but these last few weeks (in matters relating to the office) have been the most miserable I have ever spent. Do you know how it feels to go back to the office after dinner, feeling ready for any amount of work and when you arrive, having to sit there – and do nothing to work off surplus energy? Knitting does soothe one' (POST 30/4260/E4422/ 1919, 'A Telephonist (One of Many)' to Herbert Samuels [sic], Postmaster General [1911].

55 Deputation . . . *Association Notes*, I 14 (1911), p.116, speech of C. S. Howse.

56 T1/12265/50322 Pt. I/18, Committee on Recruitment for the Civil Service after the War, minutes of 34th meeting, 10 December 1918, evidence of Olive King, Civil Service Alliance.

Cornish ore-dressers of the 1860s

6

The Decline of the Independent Bâl Maiden: The Impact of Change in the Cornish Mining Industry

Gill Burke

The employment of women as mine-workers has taken various forms over time. In Britain today women work in the coal-mining industry chiefly as clerical workers in the mine offices at the surface. Only very few women go underground, and they go down as nurses or doctors in an emergency. In other parts of the world this employment pattern varies. Women in India, China and other countries in the developing world still are more closely employed in the mining process. During the 1970s in the United States, women invoked their right to equal opportunity, and are now employed as coal-miners in Kentucky and West Virginia. It is the coal-mining women of the United States who can be said to offer the strongest contemporary challenge to the view that mining is 'men's work' since they have reclaimed underground work both as a right and as a skill at a time when, in the developing countries, women are increasingly being excluded.

Women ceased working underground in the British coal-mines following the Mines and Colleries Act 1842, but they continued to work at the surface of these mines. Indeed, the last two women to be working above ground in coal-mines in Britain only lost their jobs in 1972. In this chapter I will be looking at another group of British women mine-workers. These worked in the tin and copper mining industry of Cornwall and Devon during the eighteenth and nineteenth centuries. They worked at surface, and had never worked underground. They were known as the 'Bâl Maidens' – 'Bâl' being the Cornish word for mine.

There are several reasons why these Cornish women mine-workers deserve examination. Firstly, and most importantly, because they have been very much neglected. They deserve study in their own right. Although contemporary writers discussed the work of mine women, often in some detail, subsequently they can be said to have been 'hidden from history'. Historians of Cornish mining have mentioned them, if at all, simply as an, often picturesque, part of the surface labour-force. Indeed, most historians of mining, whether of coal or of metal, have tended to focus on the *underground* face worker, the 'miner' himself. So a study of the Bâl Maidens helps to correct an imbalance and so develop a more complete mining history.

Secondly, the Bâl Maidens demonstrated an 'independence' – a lack of subservience and a pride in self. In view of many contemporary comments, and also because of their later decline, it is important that this independence is emphasized and understood. It was an independence shared with other young women workers who were employed in mills and factories. As Angela John has pointed out,[1] it is no accident that these various groups of independent young women have been largely ignored by male historians and others who inherited without question the comments of earlier writers about women's true place being in the home. The relationship between women's activity in the public sphere of the world of work and the private sphere of the domestic world of home – the former often denigrated and the latter praised by male commentators – can very usefully be examined in the context of the employment of women in mining.

Independence, particularly as manifested by single, young, working-class women, could be said to pose a particular threat to middle-class men. During the nineteenth century many such men argued that female employment before marriage should be of a kind to inculcate domestic skills, since the true task for women was marriage and work in the home as a 'ministering angel' to her husband. The independence that derived from paid employment outside the domestic sphere was not, they felt, a suitable prerequisite. Mine work, whether in coal or metal-mining, most certainly could not be said to offer a suitable training for the angelic afterlife of marriage.

Some of the nineteenth-century commentators responded to the threat posed by independent young women by offering moral arguments. These often stressed the corrupting and depraving nature of such employment. Others trivialized the women into stereotypes, often portraying them as mannish amazons devoid of any feminine virtues. Not all nineteenth-century commentators responded in this way, however. There were those who argued that women's employment, in mining as in much else, was in fact beneficial to women as a preparation for marriage, particularly in the managing of earnings and in thrift. Others went further and argued that such work was of value in itself. It is notable that the majority of such commentators were women rather than men.

Two examples of such opposing views on women's employment can help to illustrate this discussion of the Cornish Bâl Maidens. The view that mine work was not fit work for women was forcefully put by George Henwood in the middle of the nineteenth century. Henwood was deeply involved in Cornish mining, and in 1857 wrote a series of articles about the industry and the people working in it for the *Mining Journal*[2]. In these he included a specific piece about the Bâl Maidens, as well as giving them various mentions elsewhere in his text. The contrasting view that Cornish mining labour enhanced rather than degraded women was put 15 years later by an anonymous writer in the London magazine, *The Ladies Journal*. The physical and mental virtues of the Bâl Maidens' employment were described and discussed in an article that was part of a series on 'Working Women of the British Isles'.[3] Both commentators presented idealized versions of the Bâl Maidens at work to suit their arguments. Both can be said to have overstated their case. The Bâl Maidens themselves do not seem to have spoken or written anything to describe their lives. Their silence presents problems for historians since everything we know about them is mediated through other eyes. Such problems are particularly acute for those examining women's history.

Almost all the evidence there is about the Bâl Maidens is drawn from middle-class male observers, although the writer of the *Ladies Journal* articles was probably a woman. Otherwise evidence is dependent on the reports of Parliamentary Commissioners, Government Inspectors, Victorian novelists, travel writers, journalists, mining experts and medical men with rarely a woman amongst them. It is also important to remember that Cornwall was very isolated from the rest of England, an isolation which only began to end slowly with the opening of the Saltash railway bridge in 1859. Thus, despite the importance of the metal-mining industry to the growing industrial economy of Britain in the first half of the century, most commentators, male and female, approached and observed the men and women working there much as an intrepid explorer might view a strange, and possibly savage, tribe. Therefore, before exploring the images of the Bâl Maidens, it is important first to locate them in the context of the industry in which they worked.

Women and the Cornish Mining Industry

> As to the women, when they were young they rose early and were off to the mines and tin streams before the rest of the world was waking. They wore huge boots, short skirts with coarse white aprons and linen sunbonnets. At night they returned in little companies, singing very sweetly as they passed homeward through the ill lighted streets. On Sundays, or when choirs and Sunday Schools had their outings, they went gaily dressed . . . (H.D. Lowry, *Wheal Darkness: a novel*, 1906)

The metal-mining industry of Cornwall and parts of Devon, although long established, was dramatically expanded and revolutionized in the late eighteenth and early nineteenth centuries. The pumping engines of Newcomen, Trevithick and Watt enabled deep mining for copper to be successfully undertaken to meet the growing demands of newly industrializing Britain. This growth and expansion was reflected in the fact that an increasing number of women were being employed where previously few had worked. They were taken on to speed throughput of the increasing amounts of ore being brought up from below to be processed by the new and more efficient crushing machinery known as the 'Cornish stamps'.

Although by the middle of the nineteenth century Cornwall and Devon were producing over one-third of the world's copper and tin, and the industry was of major national importance, mine-work was not the sole nor the major area of employment for local women. Such work was concentrated in the ore producing districts and although these covered large parts of Cornwall (and a much smaller part of Devon) it was only in the remoter areas that mining offered the main employment opportunity. Other industrial work could be found in the dressing sheds of the china clay mines and quarries; there was also seasonal work available in agriculture and fishing – particularly with the pilchard harvests. But for women in Cornwall, and indeed in the rest of Britain, the major form of employment was domestic service and similar 'female' trades.

The number of women in mining reflected the rise and falls in the fortunes of the industry. In 1827 there was an estimated 2,276 women working in the copper and tin mines of Cornwall.[4] As the industry expanded the numbers rose to 5,764. During the 1840s and

1850s many mines began to shift their production from copper to tin. This required fewer women, and when the price of copper fell sharply during the 1860s very many more women, and men, lost their jobs as the purely copper mines closed. In 1871, however, there were still 4,450 women employed in mine work in Cornwall. This was a not inconsiderable number, but it needs to be set against the 8,167 women who were either dressmakers, milliners, seamstresses or tailoresses in Cornwall in 1871, and the 13,244 women who worked in general domestic service.[5]

Unlike the coal-mining industry, women had never worked underground in Cornwall. Indeed, Cornish evidence to the 1842 Royal Commission on the Employment of Children (which examined women's employment as well), smugly emphasized this, together with the claim that very young children did not work underground either. This latter claim was untrue – certainly by 1857 Henwood was drawing attention to the plight of boys aged ten and less who worked long hours underground when the official age for starting such work was 14[6] – but there seems no evidence to suggest that women had at any time worked underground. Possibly this helped to define attitudes to Cornish women's mine work. Discussion from the middle of the century onwards of the pitbrow lasses (the women surface workers at the coal-mines) was defined and permeated by attitudes towards women working underground. Such work was difficult, if not impossible, to justify in the light of the Royal Commissions findings in 1842.

Surface work in the Cornish mines was hierarchically organized; the hierarchy structured as much by age and sex as by skill. Children often started work at the ages of six or seven. They sorted the lumps of ore and rock into heaps of various types and qualities. Despite the passing of the Factory Acts which regulated children's employment, and despite the Education Act of 1870, there were 1,544 children aged between at least eight and 13 at work in Cornish mines in 1871. In 1890 the Chief Inspector of Factories complained that Cornish mines 'swarmed with children of insufficient age'.[7] For children, the sexual division of labour began at about the age of 12, when the girls went off to the dressing sheds and the boys began to wheel the heavy barrows of ore in preparation for their careers underground.

Women came next in the hierarchy. Their work was to break the lumps of ore and rock into suitable pieces for the crushing machines. In tin-mines they also worked the 'buddles' or separating tables. They might also do some sorting work with children and might, on occasion, wheel barrows. Since these barrows contained three hundred weight or so of ore this was heavy work, but it seems to have been exceptional. Their main task remained the 'spalling' or 'hand ragging' (i.e. the breaking) of lumps of ore. There was some degree of skill involved in the process of knocking off surplus rock from the lumps with special long headed hammers; and considerable manual dexterity required in then crushing the lumps of orestuff with large flat-faced hammers, whilst sweeping the crushed material away with the free hand.

Male surface workers were, in the main, men who, through accident, ill health or age, were unable to work underground. Their work was almost all unskilled. It involved labouring, working the stamping engines and minding the pumping engines. In the later part of the nineteenth century the Mines Inspectors were still complaining of the reluctance of Cornish mine companies to see the job of Engineman as an important occupation. One man alone might be left in charge of several engines, some considerable distance away from each other. Quite frequently the man would be unable to read the instructions, or, more importantly, understand the workings of the safety gauge. The number of boiler explosions, and concomitant fatalities, was finally lessened through legislation rather than by changed attitudes. Nonetheless, unskilled though they might be, the male surface workers earned approximately double the 1/– per day earned by women – who were classed with the boys in the Mine Account Books.

At the top of the pyramid were the skilled craftsmen. There were not many of these. They were the smiths, carpenters and masons whose task was the repair and maintenance of mine tools, plant and underground equipment. They formed an elite group amongst the surface workers, but were, however, lower in status than the underground workers. These in turn had a further hierarchy of skills which culminated in the face workers, called 'Tributers' who mined the ore.

Women's employment in Cornish mines can therefore be defined as being of low status, but requiring a degree of skill, dexterity and physical strength. Their low status was acknowledged both by low earnings and by lack of any recognition that acquiring skill could lead to promotion. Boys working at surface were clearly en route to something better – the higher status underground career. Girls could only go to the dressing shed where skills, once acquired, could only increase earnings to a given level. However, their work there was an integral part of the production process and as such, despite low rewards, was neither marginal nor marginalized.

Tin-mining required fewer women than did copper-mining, due to the greater hardness of the rock, but initially the shift away from copper to tin-mining did not substantially affect the number of women employed although there was some decline. This shift of activity was partly a consequence of the copper lodes beginning to pinch out and become difficult to extract profitably as the mines grew deeper. In part also it was a response to the winds of change that began to blow, gently at first, through the Cornish industry. It was not a shift all mine companies chose to make. The move from copper to tin involved a certain amount of re-equipping and many mines were reluctant to do this. The system by which the mines accounting and shareholding was operated – known as the Cost Book System – discouraged long-term capital investment.[8] Also, many companies preferred the flexibility of a labour-force which could be laid on or off as required rather than machinery. The latter was costly to buy and needed continual output regardless of current metal prices in order to recoup purchase costs.

The mines which remained primarily copper producers, however, were to pay the price for their conservatism in the 1860s. The growth in the production of copper from Chile brought with it a steep and devastating fall in price. Large numbers of the Cornish mines closed down. Many were never to reopen. From 1873, similar price falls occurred for tin as new deposits in Australia were exploited. The Cornish mines were faced with a crisis of survival. Those mines which remained operative did so first by labour shedding then by technological innovation and finally by restructuring. The first technical innovations were below ground. These were the drilling machines which whilst diminishing the number of underground workers required at the same time increased output. This initially increased the need for surface workers. At surface, men were laid off in preference to the cheaper women. By the 1890s, however, it was clear these changes were not enough to save the industry. By then very few mines indeed remained open – 23 in 1895 as compared with 307 in 1873 – but those few changed structurally and technologically. Most became limited liability companies, abandoning the old Cost Book System. Greater mechanization took place below ground and at surface mechanical separation tables – called Fru Vanners – were introduced. These broke and pounded the ore that had previously been broken by women. This now meant the loss of jobs for most of the few women still employed in mine work. By the early twentieth century only a handful of women remained working at the Cornish mines.

Images of the Bâl Maiden

> Though the breaking of the ore is laborious, it does not appear
> to be an injurious occupation as the women seem remarkably
> healthy . . . (*Royal Commission on Mines* . . . *the 'Kinnaird*
> *Commission'*, 1864).

The Bâl Maidens worked either in the open or in open-sided sheds.
Some mines provided a separate shed where tea could be brewed at
lunch-time, but most mines were sparsely provided. The only warm
dry place was the engine house. This was often the only place where
miners coming from underground could change and hang their wet
clothes. Separate changing rooms, called 'drys' were not provided in
any save a handful of mines until the beginning of the twentieth
century.

To all intents and purposes the Bâl Maidens' work can be
described as 'outdoor' with the added invigoration of the walk to and
from the mine, often a distance of several miles. Yet, compared to
the pitbrow women their work was not too heavy. Although they
occasionally had to wheel heavy barrows, the women in the Cornish
mines did not as a general rule have to lift heavy loads nor drag them
along on their hands and knees. Angela John has drawn attention to
the way in which 'blackness' for many in the nineteenth century was
equated with dirt, sexuality, sin, the Empire . . . the 'underside' of
respectable White Victorian Society. Yet mere lack of coal dust does
not satisfactorily explain the way some commentators 'whitened' the
Bâl Maidens. Metal-mining and its attendant surface work was far
from being a clean occupation. Tin ore in particular stains
everything a rich ochre red. The spoil tips, rivers and the seas into
which mine waste and water were pumped, the ground of the surface
workings themselves, all were of the same red colour. Yet virtually
every comment about the mine women stressed their cleanness, and
thus, by implication, their purity. Only one Victorian commentator
(inappropriately named White) differed from this, as far as I can
discover, and he was observing the *process* of the surface work rather
than the individuals involved in it. Men, women and children, he
said were: 'all red, and all busy. For here the labour goes on as in a
Factory'.[9] White was observing work in progress, where the women
had exchanged the white aprons they wore to and from work for ones
of coarse hessian. Nonetheless he was not an isolated observer.
Throughout the nineteenth century Cornwall, like many other
distant, wild and 'romantic' parts of the British Isles received

numerous visits from intrepid Victorians, many of whom subsequently wrote accounts of their travels. For these early travellers a visit to the mines was almost obligatory. Indeed, Wilkie Collins in his 'Rambles Beyond Railways' in 1851, apologised to his readers for postponing description of the mines until chapter 9.[10] The juxtaposition of picturesque moors and rugged cliffs with what was then a significant industry stirred and captured the Victorian imagination.

It was these travellers, together with the later members of various parliamentary commissions and committees who, with local commentators such as Henwood, remarked upon the cleanliness of the Bâl Maidens in their white aprons and linen bonnets. The anonymous writer in *The Ladies Journal* having opened her article in 1872 with the assertion 'There is not a cleaner, nattier, girl in England than the Bâl Maiden',[11] went on to wax positively lyrical about her subject's dress and cleanliness.

> She wears a clean print dress, cut very short, stout shoes well covering the feet, a white canvas apron with bib or stomacher, and canvas sleeves to protect her arms. On her head is perched a sensible sun bonnet . . . always kept scrupulously clean . . . Round her ankles, to save them from the inadvertent blows from the ore when swept from the table, the Bâl Maiden swathes strips of flannel, which she mostly removes when work is done. There cannot on the whole be a more suitable or practical costume . . . On washing her hands and throwing off the coarse apron . . . the Bâl Maiden is as neat and clean as if she never handled copper ore or hammer.[12]

But for all the enthusiasm shown for the apparently cleanly virtuous Bâl Maidens by the writer to *The Ladies Journal* there were other commentators who, having eulogized the neat aprons and sunbonnets, sounded notes of reservation. In the main these reservations centred upon the Bâl Maidens' 'independence' and in particular the way in which they asserted this independence with bright gaudy clothes and, what was worse, by vigorous speech and free association with the opposite sex. Fashionable dressing, particularly for Sunday chapel, drew so much adverse comment as to suggest that this form of independence posed a real threat on several levels. Social control by class, religion or gender, all were threatened by young women spending a proportion of their earnings on flamboyant dress. According to one contemporary observer in 1856 'the miners' wives and daughters are, on that day, so finely dressed, many of them in silks, that you would hardly distinguish them from Ladies'.[13]

It was noticeable that a different sort of comment was usually made about the miner in his Sunday suit. The dark sober garb was favourably contrasted with the loose, muddy workaday clothing and often commented on as evidence of miners' piety. An investigatory team from the London newspaper *The Morning Chronicle*, however, saw matters differently. Between 1849 and 1851 they travelled the country filing articles about differing occupations and the varying degrees of economic distress being experienced. They commented unfavourably on almost all aspects of Cornish mining life and work, sometimes with considerable perceptiveness, but when it came to dressing up on Sunday both men and women came in for criticism:

> The miners as a class sacrifice to a great extent their domestic comforts to their inordinate love of dress . . . To see the miners, both men and women, at church on a Sunday, or enjoying themselves at a fair at Redruth, one would not suppose there was much distress of any kind amongst them. Most of the men are attired in broad cloth whilst the women parade their finery. But many who come out covered in broad-cloth or arrayed in flaunting flounces, emerge from holes and dens more resembling pig-sties than human abodes.[14]

Even with these commentators, exceptional in their criticism of the male miners, there can be seen a greater condemnation of those who wore 'flaunting flounces'.

Yet, if the contrast between the Bâl Maiden at work and at leisure was sufficiently marked to cause comment, there was general agreement that it was employment *outside* the home that was the cause of such peacock display, and the sourest commentator on the effects of such employment was George Henwood. He deplored the lack of femininity that mine work engendered. The 'amazonian' strength of women, their coarse joking with each other and (worse) with men at work, their working proximity with men and boys together with the 'conversation and rude behaviour' this led to – all this seemed to Henwood to be highly improper, regrettable and the cause of much degeneracy. Cause and effect seemed quite clear as Henwood fulminated:

> Their being associated in such numbers and before men, a spirit of rivalry in dress . . . is soon engendered . . . To see the 'Bâl Maidens' on a Sunday would astonish a stranger; whilst at their work the pendant ear-rings and showy bead necklaces excite the pity as well as the suprise of the thoughtful. All desire to save a few shillings for after life is discarded, and nothing but display is thought of. This is carried on to an incredible extent and all the preaching in the world will never interfere with the wearing of a fine bonnet or shawl . . .[15]

Such a marked contrast with the response to the working clothes of the Bâl Maidens as described in *The Ladies Journal* quoted above, needs to be examined more closely. Clearly it was more than simply the changing in general views over the 15 years that separated the two pieces. Where the two writers differed most profoundly was on the basic issues of first, whether women should undertake paid employment and, secondly, whether this should be in metal mining.

The article in *The Ladies Journal* was one in a series written on work done by women in the British Isles. The writer clearly stated that her objective was to correct the view of 'superficial opinion, which judges that woman has but a small share in the toil of this great country.'[16] Various female occupations came under scrutiny. The writer apparently wanted to seek out and examine women's work not previously observed and tabulated through the various Royal Commissions. It must be said that this pioneering scrutiny did have an anthropological tone, with the writer presenting one 'original find' after another to her reader's gaze. But for all this, it was a perceptive scrutiny.

In contrast, Henwood's consideration of the Bâl Maidens totally opposed the notion of women having any share in the country's toil that did not specifically fit them for wifely duties in the private sphere. It is possible to suggest that this was something he had not actually given too much thought to until the time he came to consider the Bâl Maidens in detail for his article; but once examined, his opinion was quite decisive. An earlier piece in his series presented the more conventional picture of the mine women. This article was about the Setting and Pay Day at a mine – where the ground to be mined was auctioned off and the labour-force received its monthly earnings. It also covered the very good dinner held for the major shareholders and senior mine staff at the Account House afterwards. In this article, the Bâl Maidens appear only as a passing, picturesque, adjunct coming to collect their pay: 'The settings being ended, we see the modest, blushing, neatly clad Bâl Maidens' as they are called, collecting round the pay window'.[17] But by the time Henwood came to consider this 'modest, blushing' group of workers – 24 articles and over a year later – his view had changed. The neatly clad young women had been transformed into the vain creatures of pendant earrings and showy bead necklaces, employed in a wholly unsuitable occupation:

> The hard work is not the greatest calamity of which we complain, that is a mere physical evil; what we most deplore is, that when called to take upon themselves the duties of wife and

mother they are totally unfit for them. How can the moral standard of society amongst the lower orders be raised, with mothers and sisters of such education and example?[18]

Not so the writer in *The Ladies Journal*. She argued that mine work was good in itself, and to prove her point sustained throughout the article an image of the Bâl Maiden as a modest, neatly clad young woman (much like the illustration above). No pendant earrings were mentioned there. The piece ended with a description of a young woman, 'a picture of neatness and prettyness' working in tin buddles at the St Ives Consuls mine: 'She was working in a large shed, the only woman present among many men, but her young face wore the calm look of perfect modesty; it had moreover, the quiet steadfast expression which characterises a working woman'.[19]

Both writers drew a contrast between the Bâl Maidens and the women who worked in the coal industry, but they did so for very different reasons. Henwood argued that legislation should be passed to exclude women from mine work in Cornwall. He was writing at the time when such exclusion of women from pitbrow work was being debated together with the possible moral impropriety of such work. Why, asked Henwood 'if the employment of girls in coal mines be improper, why is such work not improper in mineral mines?'[20] The debate about the pit brow women was still continuing when *The Ladies Journal* writer came to examine the two groups of mining women. Although it is possible to argue that the picture of the neat, happy woman worker was a necessary idealization in a journal whose readership was overwhelmingly middle class, nonetheless the writer did not make disparaging comparisons between the Bâl Maidens and the pitbrow lasses in the way so many other commentators did. She considered instead the question of comparison of pay and working hours. The pay in Cornwall was low, she concluded, it would not serve 'to keep body and soul together' in the North of England. On the other hand the hours of work, and by implication the degree of exploitation, were less in the metal mines, 'the restraining acts of legislature have . . . never affected Cornwall nor been needed there. Gentler manners and more humane customs have been the rule . . . from the days of the Old Tinners'.[21]

The writer was not the first, nor was she to be the last, to succumb to the view that soft voices and a soft damp climate make for gentler ways. There is little evidence to suggest that, when they emerged from out of the Cornish mist, the 'Old Tinners' were noticeably any more gentle mannered than their counterparts in other mining industries. *The Ladies Journal* writer, however, extended her hyperbole to include male Cornish mine-workers as well as female, thus justifying her claim that in Cornwall mine work 'is practical proof of the blessing that work is to women'.[22]

Such a claim had necessarily to challenge the 'moral danger' theorists. The writer did so in two ways. First she emphasized the uplifting value of concentration upon work, as described above and the immunity such concentration brought from sexual harassment. Secondly, this was done by pointing to the enhancing aspects of Cornish society that distinguished it from others.

> She comes of a religious, courteous, peaceloving race . . . It is a rare exception if any slur touches her character – if it should, public opinion being Celtic not Saxon would reproach the man more than the weaker vessel. Thus, not being without sympathy and help, she would recover her station and not sink deeper into misery.[23]

This claim went much further than simply repudiating the moral danger that young women might find themselves in should they be employed alongside men. Indeed, taken in the context of much contemporary comment and opinion which argued that, should women 'fall' their virtue and station were lost for ever, it is remarkable. Examples abound in Victorian literature to illustrate the view that there could be no second chances for fallen women. A woman who repented of her 'folly' might redeem herself by dying, preferably through some form of self-sacrifice, but that was the nearest she could get. Mrs Gaskell's *Mary Barton* is one example of this;[24] as is Charles Dickens's Emily in *David Copperfield* – she, at least, got to Australia. *The Ladies Journal* writer appeared to be suggesting that whilst Cornish society was not permissive, neither was it punitive and that this was a desirable, even laudable, state of affairs.

The main stress of the article, however, was on the virtue and dignity that came from work rather than any concomitant sexual independence. The independence praised by *The Ladies Journal* writer came from economic freedom and the enhancement of work in itself. In this context, bright dresses after work (and after a proportion of earnings had gone into the family economy) were well earned. Some other commentators shared this view. J.R. Leifchild, writing at about the same time as George Henwood, had noticed the 'passion for dress' of Cornish women mine-workers in chapel. But he did not seem too outraged by this, remarking that 'Readers residing in factory or mill districts will have noticed similar propensities . . . Girls will be girls, even near the Lands End'.[25]

All these contemporary comments cannot be shorn of their biases. Nonetheless, behind all the attempts to prove particular points, a clear picture of the Bâl Maiden can be discerned. It is a picture of young women whose employment gave them some degree of economic and social freedom. They were like the pitbrow lasses and the young women factory workers in that they had sufficient control over their income to spend some of it on what might be termed 'independent clothes' – bright, fashionable, becoming, but above all not subservient. Thus they presented a marked contrast with their functional day-to-day workwear, although even there certain decorative statements could be made.

It is interesting to note that the Bâl Maidens seem to have escaped being caught in the 'double bind' that observers so often used about the pitbrow women. If the latter's work clothes were rough and practical then they were termed 'unwomanly' by middle-class observers. If further practicality meant the tucking up of skirts, then this was 'immodest'. Yet if feminine, ladylike clothes were worn these too were 'unsuitable' and seen as socially provocative and apeing one's betters. Many writers mentioned the shorter skirts of the Bâl Maidens, but no one, not even Henwood seems to have found these either shocking or provocative. Possibly the bands of flannel wrapped around the ankles served to lessen middle-class anxieties. Possibly the 'huge boots' acted as a counterweight.

It was the independence of the women that was harder to handle. It was that that made them untouchable. As *The Ladies Journal* writer put it, 'she is out in the sunshine, a free woman, mistress of herself, enjoying her work and the cheerful society of her companions and singing out of the very lightness of her heart.'[26] Yet, in the end, it was not the views of the commentators about the suitability or otherwise of women working at Cornish mines that played a part in the decline of their labour. Susceptibility to moral danger mattered little to Cornish mine companies – their view was far more direct and straightforward, although not often expressed publicly. This was that whilst female mine labour was a necessary and integral part of the production process it was utilized; when it was no longer necessary it was dispensed with.

The crises facing Cornish mining in the 1890s, when the new machinery displaced the women, were so severe and the position of the mines so desperate, that no one apparently felt any need to rationalize the removal of women from the workforce. Indeed, with most of the male workforce also unemployed, what need was there for rationalization on grounds of gender? Nonetheless, the net result of the moves that arose from the transformation of Cornish mining during the 1890s was effectively to exclude women from mine work. This also effectively ended their independence, thus bringing about the situation that Henwood had hopefully anticipated in 1857, when he wrote 'We see no present remedy for this evil, but trust machinery, and non-employment of boys underground, may produce a mighty change; and oblige those who ought to be employed in domestic duties to be so engaged, to their own honour, their husband's comfort and their children's blessing'.[27]

The Impact of Change

> Later, these women cease from labour at the mines and seem to disappear from view – so engrossing are the cares of a family to a wife who counts herself unusually fortunate if her husband earns a pound a week. (H.D. Lowry, *Wheal Darkness*)

Mine work in Cornwall, like that of the pitbrow women in the coalfields, was almost exclusively undertaken by unmarried women. Older women might be taken on again, as a consequence of widowhood perhaps, but this was exceptional. In 1871 there were a few very elderly women at work, 27 of whom were over 60, and ten over 75. More usually, the requirements of servicing the needs of husbands working the miners' rolling shift meant that metal miners' wives, like colliers' wives, did not work outside the home.

It is possible to suggest, however, that the sharing of the 'world of work' between men and women before the latter's marriage had important consequences for the structure of their social world. Although women might 'disappear from view' upon marriage, they did not necessarily nor entirely lose their 'independence'. They did not, for example, lose their love of finery; even though the consequences of this might well be indebtedness to the travelling packman.[28] Miners' wives as well as miners' daughters wore silks, if they could, on a Sunday. Even during the hard times of the 1890s when whole villages were being kept alive on money sent back by men working in the South African mines, this continued to be the case. Richard Blewett was able to comment in his memoirs on the 'tournament of fashion' in chapel on Sunday, funded out of those same remittances.[29]

It would be an exaggeration to claim that employment before marriage resulted in equality between the sexes. But what sparse evidence there is suggests that there was, at least, a lack of deference towards men. This seemed particularly true of the earlier part of the nineteenth century. During that period, there had even been notable women non-conformist preachers in Cornwall, such as Ann Mason the Bryanite.[30] In addition, the hazards of a miner's life all too frequently resulted in disabling disease or injury which necessitated a return to some form of employment by his wife. Most often this was a form of self-employment travelling round the district in a donkey cart selling sand for floors, or fish or vegetables. Most importantly, until the period at the end of the century when the mining industry was transformed and with it the whole structure of economic and social relations, the boundaries between the world of work and the world of home were less rigidly drawn for both men and women.

Although the mineralized areas of Cornwall were dominated by mines, the settlement pattern of the miners was not around the mines as such. In this they differed from the mining settlements of many coalfields. The Cornish mine companies rarely housed their workforces and, as John Rule has pointed out, the Cornish miner was an industrial worker but a rural dweller.[31] The customary practice was to lease land, or a dwelling, from a landowner – not necessarily connected in any way with the mine where the miner was presently working. Land or dwelling was leased on the 'three lives' system – that is the lease remained valid until all the three people named as 'lives' had died. Thus, although a miner might well change his workplace, he and his family remained settled at home. This leasehold practice resulted in widely spread settlement patterns. Therefore, it is more accurate to describe the Cornish mine-workers' social world as a 'community dominated by mining' than as a 'mining community'. Cornish miners, even when numerically dominant, were thus part of a wider rural community. This membership had important implications in terms of social interaction, work habits, participation in the events of the rural year and, significantly, for the role of women.

As rural or semi-rural dwellers, mining families participated in the activities, events and festivals that marked the country year. From some of these, such as crop or pilchard harvests, they gained important additions to their diet and sometimes small money wages. From others, such as market days or parish feasts, they gained the reciprocal benefits of social interaction. Such participation was possible for the male mine-workers because, prior to the transformation of the industry, control of work time came from within the work group rather than from the mine management. This flexibility enabled the Cornish miner to have the opportunity, energy and daylight to cultivate small pieces of land, to go fishing, or to help with the harvest. These activities were still sufficiently common for people to comment upon when they began to cease during the 1870s.

Almost all such rural activity was undertaken collectively. One man who had worked as a mine engineman at the end of the century remembered his childhood when such collectivity had been the norm. He recalled one such instance – the collecting of the furze (gorse) to build ricks for winter fuel;

> In the season for bringing home the furze, several men and women were employed. The men making up the bundles, which was called a truss, the women did lead the horses which were loaded with two truss . . . the women led the horses home, there the men offload the furze and build a rick. The women then jump on the horseback and gallop off for another turn. There were half a dozen or half a score of horses with women this way employed . . . I have heard my mother speak of it and the fun she enjoyed bringing home the fuel.[32]

The marking of the rural year by holidays and festivals was also collectively shared by the whole community, including mining men and women. So too were the many local fairs and markets held in the major towns. It is valid to include 'going to market' in this context since it would have counted as a major excursion for mining families from the remoter moorland districts. Camborne market on a Saturday was a crowded bustle of horses and carts, stalls and people. One woman remembered in the Market House,

> the farmers' wives in big, clean aprons with their butter, eggs and cream; poultry and rabbits, flowers and vegetables, seed stalls, boots and shoes and a stall for the big cotton sunbonnets worn by the women tin streamers . . . One corner . . . was screened off, it made a little room . . . It was the soup kitchen . . . it was the custom for miners to treat their Bâl Maiden sweethearts to a bowl of soup[33]

The celebration of patronal Feast Days were annual events. 'Feast Sunday' was primarily religious, marked by Anglicans and occasionally by Methodists. 'Feast Monday', however, and sometimes the rest of the week was more secular. Feasts were supremely drunken events for farmers, miners and fishermen alike. Henwood's description of the St Just Feast in the 1850s makes this clear: 'The public houses swarm with visitors; fiddling, dancing and revelry may be heard on every side – enjoyed by miners, their wives, sweethearts, brothers and sisters. All is gaiety and boisterous good humour, fights seldom result; or if any, at an advanced hour'.[34] Henwood's was a far from censorious account, unlike that of the writer for *The Morning Chronicle* who also witnessed the St Just Feast during the same period. Having arrived at St Just hoping to see the operations of the 'stupendous mines' of the district he was more than a little put out to discover that due to the Feast no work would be done for virtually the whole week, and attributed lax morals, early marriage and petty crime to the 'orgies' witnessed at St Just.[35]

In addition to the parish feasts, the seasonal holidays were also kept. On Midsummer Day the mine engine houses were decked with green branches. The miners would go at dawn to the top of the beacon hills and explode rows of 'Midsummer Holes'. These holes were drilled by hand in the granite rocks there, packed with gunpowder and ignited. Bonfires were lit and celebrations held. Sometimes there might be a dinner at the mine for all employees.

Shared participation in these, and other, rural activities ensured that women who left the mine workforce upon marriage were far from isolated within the home. Nor were many rural and domestic tasks undertaken by women alone. Husbands, male kin and neighbours all shared in them. Thus the overlap between public and private sphere experienced by young women working at the mines continued to be experienced, to a degree, by women after marriage – albeit with the constraints of family commitments. In addition, there were a variety of formal and informal support systems shared by women and men together in which custom played a sustaining and regulating part. And there was the important controlling role of chapel participation which was, in the main, more clearly operated along gender divisions.

Yet it is true to say that as the mining industry changed, so too did life in the communities dominated by mining. These changes were far more than simply the extreme privation suffered as mines closed and men and women lost their jobs. This is not to suggest that there was a sudden and abrupt transition from good old days to bad new times. Rather, these changes worsened those aspects of mining life that were already bad, whilst at the same time changing or eliminating customs and practices that had previously helped enhance the quality of life for both men and women.

The first consequence of the price falls – in copper in the mid-1860s, then tin in the mid-1870s – was large-scale unemployment. In addition, those miners still employed began desperately to try to increase production in order to sustain earnings that were tied to the price of metal. This meant long and greatly increased hours of underground work, with no time any more to share in fishing, harvesting or fuel gathering. Furthermore, the introduction underground of rock drills from 1875 meant that even fewer men could hold production. This technological innovation also meant increasing regulation and formalization of work time which further eroded miners' control of their working days. By the 1880s those men who still had jobs were full-time miners working an eight hour rolling shift determined by the mine company under the ever present threat of mine closure and thus ultimately unemployment. Changes were also taking place outside the mine. Amongst these was increasing agricultural mechanization which changed the nature of what had been communal tasks and relegated women and children to occasional seasonal unskilled work.

The Bâl Maidens were also affected by the loss of jobs following the many mine closures of the 1860s. However, there was a period of brief recovery from 1870 to 1872 when the price of tin rose to a boom level before it began to plunge in 1873. During this time all mine-workers began to seek to benefit from this boom by asking for higher wages. In 1872 the women at Dolcoath mine in Camborne – the most important mine in Cornwall – and at Wheal Basset mine went on strike and thereby did briefly gain a pay increase.[36] But their gains were soon overtaken by the rapid fall in tin price and the onset of depression in the industry. Initially those women working in mines that managed to stay open were less affected than the men by these price falls. The mine companies sent more boys underground and laid off expensive male labour. But this did not last, and soon women too lost their jobs in increasing numbers.

Another brief rallying of tin price during the 1880s highlighted the changed situation in Cornwall. One example of the change in relations between land and capital was the dispute over the renewal of the Dolcoath mine lease. This dispute between company and landowner brought the miners rioting on to the streets of Camborne. Further changes were shown by the election of a Radical Liberal MP by the newly enfranchised miners in 1885. This election, in the face of stiff opposition from the 'Methodist Aristocracy' of mine managers, signalled the growing class differences between the managers and the mine-workers, and an end to the old-styled 'democratic' Methodism within the chapels. Above all changes in the working day and earnings structure meant that the miners were to all intents and purposes wage-labourers with all that that implied for wider economic relations.

The impermanence of the rally in tin price was only too clear. By 1895 it had fallen to the lowest point in the century. The Cornish mines, desperate for investment capital, after years of underinvestment, were faced with two choices. They could either change or they could close. Most took the latter course. Those 23 mines that remained open in 1895 did not remain unchanged but turned increasingly from being Cost Book concerns to becoming limited liability companies. This change did little to halt the erosion of jobs. The impact of mine closures can be seen in the overall decline in the total numbers employed in mining in Cornwall which fell from 26,604 in 1872 to 5,300 in 1895. The impact of new technology at surface can also be seen in the changing proportion of surface to underground workers. In 1895 surface workers formed 49 per cent of the total workforce and this rose to 50 per cent in 1896 as even more men lost their jobs underground. However, by 1897, as the Fru Vanners were brought in to the surface workings, the number of surface workers fell to 47 per cent and by 1900 to 44 per cent. They continued to fall, and within these figures lies the fact that almost all the surface labour shed over those four years were women. The introduction of new machinery brought a virtual end to work for the independent Bâl Maiden.

Decline

The depression of the 1890s thus had special and far-reaching consequences for women who had previously worked in mining. Of course, the depression had serious effects upon everyone in the mining districts, but the changes it brought to women's lives were particularly important. Already the growing crisis of the industry had taken men substantially out of the domestic sphere. Now, they were forced out even further, forced abroad to find work. From the late 1880s men left Cornwall in increasing numbers. The majority of them went to the new and expanding gold mines of South Africa.

Migration of miners was nothing new to Cornwall. Their skills as hard rock miners were highly exportable. Throughout the nineteenth century, in good times and bad, men had sought work abroad. They had gone to Central and Southern America from the 1820s; to the United States from the 1830s and 1840s; to Australia from the 1850s. All over the world Cornishmen participated in the development of mineral mining. Indeed, it could be said that it was their labour that substantially opened up the mining frontiers of the world. These migrations, however, do not appear to have been intended to be permanent. The intention was almost always to return to Cornwall. Unmarried men would leave, return to Cornwall to find a bride and then leave again. Sometimes they would take their new wife with them; more often they would leave her behind in the newly leased cottage. Married men might send for wives and families to join them, sometimes even return to fetch them. But for many the intention to return to Cornwall failed to work out in practice. A judge on the Bodmin Circuit commented, as late as 1912, 'It is quite a common thing for them to stay away for twenty years without ever returning, and very often after being married only a few months. In the majority of cases they send money home and write the most affectionate and interested letters. They are an extraordinary people.'[37] This long-established pattern of migration was augmented during periods of severe depression – such as the 'hungry forties', the late 1860s and 1870s – by the permanent migration of whole families. Indeed, so severe was the depression of the 1870s that one third of the population of the county left Cornwall during the decade, never to return.

The migration of the 1890s, however, was of men alone. Furthermore, it was on a hitherto unprecendented scale. The mines of the Witwatersrand offered a bonanza to men faced with destitution at home. The extent of the migration can be seen by the fact that during the 1890s Cornishmen constituted 25 per cent of the white workforce in the South African gold mines. The mines in Cornwall, it was claimed, were being worked by boys and old men. The Cornish mining districts thus became a world largely without men.

Women now had control over the whole family budget, yet they were also wholly isolated now within the domestic sphere. Daughters who had previously lived at home prior to marriage and whose earnings had contributed to the household economy were now also forced away. All that was available was domestic service, hardly a form of employment that encouraged independence. Very many of these young women left Cornwall, but they went to London rather than overseas. This migration of young women seeking work in the cities can be found in all the 'Celtic fringe' areas of Britain at that time and subsequently.

The married women remaining in Cornwall relied upon money sent by their husbands and sons abroad. But, given the occupational hazards of mining, such funds were precarious even though the sums of money might occasionally be substantial. Higher earnings in the

Rand meant that often the remittances were substantially more than many women had been used to having. Blewett recounts the story of one woman who had waited many weeks without hearing from her husband. When at last a letter arrived, she tore it open, saw the Standard Bank of Africa Draft, rushed out, cashed and spent it. Only when she returned and read the accompanying letter did she learn that her husband was dead and that the money had been a last collection from his workmates.[38] More grimly, as the decade wore on, men began to return from South Africa with terminal silicosis. So many came back to Cornwall only to die, that the disease became known as the 'Africa complaint'. Between 350 and 450 men per year died in the six years 1893–9. Then, the outbreak of the Anglo–Boer War brought even more men home. In 1900 alone 500 died of silicosis.[39] Not all these men had contracted the disease in South Africa, it was just as possible in Cornwall, Australia or the United States. Nonetheless, the overwhelming majority had been working in the Rand mines. The new underground technology was the cause of this greatly increased incidence of disease. Rock drills disseminated a far more fine and more deadly dust than did hand drilling. The very much more capital-intensive mines in South Africa, where over a thousand drills were in use underground in 1895, meant a far greater concentration of risk. This was horribly clearly shown in the differing life expectation for rock drill workers in the different mining districts. In Cornwall during the 1890s/1900s, a man working a drill continuously had a life expectancy of eight years. This was bad enough, yet in South Africa over the same period a similar miner had a life expectancy of only four years.[40]

For Cornish women in the mining districts the 1890s were times of bitter and lonely hardship. They were deprived of the old ways of collective support. Some had husbands and sons either working away or else returned home ill, fighting for breath and waiting to die; others had daughters who were also working away from home. Many might be waiting for letters and money that never came. By the early twentieth century the Poor Law Inspectors were commenting on the number of elderly women left in Cornwall with no families to support them. Often these women had to enter the workhouse because no one in their family remained alive.[41] The earlier days, when independent women had 'jumped on the horseback and galloped off for another turn' were gone. The evenings, when the young employed women had 'returned in little companies, singing very sweetly' were also gone. The old days had not been good ones; life for men and women had been hard and short, infant mortality had been as high as in many industrial towns. Nonetheless, life had not been wholly without joy. The industrial changes that took place in Cornwall in the late nineteenth century and the social changes that followed from them made the lot of Cornish mining women bleak indeed.

The changes in the social world affected both men and women, and it is true to say that neither men nor women had any control over how these changes occurred. It was external factors – the price of metal and the development of the world mineral economy – that wrought such changes upon the Cornish mining districts. Nonetheless, this does not mean that the issue was not also one of gender. The economic factors that dominated were the economics of men. Male mine owners, male investors, and even male inventors of the new technology were responsible for so singularly changing the world of the independent Bâl Maiden.

Bibliographical Note

The modern sources on women in the mining industry in Britain are few and reflect the neglect mentioned in the chapter. For coal-mining women there is Angela John's *By the Sweat of their Brow* (Routledge and Kegan Paul 1984) and metal-mining women are examined in my unpublished PhD thesis 'The Cornish Miners and the Cornish Mining Industry 1871–1921' (University of London, 1982). Much more has been written about male coal-miners although, again, not a lot of recent work has been done on metal-miners. One very interesting recent book on coal-miners is *Independent Collier: the coal miner as archetypal proletarian reconsidered*, edited by Royden Harrison (Harvester Press, 1978) and there is a useful documentary-essay on de-skilling, 'Colliery Mechanisation and the Lanarkshire Miners', by Alan Campbell in *The Bulletin of the Society for the Study of Labour History*, no. 49 (Autumn 1984). From the feminist standpoint many provocative points are made about coal-miners in Ch. 7 of *'Wigan Pier Revisited'* by Beatrice Campbell (Virago, 1984). Her points about coal-miners as the heroes of the Labour Movement may help explain why Labour historians have largely ignored the Cornish miners until recently. The model of the Cornish miner as archetypal conservative was clearly drawn by A.K. Hamilton Jenkin in *The Cornish Miner* (George Allen and Unwin, 1927) and remained largely unchallenged until the last few years. In 'The Cornish Diaspora of the 19th century', ch. 3 in *International Labour Migration: Historical Perspectives* edited by Shula Marks and Peter Richardson (Temple Smith, 1984), I have argued that Cornish miners were every bit as concerned with issues of industrial relations as any group of working people, but that they had more freedom to organize and unionize abroad than in Cornwall. At a more general level, John Rowe's *Cornwall in the Age of the Industrial Revolution* (University of Liverpool Press,

Liverpool, 1963), provides a basic introduction to the importance of Cornwall to the growing British economy of the early nineteenth century, and sets the scene for the changes and decline which was to follow.

As mentioned in the chaper there seems to be no record of what the Cornish mining women *themselves* felt about the events of their time and contemporary accounts by male mine-workers are also very sparse. One way of discovering the 'feel' of a time is through novels of the period, although it is important to remember that these too have class and gender biases as well as the needs of the author to fulfil the plot. At the turn of the century a series of genre novels about Cornwall were written by Henry Dawson Lowry which provide a vivid picture of life in the mining districts. The stories centre round the fictitious town of Tallywarn, which contemporary observers identified as Camborne, and reveal acute observation and a high degree of sociological awareness particularly with regard to the lives of women. *Wreckers and Methodists* (Heinemann, 1893), and *Women's Tragedies* (Heinemann, 1895), both construct a social world clearly based on observation of everyday life. It is a world of racing pigeons, of Friday evening marches with the Volunteers, of Saturday evening markets, of drink, adultery, of chapel going and chapel based socializing; a world where women's lot was almost inevitably unhappy as a consequence of poverty, drink, migration or mine disaster. Lowry could be said to have written 'faction' rather than simply fiction, and his last novel *Wheal Darkness* published after his death (Hutchinson, 1927), is the clearest example of this. The events in the novel take place within the context of the dispute over the lease of Dolcoath mine in the 1880s and draw attention to various underhand occurrences – share dealing based on 'insider' information for example – which took place during that time. It must be admitted that as stories they are probably not to current taste, but they were extremely popular at the time. I do recommend them, however, if readers can stomach the dollops of sentimentality that overlay the social realism, as evocations of a world that had almost vanished by the time Lowry wrote of it.

Notes

1 John, *By the Sweat of their Brow.*
2 George Henwood, *Cornwall's Mines and Miners,* first published in a series in *The Mining Journal* between 1857 and 1859. Reprinted (Bradford Barton, Truro, 1972).
3 *The Ladies Journal of the Court, Fashion and Society.* vol. ii no. 29 (12 October 1872). 'The work done by Women in the British Isles: The Bâl Maiden.'
4 The mining districts of Devon were far smaller than those of Cornwall. They were located mainly around the Tavistock area on the edge of Dartmoor, and along the edge of the river Tamar. In many cases the lodes ran underneath the river and shafts were sunk in Cornwall to reach them. The principal mine was Devon Great Consuls which continued to produce arsenic after the fall in copper prices ended production there and closed most of the Devon mines. The relative smallness of the Devon

mining field and its virtual demise in the 1860s meant that it was simpler for me on the whole to limit my discussion to Cornwall.

5 *General Census of England and Wales*, PP 1871, III, pp.253–5.

6 Henwood, *Cornwall's Mines and Miners*.

7 *Report of the Chief Inspector of Factories and Workshops for the Year ending 1889*, PP 1890, XX Cmd. 6060.

8 Gill Burke and Peter Richardson 'The Decline and Fall of the Cost Book System in the Cornish Tin Mining Industry', *Journal of Business History*, vol. xxiii, no. 1 (1981).

9 Walter White, *A Londoner's Walk to the Lands End and a Trip to the Scilly Isles* (first published in 1855, first printed Chapman and Hall, 1861).

10 William Wilkie Collins, *Rambles Beyond Railways; or Notes in Cornwall*, (Richard Bently, 1851)

11 *The Ladies Journal*, 'The Bâl Maiden'.

12 Ibid.

13 J. Roberton, *On the Insalubrity of the Deep Cornish Mines and, as a Consequence the Physical Degeneracy and Early Deaths of the Mining Population*, paper presented to the Manchester Statistical Society and published in pamphlet form (1859), p.3.

14 P. E. Razzell and R. W. Wainwright, *The Victorian Working Class* (extracts from *The Morning Chronicle* 1849–1851), (Cass, 1973), 'The Mines and Miners of Cornwall', letter xi, pp.21–9

15 Henwood, *Cornwall's Mines and Miners*.

16 *The Ladies Journal*, 'The Bâl Maiden'.

17 Henwood, *Cornwall's Mines and Miners*.

18 Ibid.

19 *The Ladies Journal*, 'The Bâl Maiden'.

20 Henwood, *Cornwall's Mines and Miners*.

21 *The Ladies Journal*, 'The Bâl Maiden'.

22 Ibid.

23 Ibid.

24 Elizabeth Gaskell, *Mary Barton: a tale of Manchester life* (first published Chapman and Hall, 1848; Many subsequent editions including Penguin, 1970).

25 John R. Leifchild, *Cornwall: Its Mines and Miners, by the Author of Our Coal and Our Coal Pits*, The Travellers Library, vol. 23 (1856).

26 *The Ladies Journal*, 'The Bâl Maiden'.

27 Henwood, *Cornwall's Mines and Miners*.

28 *Report of the Commissioners appointed to enquire into the conditions of all Mines to which the Provisions of the Acts 23 and 24 Vict Cap 115 do not apply* (*The Kinnaird Commission*), PP 1864, xxiv, Cmd. 3389 vol. iii

29 Richard Blewett, *The Village of St Day in the Parish of Gwennap*, Paper given at a Board of Education Short Course for Teachers in Public Elementary Schools on 'The Citizen in the Modern World', July 1935.

30 I acknowledge the unpublished work of Deoborah Valense of Boston, on women Bryanite preachers in Cornwall.

31 John Rule, *The Labouring Miner in Cornwall 1740–1870*, unpublished PhD thesis (University of Warwick, 1971).

32 *Reminiscences of Old Times by J. H. a Mine Engine Driver 1871–1908*, Cornwall County Record Office, Truro, DDX 152/11 (1930).

33 Murial Sara, *Cornwall Remembered* (privately published, 1969).

34 Henwood, *Cornwall's Mines and Miners.*

35 Razzell and Wainwright, *The Victorian Working Class.*

36 *The Royal Cornwall Gazette*, 27 January 1872, pp.4–7.

37 *Royal Commission on Divorce and Matrimonial Proceedings*, PP 1912–1913, xix, Cmd. 6480, vol. iii # 12838.

38 Blewett, *The Village of St Day.*

39 *Cornwall County Council Sanitary Returns 1893–1903*, Rashleigh Papers, Royal Institution of Cornwall, Truro.

40 *Report on the Health of Cornish Miners, Appendix III.* PP 1904, xiii, Cmd. 2091. See also Gill Burke and Peter Richardson, 'The Profits of Death: a comparative study of Miners' Phthisis in Cornwall and the Transvaal 1876–1918' *Journal of Southern African Studies*, vol. 4, no. 2 (April 1978).

41 *Royal Commission on the Poor Laws, Appendix IX, pp. 1909, xvi, Cmd. 4653. 'Final report on the relation of Industrial and Sanitary Conditions to Pauperism'* by A.D. Steel-Maitland and Miss Rose E. Squire.

Part III

Women and Organization

The Manningham Strike Committee, 1891

7

Lost Leaders:
Women, Trade Unionism
and the Case of the General Union
of Textile Workers, 1875–1914*

Joanna Bornat

In 1900, the Women's Trade Union League, which had been formed in 1874 to encourage women to form and join trade unions, carried out an enquiry into the problems of organizing women. Men and women trade unionists, leaders in the main, replied with a wide variety of explanations. There was a shared assumption that women were a problem. Their apathy, lack of interest and instability were generally seen as presenting special difficulties for organizers and officials. The most positive responses came from those who recognized that women's position in society forced submission but that with education and encouragement a woman could be as committed as any man, often more fiercely so.[1]

Women's willingness to join trade unions was *not* the main issue. Following a wave of militancy in the late 1880s more unions had begun to open membership to women. And women had formed their own unions. The Women's Trade Union League helped to start about 60 of the 80 or 90 women's societies formed between 1886 and 1906.[2] What was at issue was the turnover in women's membership, an apparent lack of staying power and interest which seemed to

*The General Union of Textile Workers was only adopted as a title for the union in 1912. Prior to this it had gone under various names, as Huddersfield and District Power-Loom Weavers' and Woollen Operatives' Association, and, in 1899, General Union of Weavers and Textile Workers. As the GUTW it became more widely known as a general union for textile workers. It is the name which I prefer to use in this essay.

suggest a lack of enthusiasm and which meant that few women rose to positions of leadership within unions.

By looking at one union, the General Union of Textile Workers (GUTW), during the years 1875 to 1914, we may be able to identify the factors which apparently held women back from sustained membership and which prevented them from taking leading roles. As an organization, the General Union of Textile Workers presents a particularly strong case against which to test ideas. Outwardly, at least in terms of its origins and leadership, it provided a favourable context for women's trade unionism to flourish. Its origins lay in women's collective initiatives. It recruited equally amongst men and women workers in the wool textile industry from the start. Women comprised slightly less than half the membership in the years up to 1914 when the total reached 12,950, and it was led by two men, Ben Turner and Allen Gee, who were committed to adult suffrage. Both were well known for their advocacy of equal political rights for men and women.[3]

It is in relation to this last point that an explanation for women's trade union role will be developed. It will be argued that the segregation of women's political and economic roles meant that while women's suffrage was promoted, women's role in production was consistently portrayed as marginal. Segregation and marginalization were sustained by social and ideological controls which were imposed by employers and leading trade unionists. These had a direct effect on women's levels of participation in the GUTW.

Women in the wool textile industry of West Yorkshire, though in a slight majority numerically, were typically restricted to jobs which guaranteed more skilled employment and higher earnings for men. This sexual division of labour was maintained by social controls which were rooted in assumptions about women's lesser economic needs and lower productive potential. Women's needs as workers were generally defined in domestic terms. Though the most extreme situation and consequent marginalization was reserved for married women, those who were single also tended to have their needs as workers defined in terms of family relationships. This is not to say that the main union, the GUTW, was unconcerned about women's levels of pay nor that it failed to seek solutions to problems of low pay. Rather it was a question of reinforcing often fixed assumptions about women's lesser financial need: an implicit marginalization of women in relation to issues of economic production.

Notions of man as breadwinner and woman as dependant

pervaded, and still pervade, discussions of work and domestic relationships, affecting women's status as workers throughout their lives. As young girls, notions of expected domestic role tended to determine the moment and point of entry into employment.[4] Skilled occupations were less likely to be sought if marriage and childbearing were considered the main careers for a young woman. And if employers, managers and foremen shared this view then skilled jobs would not be provided.

Inequalities of need were further supported and matched by a second set of judgments, those relating to women's productive potential. Assumptions about women's lesser productive potential, whether expressed in terms of suitability for different types of work, or lower output, were to be found in statements, articles and even the actions of key figures in the trade union movement. In 1877, Broadhurst spoke for a majority of men delegates at the Leicester TUC when, as president he pronounced that 'it was their duty as men and husbands to use their utmost efforts to bring about a condition of things, where their wives would be in their proper sphere at home, instead of being dragged into competition for livelihood against the great and strong men of the world.' Even during the war years when women's ability to match the output of men in 'quite 'new' areas of work became obvious, arguments which centred on suitability for certain types of work only were still being advanced.[6]

The wool textile industry, in the years before the First World War, provides a clear example of the effect of social and ideological constraints on women's role in production. The woollen and worsted industry was a part of that great band of industries, textiles, in which the wages earned by women workers were higher than in most other areas of employment. 1906 figures showed that on average women's earnings in the wool textile industry were, at over 56 per cent, in greater proportion to men's earnings than in any other industrial group.[7] Within and between various occupations, however, there were wide differences and, of course, such figures conceal the fact that earnings were determined largely by the occupations which were open to women.

All pre-war observers were struck by the problems of attempting some form of representative statement of earnings in the wool textile industry. Average earnings for both sexes varied between districts though there tended to be greater consistency amongst men than amongst women. Men's earnings varied from 26/– to 29/– while women's earnings varied from 12/– to 17/–.[8] One relationship is clear; in towns such as Bradford, where women predominated in the industry, wages tended to be lower, in places like Huddersfield, where the numbers of men and women were more equal, wages tended to be higher. This might suggest that sections of the industry which had become identified with women's employment were consequently marginalized into a downward spiral of low pay and fewer opportunities for women.

Differential earnings for men and women in the industry were maintained through periods of rising and falling prices. Throughout the depression years of the 1870s and 1880s, the differences in some occupations between men's and women's earnings were maintained. In Huddersfield, women weavers actually took a proportionately greater reduction than men.[9] There were well-established norms by which a distinction was maintained between men's and women's earnings within different districts. In the heavy woollen and fancy woollen trades of Dewsbury, Batley and Huddersfield, there was said to be no particular advantage in employing a man or a woman in weaving. Men and women could be found side by side on similar work and machinery in some mills. In the Huddersfield area, however, women were paid at rates which were between 10 and 15 per cent less than those of men. Those who supported this inequality claimed that it was due to the fact that women weavers needed more help from tuners, in preparing looms and carrying finished pieces from the looms. At the Royal Commission on Labour, in 1892, Allen Gee, general secretary of what was later to become the GUTW explained that:

> a woman will have to wait occasionally for a tuner to attend to the loom, where the man would not wait, and he would therefore get on with the work a little quicker. There are exceptions, I had better say, where women will turn out quite as much work as men, but they are very rare exceptions indeed.[10]

Recalling their working lives, women weavers had different views:

> When you finish your job the men used to be able to lift their own beams out and a woman wasn't expected . . . that was about the only thing they did more than we did . . . And they used to get many a shilling a cut more than we did for that . . . All the time the women grumbled about the men having more than them you see for doing the same type of job. Because lifting the beam out it was a hard, heavy job, but it was only a matter of two or three minutes you see.[11]

Setting aside such obvious inequalities, there were other issues which helped to establish lower earning levels for women. Average figures mask factors of skill, age, and type of cloth woven. For example, men might weave throughout a working life, up to age 55, whereas the majority of women weavers were below 25 years of age. Although the basic skills of a weaver were learned in a matter of weeks, experience and length of service could make crucial differences. Older women who stayed in the industry as weavers, without a break, were frequently noted for, and justly proud of, reputations for skills in teaching, efficiency, and, quite frequently, tuning their own looms. Length of employment could therefore affect earnings levels.

Within mills, tendencies to allocate the heaviest and most complex looms to men could also mean greater earnings for men. Prices were determined by complex computations of calculations based on numbers of shuttles and picks, or threads, to the inch. Each additional shuttle was paid for as were any other extras on a loom. As weavers were paid by the completed piece, the ability to complete pieces without having to wait for a tuner to fix problems could also affect pay. Inequalities in earnings and in access to jobs which offered better pay played their part in delimiting women's scope of action in the pre-war years. Such factors need to be remembered when considering women's record as trade union members.

The earliest textile unions in Yorkshire have left very little evidence of their scope and activities, nor is it clear to what extent, if any, women took out membership in organizations such as the West Riding Fancy Cloth Weaving Union and the General Union of Weavers and Spinners of the 1820s.[12] Women had been actively involved in all the different periods of militancy from the beginning of the nineteenth century. As handloom weavers in 1832 they had established large co-operative workshops in Huddersfield. Women, with men, were active in the Owenite Grand National Consolidated Trades Union, but following the collapse of this first general union, women textile workers were to take no leading role for some decades.[13] Outside the skilled men's societies, dating mainly from the 1850s and 1860s,[14] there were no successful attempts at organization among less skilled sections of the industry. Groupings emerged in towns and villages, but tended to centre around individuals or incidents and failed to secure more enduring bases. Organization among woollen and worsted workers did not match the achievements of the cotton, hosiery and boot and shoe industries during these years.

A standard text for trade union history[15] attributes poor levels of organization in the wool textile industry to two main factors. There was the late arrival of mechanization in the industry in comparison with cotton. Secondly, the effects of the depression years of the early 1880s meant that there was a shift away from men's employment as cheaper labour and cheaper products were sought. Such an explanation assumes that mechanization and men's employment were prerequisites for organization. Of course lateness of mechanization in industries such as quarrying and mining did not prevent organization, nor did low wages which were also characteristic of these industries.

This apparent failure on the part of the woollen and worsted workers was not due to any lesser trade union consciousness amongst women workers. In fact the first successful attempt to organize in Dewsbury took place amongst women workers, as did the momentous Manningham strike in Bradford. In Dewsbury, a wage reduction imposed by the employers was rejected by women weavers, who, in 1875, left work and formed an all-women strike committee.[16] During the strike, large meetings, some 7,000 and 9,000 strong, were addressed by the strike committee members and their supporters. All the leading Dewsbury manufacturers were involved in the dispute, which lasted several weeks during February and March of 1875. The strike was financed by contributions made to a strike fund by groups of weavers at various mills in the district and further afield. The Women's Trade Union League, formed the previous July in London, was certainly involved from the outset, though it is not clear to what extent. A Miss Ashworth of Bath, a niece of John Bright,[17] donated £10 to the strike fund. The strike ended in compromise: the actual cut imposed by the employers was reduced. Signatories to the agreement were the local Manufacturers' Association and Mrs Hannah Wood, president of the Weavers' strike committee.

Perhaps more significant than this agreement was the decision taken after the strike to form the Dewsbury, Batley and Heavy Woollen District Woollen Weavers' Association. A mixed union of men and women had originated from action taken initially by women. Although men had played a part, chairing and speaking at meetings, surviving documentary evidence shows that the origins and drive had come from women weavers. The new union drew its strength directly from weavers in mills in the district. Meetings were held initially at the Old School, Batley Carr, somewhat in contrast to the normal place for union meetings, the public house. The strike made its mark locally as women speakers stood at mill gates addressing groups of workers.

Though at first the new union consisted entirely of women, including the four auditors and a subcommittee active in the suffrage campaign, leadership gradually came to be concentrated among the men members. By 1881 the committee was entirely led by men. Problems with a full-time collector of union subscriptions who apparently failed to hand over money he had collected[18] could not have helped. The union struggled on, trying unsuccessfully to extend membership to other grades, but finally voted to amalgamate with the coexisting Huddersfield and District Power Loom Weavers' Association in 1883. After the amalgamation, women took even less of a leading role. The new organization, the Huddersfield and District Power Loom Weavers and Woollen Operatives' Association, elected three Huddersfield men to the leading posts. Of the ten committee members, only four were women, one of these being Mrs Ann Ellis of the original Dewsbury strike committee.

Ann Ellis had been treasurer of the strike committee and a frequent speaker at public meetings during the strike. Her career in the union and later illustrates rather well the opportunities which trade unions could offer to someone with determination and conviction, but also the frustrations of employment in the textile industry. Soon after the amalgamation she was elected, with Allen Gee, the chairman of the new union, to go to the forthcoming TUC at Nottingham. This was her first TUC, Allen Gee's second. At the 1883 and 1884 TUCs she played an active part. She identified herself clearly with the feminist wing of the women's trade union movement in her opposition to limitations on women's employment, this being advocated by those delegates who sought to exclude women from what were thought of as dangerous occupations.

Attending the TUC was to bring Ann Ellis into contact with suffragists, feminists and others who were outspokenly in favour of a more emancipated and equal role for women, both politically and in production. In the 1883 TUC she stood for the Parliamentary Committee, but received only 24 votes. Despite this defeat, she played a forceful part in the proceedings, speaking against the extension of the Factory Acts to cover girls under 14, on the grounds that these should be applied to boys too. In opposing the exclusion of mothers of young children from factories and workshops, she argued that inequality in piece-rate earnings between men and women woollen weavers was the result of restrictions on overtime and night work. At the following year's TUC in Aberdeen, Mrs Ellis made an even greater impact, clashing with the president, Broadhurst, over the exclusion of young girls from ironworking and identifying herself clearly with those sections of the women's movement which were opposed to fixing limitations solely on women's employment. Allen Gee, her co-delegate at Aberdeen, disagreed with this. He favoured placing limits on women's hours of work in the textile trade; nevertheless, he joined with her in demanding the same franchise for women as for men.[19]

Ben Turner, later president of the textile worker's union, its historian and chief spokesperson for over 40 years, later described Ann Ellis as being at this time, 'the recognised women's textile leader in Yorkshire'.[20] In a small union which emerged from the amalgamation, she occupied a position of some local importance, attempting to help other women's associations to form elsewhere in the West Riding. In Leeds she had had some success starting a society of Female Machinists,[21] and she also tried to set up a union for women weavers.

In 1885, after having attended and spoken at a conference in London, she returned to work in Dewsbury to find that she had been sacked on a pretext. Without work in the textile trade, as a known activist, she was forced to leave the area and went into service as a housekeeper in Brighton. While there she threw her energies into organizing laundresses and agitating amongst the Brighton unemployed. She eventually returned to Bradford, where she worked as a foster mother for the Bradford Board of Guardians. In the early 1900s she was involved in the campaign for women's suffrage, collecting signatures for the Yorkshire section of the women textile workers' petition for the vote presented to parliament in February 1902.[22] Although she remained an honorary member of the union until her death,[23] she no longer played an active part and her going seems, as Barbara Drake argues, to have led to a general loss of confidence by women in union affairs.

The events surrounding the foundation of a weavers' union in Dewsbury show that women were not lacking in militancy nor in the ability to organize in defence of their interests as workers. But the founding and the running of a union seem to be differently ordered activities. What was to become the nucleus of the union, the centre of organization for weavers in Dewsbury and Huddersfield, had lost women's leadership by 1885. The Huddersfield union had been an entirely men's union from inception to amalgamation. Though women were never again to hold positions of leadership in the union, the amalgamation ensured the dominant role of two men, Allen Gee and Ben Turner, who were, during the next 40 years to earn a deserved reputation nationally in the trade union movement for their commitment to women's rights.

Publically this commitment began with the new union's affiliation to the Women's Trade Union League in 1889. At about the same time, Allen Gee was one of a group of trade union members who were invited to join the League's 'Committee of Counsel', a grouping of men and women who, it was felt, could advise women on trade union matters.[24]

Despite the growing tendency for men to dominate the leadership of the union in these early years, women did appear, though typically at lower levels. New branches opened in the 1890s in Halifax, the Heavy Woollen District, Slaithwaite, Haworth and Bradford. All included women committee members. The Haworth branch opened in 1893 with three women amongst the seven committee members, but failed to survive. In Colne Valley, the first committee, based in Slaithwaite, met in 1894 and included three women. Following amalgamation with a branch at Marsden to form the Colne Valley District in 1899, the new committee and officers were all men. Halifax had, for a while, a woman secretary and a Laura Buckley on the committee who was noted for her membership in Halifax ILP, but she resigned in 1900 when she married. The Heavy Woollen Branch had a majority, five out of eight, on its committee, who were women members, but the officers were all men. The teetotalism of the branch secretary, Ben Turner, was perhaps responsible for the fact that the branch met at the Exchange Coffee Tavern in Batley. Perhaps this was an encouragement to women who might not like to attend meetings in a public house.[25]

In Bradford, events were to take a more dramatic turn. The Manningham strike of 1890–1 was to have an immense impact on labour politics in that town, though as far as women's trade union membership was concerned, the strike was to be less memorable. When the strike began in December 1890,[26] there was no strong local organization of weavers and spinners, although the all-men dyers' union, with three Bradford branches was well established, as were a number of craft unions and societies. The strike followed the introduction of wage reductions in December 1890 and affected 11,000 employees of Lister and Co. Ltd. Using the excuse of the US McKinley tariff and depression in the industry, the employers argued that wages in the firm's Manningham mills were 'not natural'. The strike lasted five months and attracted countrywide interest with a large sum being collected or raised in support of the workers. As soon as the wage reductions were announced, Ben Turner, Allen Gee and the local Bradford representative of the weavers' union, William Henry Drew, were drawn into organizing the strike, publicity and fund-raising. The majority of the strikers were women plush-weavers and few, if any, had been trade unionists at the beginning of the strike. What began for the employers as an apparently straightforward price reduction in the interest of competition, became a widely based symbolic struggle with far-reaching repercussions. Although finally ending in defeat, the impact of the strike on Bradford was great enough to create a strong basis for local independent labour politics. As Ben Turner later recalled, the strike was significant 'in making or paving the way for the present Labour dominance on the public bodies and public life of Bradford. This great strike was a hurt to those in it, but it was a blessing to humanity in general.'[27]

As at Dewsbury, women played an active role in the strike. A photograph of the strike committee shows a large group of 27 people, of whom 16 are women (see illustration at the beginning of this chapter). Women collected money, carrying round cigar boxes slit open to receive money and displayed Lister's wage slips as proof of identity. They took part in street processions, sold draw tickets and prepared food for the soup kitchens. £11,000 was raised during the strike, with donations presented from groups of workers in all parts of England, Scotland and Wales.[28]

Well-known women such as Lady Dilke and Isabella Ford (whose father was a Leeds silk manufacturer and who herself was a popular speaker at local trade union and socialist meetings) helped in the organization of the strike. But despite Isabella Ford's success amongst women workers in Leeds where permanent organizations of women clothing workers had been formed, and despite general sympathy and interest during the strike, there seems to have been no lasting effect on women's organization in Bradford. Following the strike, a 2,000 strong branch of the union was formed. In 1892, its membership was put at 800. By 1900, at the Huddersfield TUC, it had shrunk to only 284. Six years later Board of Trade returns calculated Bradford's textile workforce as just over 39,000.[29]

The Manningham Mills' strike politicized a town's working class, but although W.H. Drew of the weavers' union was arguably the founder of the Bradford Labour Union, the organization which became the Independent Labour Party in May 1891, the impact on weavers' and spinners' organization in the town seems to have been minimal. Nevertheless Bradford was to become, in the early years of the twentieth century, a fertile base for mass organization amongst members of its working class. Margaret McMillan, who was to be the leading spirit in educational reform in Bradford and later earned a national reputation as an educationalist, sensed something of the special nature of Bradford's political life. On her first visit in 1893, addressing a meeting at the Labour Church, she had determined to make the town her home.[30] A well-informed and well co-ordinated band of labour activists were to bring about some of the first successes of municipal socialism in the town. School meals, milk, school baths and clinics were introduced during the two decades before 1914. On the trade union front, dyers and combers had taken pioneering steps in the direction of the closed shop.

Bradford was also to witness growing support for adult suffrage amongst a broad section of the population. The *Woman Worker* reported a franchise meeting of 60,000 women at Shipley Glen in 1908. The history of the suffrage movement in West Yorkshire is yet to be written and it is difficult, lacking the kind of documents which exist for Lancashire, to reconstruct events and networks of support amongst the various groupings in Yorkshire. Lancashire textile workers, as Jill Liddington and Jill Norris have shown, were deeply and enthusiastically involved in the women's suffrage issue. A petition organized in 1900–1 calling for the right to vote had gained 29,359 votes in Lancashire. This success had led women activists to draw up a petition for other groups of workers, including those in wool textiles. In 1901, a Mrs Green from Beswick spoke at 18 meetings in the Colne Valley and Huddersfield area. Interest and enthusiasm was immense, petition workers reported. In Batley 'whole streets of women engaged as rag-pickers wanted to sign in many other towns dressmakers, laundresses, and others were disappointed that they must not add their names'.[31]

Despite the enthusiasm with which women in the wool textile industry greeted the 1901 petition, there is little evidence of any persistent organization around the suffrage issue amongst working women. The lack of surviving documents may mean that we are not able to do them full justice, but there is one significant factor in Yorkshire which may provide a key to this apparent lack of involvement. In Yorkshire, in contrast with Lancashire, those who were active in the suffrage movement were almost all members of the ILP. Pioneering figures such as Isabella Ford and Ben Turner embraced both ILP politics and the suffrage issue so that, from an early period, the suffrage campaigns took on a rather different development. This containment of a women's issue within labour politics may have had the effect of neutralizing women's special concerns. The petition which the Lancashire women had signed linked political and workplace demands,

> That in the opinion of your petitioners the continued denial of the franchise to women is unjust and inexpedient.
> In the home, their position is lowered by such an exclusion from the responsibilities of natural life.
> In the factory, their unrepresented condition places the regulation of their work in the hands of men who are often their rivals as well as their fellow workers.[33]

In Yorkshire, despite, as we shall see, sympathy and understanding for the working woman's burden of responsibilities, the suffrage issue retained a purely political profile.[33] Even if the extent of the working women's involvement in the suffrage campaigns is underestimated here, it remains significant that the impact on the union of women's politics appears to have been modest. During these years women outnumbered men as GUTW members. Figures which were given to the Royal Commission on Labour confirm this. Ben Turner himself, in a curiously revealing statement described his 1,000 strong Dewsbury branch as having '190 men, and the remainder are women'. According to Allen Gee, in Huddersfield the 2,000 membership was equally divided between men and women, while overall in the union, 60 per cent of members were women. In Bradford, William Drew gave figures which showed that, just after the Manningham strike, three-quarters of the 2,000 members were women. By 1907, men had a slight majority of 2,200 out of a total union membership of 4,200 men and women.[34] Despite this respectable level of membership in an admittedly small union, there are only a few instances of women taking a leading role and there is little evidence that women were being given any speical consideration as workers or as union members.

Julia Varley highlights the frustrations and limitations encountered by those women who succeeded in winning their way to positions of responsibility in the union. She came from a long line of Bradford radicals. Her great grandfather had been a Chartist and she had from an early age been brought up to think and talk labour politics. Joining the union before the Manningham strike in 1891, she soon became a branch officer and was elected to the Bradford District executive in 1895, apparently serving on Bradford Trades Council at the age of 14. It may have been symptomatic of a struggling new union that such a young worker was to take on these responsibilities, nevertheless, she was able and hardworking, remained Bradford District Secretary for 15 years and attended the Trades Union Congress on three occasions in the 1900s as branch delegate.

An appreciation of Julia Varley appeared in the newspaper of the wool textile trade union, the *Yorkshire Factory Times*, almost certainly written by Ben Turner. This was one in a series of 'Pen and Ink Sketches of Notable Trade Unionists',

> She is a Yorkshire young lady all through, though from her refined way of talking one would never gather that she understood and could read, write and talk the dialect . . . Miss Varley learnt to weave when she first began work as a full-timer and she joined the Weavers' Association nearly as soon as she commenced working . . . No one is better known in the trade union clubs, for she has addressed numerous meetings with the object of trying to urge the men to enrol the women workers of their families in their trade unions . . . Miss Varley had found out how hard it is to get trade union fathers to make their daughters into trade unionists . . . For her own part she had been trained to be a trade unionist. The family comprises eight, six of whom are in the union, and two cannot be.[35]

Julia Varley, in company with certain male officials of the union, was an active member of the ILP, and was elected, together with other members of Bradford ILP, to the Board of Guardians in 1901. She took an independent role, investigating women's conditions, tramping from Liverpool to Bradford, finding out what life was like on the road for unemployed women and even spending five weeks in a central London lodging house. But whatever local use the GUTW may have had for the skills of Julia Varley it is perhaps significant that in 1908 an invitation to work for the National Federation of Women Workers was to prove a more attractive alternative. She left Bradford that year, never again to work for wool textile workers.[36]

The surviving minute books of the GUTW do not reveal a prominent role for women in terms of union policy or organization during the years after 1900. Bradford district of the union presents the one exception, though even there opportunities were limited. The first woman to be elected to the executive of the union, Helen Hillas, was nominated by Bradford District in 1914. Outside Bradford and Leeds, in the smaller Yorkshire towns of Huddersfield and Dewsbury, women appear to have played an extremely minor role within the union. Huddersfield had no women district committee members until the war years, nor had Colne Valley. Minute books provide no evidence of any attention to issues relating to women, nor of any special concern to attract women as members in under-unionized areas of the industry until the years of militancy which immediately preceded the outbreak of war. A reading of the minute books for the years up to 1912 and 1913 might give the impression that women's membership in the union was insignificant were it not for the fact that membership figures belie this.

A general growth in radical activity and militancy is apparent in 1912 and 1913. As a part of this broadening and radicalizing, Huddersfield (but not Colne Valley district with its radical reputation),[37] turned its attention to the question of recruiting and organizing women members. In April 1913, Huddersfield District asked the union executive for 'a woman organizer for a week or two'. A Miss Newton was taken on for a week and six meetings were arranged in different parts of the district on successive days.[38] The following year, the district considered the appointment of a woman organizer for an initial 12 month period. Letters were sent out to other unions enquiring as to the terms and wages typically offered for such a post. It was eventually agreed to offer an appointment at between 40/– and 45/– a week. Preparations were under way, the decision had been ratified by the biannual members' meeting, when war was declared. The appointment of a woman's organizer was then immediately suspended.[39] It is interesting to note that when, in 1916, the union finally decided to take on a full-time woman organizer, a Lancashire woman, Mary Luty, was appointed, no candidate from within the industry was either forthcoming or thought suitable.[40]

Julia Varley's departure and the minimal involvement of women in trade union affairs suggest that for women there was an element of blocked mobility. This mirrored the situtation which existed within mills. That this was not untypical even in areas of majority membership and organizational strength, such as cotton weaving, has been graphically described elsewhere.[41] What is unusual in the case of wool textile is the fact that leading men in the union had for decades supported women's suffrage and a minimum wage for women workers.

Allen Gee and Ben Turner had been consistent champions of women's suffrage and had taken part in various activities and functions which sought to improve women's civic and economic powers. Ben Turner and Elizabeth Turner, his wife, had both been keen and active supporters from the early days of 1884 when the union had its own petition on the issue of the vote and had taken part with its own banner in one of the mass demonstrations organized by the National Society for Women's Suffrage. As he was to recall years later, 'We had numerous demonstrations in Yorkshire for Women's Suffrage, and many of the leaders stayed at our house, where every one of us [Turner had five daughters] were ardent supporters of the cause.'[42]

It was Ben Turner in particular who kept the issue of women's as opposed to adult, suffrage before ILP and Labour Party conferences through the pre-war years.[43] Year after year, Ben Turner put resolutions calling for a vote for women on the same basis as for men. In doing so, he (with Keir Hardie), was going against majority opinion in the organized Labour movement. It was not until 1912 that, after persistent betrayals by Asquith and the Liberals, a resolution pledging the Labour Party in parliament to support only those franchise bills which included women was passed at the Labour Party annual conference. Ben Turner, as chairman of the conference that year spoke strongly in favour of women's suffrage, 'I trust that manhood suffrage may not be accepted by men, unless sex disabilities are removed. Fight for the whole, but have something like fair play for women or refuse the half load of manhood suffrage'.[44]

Despite their national reputation, the GUTW's leaders appear to have had a marked lack of success in mobilizing or supporting women in their own industry. Part of the explanation for this may lie in the division which Allen Gee and Ben Turner appear to have maintained between women's civil and production rights and in the persistently paternalistic language in which women's membership was discussed. From the 1890s onwards, when questioned about women's poor showing in their union, Allen Gee and Ben Turner stressed the need for education, the importance of men's example and the problematic aspects of women's involvement.

As witnesses at the Royal Commission on Labour in November 1891, a few months after the Manningham strike, the all-male witnesses could remember few examples of women on mill committees. It was suggested that women were unwilling to take on committee work, preferring to leave this to the men. Ben Turner was asked to account for the fact that, unlike other unions, the woollen weavers had made little progress. He explained, 'It is easier to organise men than women, because the women imagine that they will leave the mill some time'. Just over 20 years later, after a period of upturn in union growth, the explanation for Bradford's failure to match other districts' expansion was that 'it is difficult . . . because of a large number of women employed in the textile industry'.[45]

In his response to the Women's Trades Union League inquiry (see above) into unions' problems with women members, Allen Gee stressed the important role of education. But he also emphasized that 'the men-folk have been to blame in not educating their sisters and daughters' Within this rather patronizing and limiting perspective he was none the less positive in his approach,

> When the idea has permeated their minds thoroughly, and they have given in their names to join a union, women have been as loyal as men . . . one reason, which, I think tends to keep women out of the union is the lack of training which women have had in managing such an organization as a trade union . . . When they have been educated sufficiently to do the work of negotiating with employers, and also in keeping the accounts, I think that women will be far better organized than they are to-day; for after all, it must be admitted that women can understand women's grievances better than men can.

There was no question of course as to who had undertaken the training of men such as Gee when they embarked on their union careers and no reference to the initiative of the Manningham women, only eight years before.

In contrast to Allen Gee's explanation was that of Isabella Ford, who in 1900 was Honorary Secretary of the Leeds Society of Workwomen. She emphasized the fact that women were conditioned into submissiveness by society. To be a trade unionist was, for a woman, to be something of a rebel. This was contrary to women's social training, 'The political world preaches to women submission, so long as it refuses them the Parliamentary franchise, and therefore ignores them as human beings. Society encourages selfish indifference amongst women, in that it considers a woman's home must make her sacrifice to it everyone else's home and all public honour'.[46]

The language of paternalism and marginality which men such as Allen Gee and Ben Turner employed and their emphasis on the problematic nature of women's trade union membership provided no encouragement to recruitment of, and participation by, women members. And there was one issue in particular which, more than any other, detracted from what was otherwise an exemplary attitude towards women's rights. This was the question of married women's work, Then, as today, women's status was specified in terms of dependency both before and after marriage. The issue is crucial since attacks on married women's employment have direct implications for women's workplace status. If married women's right to work is questioned then, by implication men's rights are exalted and emphasized.

Trade union witnesses at the Royal Commission on Labour of 1891 had been particularly critical of married women's work. A Mr J.W. Downing of the West Riding Power Loom Weavers' Association (later to become the GUTW) complained that in his district, Huddersfield, there were

> scores, hundreds, of able-bodied men walking the streets, good weavers, who cannot get employment in consequence of women's labour. I should like to speak more particularly of the married women's labour. I think myself . . . that it is a disgrace to humanity to see married women pulling their children out of bed in the morning, wrapping them in shawls, and taking them in all kinds of weather – in some cases half-a-mile – to nurse, so that they can go to the mill, and in the long run they take the men's places and throw the men into the street.

William Drew explained that both women and men could be helped to support the exclusion of married women if men were able to earn enough to 'keep their wives at home'. In his view, wages could be increased if married women's labour were restricted. Neither Allen Gee nor Ben Turner went as far as to call a ban, though both deprecated married women's work.[47] Those who opposed the employment of married women were supported by employers in the industry. Allen Gee was a director of a co-partnership firm, Thomson's of Huddersfied, which wholly excluded married women. At Mark Oldroyd's, one of the leading firms in Dewsbury, married women were not encouraged to seek employment.[48]

Ben Turner was noted as a local dialect poet. His lines not only appeared weekly in what was to become the union's own newspaper, the *Yorkshire Factory Times*, but he also published two volumes of poetry. Through his poetry, Ben Turner expressed his feelings about the men and women amongst whom he lived and worked. One of his most telling poems in the context of this discussion is his 'The Folks I like':

> The manly man is he I like
> One not too proud or humble,
> Who won't too freely show dislike,
> Nor yet too freely grumble;
> Who is not sad
> When times are bad,
> And not afraid to stumble.

The womanly woman I can prize,
The one you talk to proudly,
Who'se not too over wordly wise,
Yet doesn't talk too loudly;
Whose love is great
For home and state,
And faces danger boldly.[49]

Though affiliated to no church,[50] Ben Turner was a highly religious man who often used Christian texts to illuminate his speeches. In 'If Christ came to Dewsbury' he used a powerful imagery to advocate his own views on the situation of local textile workers:

He'd point to women's wages, and ask if it were true
That married women's toil was sought and children left to roam
Without a mother's guiding hand, and spoiled was many a home?. . . .

He would not feel surprised because some homes were not as clean
As houses He would like to see where human beings live.
He'd know the women could not work, and to their houses give
That full attention they should have.[51]

Ben Turner had a long and happy married life. Elizabeth and their five daughters played active roles in most aspects of his public life as mayor, trade union president and lecturer. Living in Batley, he witnessed the low wages, poor living conditions and double workload of the married woman worker. This was to make him keenly aware of the cruel contradictions faced by many working wives and mothers. In his poetry he calls up an ideal existence, in which married couples are portrayed as partners in life, mates in a joint endeavour. His husbands are not portrayed as masters or supermen, nor his wives as mindless submissives. Nevertheless the implicit segregation of spheres of interest and competence is clearly expressed.

Within the union there were differences in the emphasis placed on the impact of married women in the labour market. While Ben Turner and Allen Gee expressed regret at the double workload of the working wife and mother, they still tended to advocate raising wage rates, both men's and women's as a means to making paid employment for a mother less essential. For them, married women's work was a characteristic of general low wages, uncertain earnings and poor working conditions.[52]

Others in the union took an even less tolerant view. Well after the worst aspects of the Great Depression had been overtaken, references to married women in union minute books betray critical attitudes which imply exclusion. In Colne Valley, the only reference to women workers as such in the district minutes between 1910 and 1914 is in relation to an item on an agenda for discussion with employers in July 1914. The question of married women's labour was earmarked for discussion when establishing priorities amongst workers being laid off during a depression in trade.[53] In Huddersfield, the minutes record that during 1909 weavers at a mill objected to a man being appointed as collector, and thereby being entitled to a collector's commission, 'owing to his wife working'. The District Committee gave the weavers permission to call a meeting and suggest another collector.[54] During 1915, articles in the union newspaper the *Yorkshire Factory Times* written by a woman, a weaver and ILP member, outspokenly criticized married women's employment, holding married women responsible for low wages and problems for organization in the Bradford area. In 'Married Women's Labour. A Blessing or a Curse?', she advocated a three-point programme for Bradford women workers: to build the union, abolish child labour and end married women's labour. The union's executive was taken to task for not taking a stand against married women's labour.

The articles in the *Yorkshire Factory Times* were part of a debate within the union which followed Huddersfield District's decision to advertise for a woman organizer, but which stipulated that no married woman need apply. Jessie Cockerline's articles praised the union for taking this stand, opposing demands that employers should provide for married women workers and claiming that working women drove their husbands to the public house by baking and doing housework in the evenings.[55]

The 1911 census reveals that there were relatively few married women in the textile industry, far fewer than critics such as Jessie Cockerline seemed to be suggesting. Only 10.3 per cent of all women workers nationally were married. In Yorkshire as a proportion of *all* textile workers, figures varied from 11 per cent in Dewsbury and 12 per cent in Bradford to 9 and 7 per cent respectively in Halifax and Huddersfield.[56] As a proportion of all workers in wool textile manufacturing, married women seem to have been a relatively small group. Beliefs in the depressive role of married women's earnings played a greater part in shaping policy than hard facts about the reality of their work. What seems most significant is the contribution of such arguments to assumptions about women's status. Allegations about less eligibility and 'greed' only helped to further marginalize women in production.

Many women enjoyed working outside the home for a wage which was their own and were fortunate to encounter no obstacle to this, before or after marriage, with or without children. Others had no choice in the matter; faced with low earnings, large families, illness or unexpected expense, work was a continuous necessity. The frustrations of Ben Turner, Allen Gee, Julia Varley and Jessie Cockerline were born out of real situations as were the fears of men workers, supporting families, who had seen their wages decline through the 1880s and 1890s. But there seems to be no evidence that it was married women's work which kept wages down or that they had any impact on union recruitment figures amongst women.

To draw a distinction between the married woman wage earner and other women, whether single or in unpaid work was, in practice, not as simple as it might have seemed. For example, the historian Eric Hobsbawm has shown the contradiction which existed between the symbolism of trade union banners and decorative art, with its emphasis on sexual equality and emancipation and the practice of exclusion from full membership of the labour force.[57] He goes on to criticize 'feminist historians' for failing to accept that few married women were in paid employment and that the pattern of the male breadwinner and dependent wife was not simply an ideal, but a fact of life. But estimates of the contribution of a wife's earnings and the extent of married women's part-time employment are hard to fix exactly. Such evidence as does exist suggests that women's contributions to family finances may have been greater than Eric Hobsbawm claims. Documentary evidence is well-known for its neglect of women's activity. Thus the census provides few references, if any, to taking in washing, child-minding, cleaning and the many other jobs taken on by women in and around the home. Oral evidence is more reliable, as Elizabeth Roberts has shown, women's ingenuity in stretching the family's finances was often a vital necessity and might determine the survival of the family members as a unit.[58]

Earlier attempts to assess the financial contribution of women's work to family finances included that of Ada Heather-Biggs who, in 1893, wrote about domestic employment where several members of a family were involved. After observing such industries as the Staffordshire nail trade, where a man's 'stint' included the labour of a wife and daughter, though only his name appeared in the master's book, she concluded that 'a great deal of woman's work in the past has escaped the notice of economic inquirers through this practice of *throwing in* [her emphasis] her work with her husband's.' Ultimately, she argued that 'at no time in the world's history has the man's labour alone sufficed for the maintenance of his wife and children.'[59]

The domestic system of production had almost died out in the wool textile industry by the turn of the century but the contribution of women's earnings was still significant. By singling out married women factory workers for criticism, the union was helping to enforce a segregation of roles in home and work. This was, inevitably, to lead to limitations on women's activity within the union, as an extension of the workplace.

Barbara Drake documents the ways in which, though numerically dominant, Lancashire women in the cotton unions rarely rose to positions of responsibility.[60] Many of the points she makes also apply to the Yorkshire women. By holding meetings in working men's clubs where women were not equal members, and after working hours when women had to take up domestic tasks, unions were unwittingly excluding women from active membership. And though the house-to-house collection of union dues encouraged family membership and provided a check on members' movements between mills, it had the effect of locating membership alongside other forms of insurance which families took out on behalf of members. It does not seem to have helped to support collective action based on the place of work and tended to identify women members in terms of their family relationships rather than in terms of their jobs or earnings.

For women, definitions of socio-economic role in terms of domesticity meant that they tended to be regarded as both problematic and marginal in the workplace. Such definitions, both imposed on women and internalized by them, had inevitable implications for their power and status as wage-earner and therefore for their participation in trade unions. Dependence for women carried with it the superior rights of men. The family's survival line, linking it to the wage, was traced exclusively through the external and worldly representative of the family, the husband and father. For men, unions were a matter of defence of their right to work and improve their conditions of labour. For women, work experience was shaped by more conflicting pressures from work and home.

Documenting women's history, or a history in which women feature as whole and active beings, is well accepted to be a difficult task. Using oral evidence together with statistics and the writings of those involved in labour politics at the turn of the century, I have tried to recover some of this 'hidden history'. What has emerged is a record of loss, in itself an elusive story. Finding out why things fail to happen is not obviously worthwhile, when there are so many victories and worthwhile achievements to record. But much of history is the story of compromise and slow progress, if not retreat. We need to know when and why what promised so much, yielded so little. In the case of women in the wool textile industry of West Yorkshire, the explanation comes through a complex interweaving of general socio-economic factors and individual action. Certainly, the key role of the union leaders, Ben Turner and Allen Gee should not be underestimated. For 40 years they placed a personal stamp on wool textile trade unionism.

I have tried to show how a certain ambivalence towards the role of women in the industry explains why, though committed to the cause of women's civic rights, they were less successful at involving women in their union's own leadership. While women's role in production outside the home was not clearly established, while men in key positions, and women too, continued to speak in paternalistic tones and while women's collective spirit was questioned rather than supported, trade union membership was bound to be equally marginalized and diminished by women themselves. It was not sufficient for women to be led by men who committed themselves to political rights while inequalities in production and in trade union organization were allowed to persist without even critical comment.

I have chosen to end the story at 1914.[61] Historians describe this as the watershed year. Nothing afterwards is seen as ever being the same as it was before the outbreak of war. Certainly the war years were to bring wool textiles into a more central role, as munitions of war. Leading trade unionists were co-opted into powerful positions, they became controllers and suppliers of dependable labour. Women found themselves much in demand as workers, consequently earning vastly more than they ever could in peacetime. Union membership expanded at an unprecedented rate and women rose to occupy executive positions in the union. Ultimately, such gains were to be short-lived. As the men returned for what were seen as their jobs, and as the industry contracted to serve the needs of peacetime recession, women once again found equality slipping out of reach.

What had remained virtually unchanged were women's rights in industrial production. Wartime production demanded the temporary promotion of women to indispensablity. Peacetime saw a return to marginality, dependency and domesticity. The continuity between 1914 and 1919 is clear. Not simply a continuity of leaders,

Ben Turner and Allen Gee were to cease to have direct influence after 1922, there was of course a continuity of social relationships and ideology which was to be more powerful and enduring. These have been the determinants of women's sphere of power and competence and it is these which make the identification of lost leaders so crucial to an understanding of our history.

Bibliographical Note

In the absence of any detailed history of the wool textile industry or of any thoroughgoing analysis of women's place in trade union history the most useful sources for further reading are mainly comparative. My own thesis, 'An Examination of the General Union of Textile Workers: 1883–1922' (University of Essex, 1980) covers the pre-war years and the experience of wartime work in the industry. Earlier and later periods await further research. Barbara Drake's recently reprinted *Women in Trade Unions* (Virago edn. 1984), remains the most detailed and painstaking attempt to examine women's trade union history. Published in 1920, it reflects the concerns of a particular period, but is nonetheless valuable. More recently written histories include those of Norbert Soldon, *Women in British Trade Unions, 1874–1976* (Gill and Macmillan, Dublin, 1978) and Sheila Lewenhak *Women and Trade Unions* (Ernest Benn, 1977). These, however, are straightforwardly chronological accounts and make no attempt to link social issues to trade union history. More rewarding are accounts of particular industries, similar to wool textiles, but which, by concentrating on family structure, social ties and inequalities, bring out the contradictory forces which determined women's trade union role. The history of the struggle for the vote amongst Lancashire textile workers provides an interesting comparison with wool textile workers. This particular issue is traced in Jill Liddington and Jill Norris, *One Hand Tied Behind Us* (Virago, 1978), and a comparison with the wool textile workers of North America is provided by Tamara K. Hareven and Randolph Langenbach in *Amoskeag: Life and Work in an American Factory-City in New England* (Methuen, 1979). Tracing the antecedents of the women described in this essay also provides interesting insights. Barbara Taylor's, *Eve and the New Jerusalem* (Virago, 1983), explores the radical movements of the early nineteenth century which provided a field of action for the grandmothers of the women whose industrial lives are described here.

Notes

1 Drake, *Women in Trade Unions*, pp. 41–3.
2 Ibid, pp. 28–9

3 A more detailed account is given in Joanna Bornat, 'An Examination of the General Union of Textile Workers: 1883–1922', unpublished PhD thesis (University of Essex, 1980).

4 This argument is developed in Joanna Bornat, 'Home and Work: a new context for Trade Union history', *Oral History*, vol. 5, no. 2 (1977). Interesting confirmation of the identification of young women workers with a domestic role comes from another industry, the potteries. Richard Whipp's article '"Plenty of Excuses, No Money": The Social Bases of Trade Unionism, as illustrated by the Potters', *Society for the Study of Labour History, Bulletin*, no. 49 (Autumn 1984), uses union collectors' notebooks as a source and establishes the close ties linking trade union membership to family relationships.

5 *Report of the Tenth Trades Union Congress*, Minutes of Proceedings, 1877.

6 See in particular evidence given to the War Cabinet Committee on Women in Industry, minutes of evidence in Lab 5/1, 1917–19.

7 Guy Routh, *Occupation and Pay in Great Britain, 1906–14* (Cambridge University Press, Cambridge, 1965), pp. 57, 59 and pp. 86–9.

8 *Report of an Enquiry by the Board of Trade into the Earnings and Hours of Labour of Workpeople of the United Kingdom. 1. The Textile Trades.* PP 1909, Cmd. 4545.

9 Rough calculations based on a table in G. H. Wood's 'Wage Notes', B383 to B637 give a 29 per cent drop for women and a 19 per cent drop for men weavers in Huddersfield and district. G. H. Wood, 'Wage Notes' (1908), G. H. Wood Papers.

10 *Royal Commission on Labour*, PP 1892, Cmd. 6708, q. 4827–4835.

11 Colne Valley interviewee no. 11. Twenty-one women and men who worked in the wool textile industry were interviewed and the resulting data included in Bornat, thesis (1980).

12 See Ben Turner, *Short History of the General Union of Textile Workers* (Heckmondwike, 1920), pp. 7–8.

13 Taylor, *Eve and the New Jerusalem*, p. 91.

14 For example, the Huddersfield, Bradford and Barnsley Dyers, later the National Association of Dyers and Finishers, formed in 1851, the Leeds Cloth Pressers formed in 1864, the Huddersfield Power Loom Tuners Society formed in 1861, the Halifax Power Loom Overlookers formed in 1866.

15 H. A. Clegg, Alan Fox and A. F. Thompson, *A History of British Trade Unions since 1889*, vol. 1. 1889–1910 (Clarendon Press, Oxford, 1964), 'whereas in cotton the male weavers organized the women and brought them up towards men's standards of wages, in wool the women dragged the men down to their's,' p. 34.

16 Turner, *Short History*, ch. 1. 'The Foundation of the Union in the Heavy Woollen District'.

17 John Bright was Liberal MP for Rochdale.

18 This man had secured more votes than Kate Conran, one of the original strike committee, in a ballot for the post of full-time collector. Soon after, he appeared in the County Court 'for monies he had received'. Allen Stringer, whose daughter Grace had been treasurer for a short time, was

then appointed. He was to keep this position for some years. A. Turner, *Short History*, p.105. Maria Bottomley, 'Textile Trade Unionism in the Heavy Woollen District', unpublished paper, traces the strike in some detail and shows how the experience of the strike gave the women weavers self-confidence, but that in the years which followed, lack of support weakened resolve. Nevertheless in the amalgamation, it was the Dewsbury and Batley workers who provided the bulk of union funds and enabled the union to invest in permanent premises.

19 *Report of 1884 TUC*, Drake, *Women in Trade Unions*, p.21.
20 Turner, *Short History*, p.119.
21 Ibid., pp.119–20
22 See Liddington and Norris, *One Hand Tied Behind Us*, pp.149–53, and below for a description of the petition and collection of signatures in Yorkshire.
23 Turner, *Short History*, p.109.
24 Drake, *Women in Trade Unions*, pp.30–1.
25 Turner, *Short History*, pp.115, 154, 156, 159–60.
26 The strike is described in some detail in Turner, *Short History*, chs 20 and 21 and in Cyril Pearce, *The Manningham Mills strike Bradford, December 1890–April 1891*, University of Hull Occasional papers in Economic and Social History, no. 7 (1975).
27 Turner, *Short History*, p.129.
28 Ibid., pp.132–7.
29 *Report of 1892 TUC*. Membership of the Amalgamated Society of Dyers was 3,000 at this time, while the Woolcombers numbered 1,500. Reference to a comment by Will Thorne of the Gasworkers to a 'new, a poor organisation' of Bradford weavers is made in Yvonne Kapp, *Eleanor Marx*, vol. 2 (Virago, 1976), p.428.
30 Fenner Brockway, *Socialism over Sixty Years, the Life of Jowett of Bradford* (George Allen and Unwin, 1946), pp.60–2.
31 Liddington and Norris, *One Hand Tied Behind Us*, p.148.
32 Ibid., p.145.
33 I am grateful to Gloden Dallas, who is sadly now dead, for discussing these issues with me.
34 Cmd. 6708, q. 5692, 4785, 5383; *Report on Trades Unions 1908–10*, Cmd. 4651.
35 *Yorkshire Factory Times*, 22 July 1904.
36 It was her organizational skill and her eye for impact which helped the women chain-makers at Cradley Heath to win acceptance of Trades Board rates from employers. She became the first women executive member of Birmingham Trade Council and, in 1912, the first full-time woman officer of the Workers's Union. In the two years before the outbreak of war she was a leader in the successful Black Country strike movement for minimum wages for men and women. She later became a pillar of the moderate group within the trade union movement, occupying the post of Chief Woman Officer in the Transport and General Workers' Union at the time of her retirement. See this volume, chapter 9.
37 Colne Valley returned to parliament the independent and radical socialist

candidate, Victor Grayson, in 1907. He won his contest against the Liberal candidate with an outspokenly socialist manifesto. His parliamentary contests and subsequent career are described in Reg Groves, *The Strange Case of Victor Grayson* (Pluto, 1975).

38 Minute books of Huddersfield District of the GUTW, 9 May 1913, deposited in Huddersfield Local History Archive at Kirklees Libraries and Museums Headquarters.

39 Ibid., 9 July 1914, 10 August 1914.

40 The two candidates who came before the appointment committee were Lancashire women, Nancy Shimbles of Nelson and Mary Luty of Rawtenstall. Mary Luty left two versions of her biography: 'My Life has sparkled', an unpublished, undated manuscript now deposited in Rawtenstall Public Library, and *Penniless Globetrotter*, published by an Accrington firm in 1937.

41 See Drake, *Women in Trade Unions*, the personal account of Alice Foley, *A Bolton Childhood*, (Manchester University Extra-Mural Department & North West District of WEA, 1973), and Liddington and Norris, *One Hand Tied Behind Us*, ch. v 'Weavers and Winders', which contains a valuable examination of women's position within the various cotton unions.

42 Ben Turner, *About Myself* (Humphrey Toulmin, 1930), p. 278. At about the same time, G.H. Wood of the Employers' Association was a supporter of Full Adult Suffrage, speaking in defence of this principle at the Northern Fabian Conference of 1911.

43 Liddington and Norris, *One Hand Tied Behind Us*, pp. 237–8.

44 Quoted in Marion Ramelson, *The Petticoat Rebellion* (Lawrence and Wishart, 1972), p. 158.

45 Cmd. 6708 q. 5189–5194, 5816; *Annual Report of the GUTW*, 31 December 1914.

46 Quoted in Drake, *Women in Trade Unions*, pp. 41–2.

47 Cmd. 6708, q. 4999, 5442, 5586, 5711 ff.

48 Woods, 'Wages Notebooks', p. 1686.

49 Ben Turner, *Pieces from a Yorkshire Loom* (Published by the author, Heckmondwike, 1909) p. 78.

50 E. P. Thompson, 'Homage to Tom Maguire', in *Essays in Labour History* (Macmillan, 1960), p. 289, quotes Norah Turner, Ben Turner's daughter, as saying that he 'never belonged' to any church.

51 Turner, *Pieces*, pp. 90–1.

52 Towards the end of his life, Allen Gee seems to have adopted a more tolerant, perhaps more realistic attitude towards the situation of married women workers. In an interview reported on the occasion of his golden wedding, Allen Gee spoke of 'the employment of women in the mill, Mr. Gee was not prepared with wholesale condemnation, though he admits that it has a tendency to keep down wages, while married women in particular are tempted, when there are men's wages coming into the house, to accept terms which a single woman would not, and could not accept. But he does not see any harm in a young married woman going to work, when there is no family, or perhaps one or two babies that can be

left in Granny's charge; they can often that way save the money for furnishing a house, which he has often known to be done', *Leeds Mercury*, 9 May 1925.

53 Minutes of the Colne Valley District Committee of the GUTW, 15 July 1914 deposited in Huddersfield Local History Archive.

54 Huddersfield District Committee Minutes, 9 June 1914, 11 June 1914.

55 *Yorkshire Factory Times*, 12 November 1914.

56 PP. 1909, Cmd. 4545.

57 Eric Hobsbawm, 'Man and Woman in Socialist Iconography', *History Workshop*, no. 6 (1978).

58 See E. Roberts's contributions in J. Lewis's companion volume.

59 Ada Heather-Biggs, 'The Wife's Contribution to Family Income', *Economic Journal*, vol. iv (1894).

60 Drake, *Women in Trade Unions*, pp. 61–2.

61 The argument is taken further in chs 7–10 of Bornat, thesis (1980).

Clementina Black

Margaret MacDonald

8

Strategists for Change: Social Feminist Approaches to the Problems of Women's Work

Ellen F. Mappen

Social feminists were especially concerned about the problems of women workers from the late 1880s.[1] To solve these problems and at the same time to create a political role for women even before they had the parliamentary franchise, they formed pressure groups which had the express aim of achieving economic and social rights for women. Bringing about social reforms was central to their efforts to better women's overall position in society.

As a result of extensive investigations into women's life and work, social feminists concluded that one of the root evils of women's employment was the low wages received by women. How to improve these wages was therefore a matter of great concern as can be seen when looking at two social feminist organizations, the Women's Industrial Council and the Women's Labour League. While some of the leaders were, or had been, active in forming trade unions for women, the consensus was that trade unionism alone could not ameliorate working and living conditions.[2] Various remedies were considered over the years, culminating in the acceptance by most of the leaders that a legal minimum wage was a necessary first step in achieving economic rights for women workers. After reaching this conclusion, many were then involved in efforts to secure a minimum wage through Trade, or Wages Boards.

Since the leading women actors in the agitation for Trade Boards were affiliated at one time or another with either the Women's Industrial Council or the Women's Labour League, this essay will first look at their formation. It will then focus on the search for a solution, highlighting the efforts of Clementina Black and Margaret

MacDonald's efforts as social feminists within the framework of their organizations. Black, one of the Council's founders and long–time leader, was an advocate of Trade Boards. MacDonald, also a member of the Council and a founder of the League, was, on the other hand, the leading opponent, although the Women's Labour League supported them.

The Formation of Two Social Feminist Groups

In their work, social feminists took the advice of Lady Ishbel Aberdeen, president of the Council, who, speaking at the 1893 Chicago World's Congress of Representative Women, concluded that it was 'not required that women should possess the franchise before beginning to make their influence felt'. In fact, she said, women had to become 'intelligent politicians' if they were 'to become real social reformers and undertake to do earnestly with the betterment of the people'.[3] It was within their social feminist groups that a number of women, including Black and MacDonald, gained experience and established themselves as experts on women's work.

While 'social feminism was social reform as a gender-related mission', social feminists did share some common beliefs and practices with other reformers who were not feminists.[4] For instance, social investigation, as pioneered by Charles Booth, was considered the basis of the knowledge needed to influence policy makers.

Social feminist groups were more influential than they otherwise might have been because of an overlapping of membership, particularly among the leaders. MacDonald and Mary Fenton MacPherson, the latter a London journalist and honorary secretary of the Railway Women's Guild, were both founders of the League, but belonged to the Council as well. Margaret Bondfield, of the Shop Assistants' Union, was also a member of both groups. Frequent contact and shared concerns usually led to co-operation and mutual support. This is not to say that there was not disagreement over the best method to ameliorate the evils of women's work.

Both the Council and the League had their origins in the labour movement, but while the former was 'wholly unsectarian and independent of party', the latter wanted to be seen as a section of the Labour Party.[5] Although sharing with the League the basic social feminist goal of improving women's economic and social position in society, the Council identified its task in relation to women in the industrial world while the League looked more broadly at women's lives, though still considering women as workers. The Council did not, however, ignore women's position in that sphere as well. In terms of strategy, the Council placed more emphasis on social investigation as the first step in asserting pressure on public authorities than did the League. In the end, both groups succeeded in keeping women's issues before the public eye by, most importantly, making women's private sphere an issue for public concern.

The Council, founded in London, was an outgrowth both of the concern felt by middle-class reformers about working-class life, and the trade union movement of the late 1880s. The women who joined to create the Council had earlier attempted to organize women workers through the Women's Trade Union Association which had been formed in October 1889. Finding that women's trade unions were proving themselves unstable and thus unlikely to bring about permanent social change, the leaders of the Association turned from trade unionism to become a political pressure group in the hope that they could attract wider support.

The Council was thus created 'to watch over the interests of women engaged in trades, and over all industrial matters which concern women'. Its approach included the investigation of 'the actual facts of women's work' and the publishing of collected information, the scrutinizing of parliamentary bills, official reports, etc., as they affected women's interests; the organizing of petitions and deputations in connection with legislative or local government matters; and various other activities all aimed at promoting the interests of 'industrial' women. Underlying all its activities was the basic belief that 'without full investigation' it was 'impossible either to legislate or to organise wisely'.

Although its base was in London, the Council's membership consisted of people who lived outside the metropolis and who were 'engaged in every variety of social work'. Its more well-known women members included, in addition to Black, Bondfield and MacDonald, the Fabian B.L. Hutchins, Catherine Webb, a Liberal and a member of the Women's Co-operative Guild who was Secretary of the Council for most of its first seven years of existence, and, in its early years, Mary Macarthur, secretary of the Women's Trade Union League. The Council was never a large organization. By 1906/7, it claimed 244 members, many of whom were far from active.

Council members saw their investigative work as practical in nature. The Council worked for 'remedial legislation' and became as Sheila Lewenhak has observed, 'a powerful parliamentary lobby'.[6] The members did this, in spite of the fact that 'the absence of Parliamentary representation made it difficult for women's wants to be adequately discussed when measures concerning them were before Parliament.' Women like Black and MacDonald sought to achieve their goals in the Council by first collecting data about women's work and then attempting to influence 'public, Parliamentary, and Cabinet opinion'. The League was founded, on the other hand, because MacDonald and her friends wanted to ensure that women had a voice in the Labour Party and also to further their feminist and socialist programmes. The idea for a women's section had first surfaced in November 1904 when MacPherson wrote to Ramsay MacDonald that she and Bondfield thought 'the time was opportune for something definite to be done to bring together women who believe in the Labour movement'. The Executive of the Labour Representation Committee advised her to go ahead on her own. MacPherson did this and after some delay, a meeting to discuss the formation of 'a Women's Section' was held in the MacDonalds's home at 3 Lincolns Inn Fields on 9 March 1906.[7]

From its inception, the League's leaders emphasized the importance of women for the new party. As MacDonald noted in her address from the chair at the League's first conference in June 1906, League women would no longer just sit and wait but would now 'fight side by side with the men'. They had established the Women's Labour League 'so that they might be enabled to make more progress in the new crusade against the evils of society – against 'the great giants of competition and capitalism'.

At the same time, the founders did not ignore the importance of the League and the party for women. They hoped the League would become more than an adjunct to the party; the League was to work not just for 'independent Labour Representation' but also 'to obtain direct Labour Representation of women in Parliament and on all local bodies'.

The League's initiators also emphasized that through the League, women could 'set about to do something for themselves' and 'express their opinions as women on all matters of which they had special knowledge'. They would thus correct the 'lopsided' state of the Labour Party, which, as MacDonald said, accepted women as members but did not let them share equally with men in the party's work.

The League's founders believed that a women's pressure group was essential to ensure that the Labour Party kept women's interests in mind. Speaking in 1909, MacDonald noted that 'if the party was not to be a feckless masculine affair we saw that a special effort must be made to organize ourselves separately from the men . . . '. She went on to say, echoing the words of Lady Aberdeen spoken over a decade earlier, that while they could not do much as individuals, they could 'by political methods . . . win freedom, economic and spiritual, for ourselves and for the generation . . . growing up around us . . . '.

To do this, the League opened its membership to virtually all women, appealing to the wives, mothers, sisters or daughters of men in the labour movement but also encouraging women trade unionists, women on public bodies and even women of leisure and education to join. It was felt that the League would be attractive to professional women (teachers, nurses, doctors, inspectors, post office clerks, etc.) because, according to MacDonald, 'the facts of life have driven them to make common cause with the wage earners and they see in our movement the only hope for real social reform'.[8] As Bondfield said when she chaired the fourth meeting of the League in 1909, 'the Women's Labour League provided a common platform, a uniting ground for the women who were free to study, to plan, to execute, and the house mothers, wives of trade unionists and wage earning women who brought their practical experience of life's difficulties . . . '.

Thus women had a common goal even if they came from different backgrounds and classes. Further, public life was no longer separate from home life for the issues that were being dealt with by public bodies affected the home and the family. Women dealt with these issues as wives and mothers in the home; they could also deal with them in the public sphere in 'a sort of municipal housekeeping'.

Although the National Women's Labour League was, like the Women's Industrial Council, centred within London, it also organized local branches around the country and in London. The purpose was to get more women involved in the Labour Party and to show that women were useful to its work. By its fourth meeting in 1909, the League had 40 branches, each engaged in a variety of different kinds of work ranging from social events to campaigning for labour candidates at all levels of government. Branch meetings gave women the chance to educate 'themselves by watching both local and parliamentary politics'. The importance of the League was noted by one of its organizers, Mrs Simm, who could claim to know 'something of the mining villages, where the WLL weekly meeting was an event in the lives of the miners' wives, some of whom walked miles to attend the meetings'.

Despite its relationship to the Labour Party and its interest, as a group, in suffrage efforts, the League's objectives were not dissimilar from those of the Council. They included such social feminist goals as educating League members and others on political and social questions (the latter ranging from issues of unemployment and old age pensions to child welfare matters); taking an active interest in the work of local and parliamentary officials; watching 'the interests of working women in their own neighbourhood', and striving 'where possible, to improve their social and industrial conditions'. In carrying out their objectives, the League used methods similar to those employed by the Council. Like other social feminists, League activists believed that women had 'an important and useful part to play in politics'.

Social Feminist Remedies to Sweated Labour

Their investigations and discussions about women's paid employment helped social feminists to realize the complexity of the problem they sought to tackle. Whether talking about women workers in London or the country as a whole, remedies to improve conditions in the workplace could not be separated from women's role in the family. That most working-class girls did not plan to work for more than a few years and were consequently not prepared to support themselves adequately in later years was taken as a fact. That many would need to re-enter the job market because of the unemployment or underemployment of their husbands, or because they were deserted or widowed, was also accepted. Many social feminists concluded from their own experience that the low, or sweated, wages paid to women, and to men, were at the core of the problem although poor working conditions and long hours of labour were also considered.[9] How to provide women with a decent and 'living' wage was thus the main question.

The issue of sweated labour first surfaced as a public concern in the late 1880s as part of the increased interest in working-class life. Social feminist investigations were part of a broader concern but with a particular focus on the conditions and problems of women's work. In the 1890s and even more so in the first decade of the twentieth century, efforts to alleviate the worst evils were intensified because of the stimulus provided by social feminist groups.[10]

Leaders like Black, Hutchins, Macarthur and MacDonald identified from personal experience various aspects of the problem. Over the years, they proposed different remedies, ranging from trade unionism, consumer action, and more factory and other types of protective legislation to trade training for working-class girls and the legal establishment of a minimum wage. Since the issues were considered to be complex and interconnected, it is helpful to look briefly at the proposed remedies, concentrating on the efforts of Black and MacDonald. The common ground was to help women workers but, in the end, these two leaders differed over the best strategy.

In the mid to late 1880s, Black became involved in attempts to organize women workers, first through the Women's Trade Union League and subsequently through the Women's Trade Union Association. She began writing on social issues to publicize the plight of working women. Her articles give her impressions about the state of women's work in London and show that at least as early as 1889 she had concluded that low wages were 'at the root' of working women's problems. At the time she thought that workers could only resist wage reductions by forming unions. She saw her role as an 'outsider' who could show workers how to organize. Soon she and the other leaders of the Association changed their minds and formed the Council. In later years, Black still supported trade unionism but not as the first step in ameliorating 'the effects of economic competition' on women's work.[11]

While identifying the central issue as one of low pay, Black also outlined the gist of an idea for what would later become the basic mechanism for the operation of Trade Boards. She thought that 'two organizations, both resolved to resist that undue competition which destroys a trade and threatens both classes alike with ruin, might fairly exist and work harmoniously, the employers fixing a selling price for themselves and agreeing to pay the minimum rate of the employees union.[12] That is, both employers and employees would negotiate an acceptable rate of pay in a particular trade. Here she suggested it be through voluntary organization; later she believed that government intervention was necessary.

Black also considered consumer action as a possible solution to low pay. In 1887 while still the secretary of the Women's Trade Union League, she published a brief list of employers who dealt 'fairly' with their employees. In the same article, she raised the question whether there should be a consumer's league to scrutinize places of employment and publish its findings so that, as she wrote in 1890, consumers would know who were the 'good employers'.[13]

Although she believed it was the consumer's 'duty to pay something more than a starvation wage to all those who work directly or indirectly in our service', she did not think that a consumer's league could be in a strong enough position to remedy 'the poverty of the worker'. By 1908, she was far from optimistic over the results of consumer action to help the victims of unrestrained competition.[14]

The leaders of the Women's Trade Union Association, the Women's Industrial Council, and later the Women's Labour League supported effective protective legislation (such as the limitation of hours and health and safety regulations) as another remedy for the poor conditions under which many women worked, as long as such measures did not restrict women workers and put them at an unfair disadvantage. They also believed that women workers needed knowledge of the legislation that protected them.

First the Association and then the Council sought to assist the Factory Inspectors in their work and to educate working-class girls about their rights. The annual reports of both groups provide numerous instances of vigilance in reporting breaches of the Factory and Workshop Acts to the Inspectors. In 1905–6, for example, 36 complaints were sent to the Home Office by the Council; of these, 26 dealt with sanitation and safety violations and eight with illegal employment.

Both groups also campaigned to increase the number of Factory Inspectors. In 1892, the Association held a meeting 'to urge upon the Home Secretary the desirability of appointing women, and especially working women as Factory Inspectors'. When May Tennant left the Inspectorate, the Council passed a resolution urging the government to appoint a woman to succeed her. The League also devoted some time to the same subject when, at its second conference in 1907, it passed a resolution urging the government to increase the number of women employed as factory as well as School Inspectors.

As usual, Black was the voice of the Council in publicizing its efforts in this direction. She both lectured on and wrote about factory legislation for women workers. In the late 1890s, she wrote a poem, 'The Rhyme of the Factory Acts' which the Council hoped would convey 'the essence of those clauses of the Factory and Workshop Acts which apply to women and girls'. Her 'Rhyme' was updated and reprinted after the 1901 Act.

Although they accepted the concept of protective legislation, social feminists offered constructive criticism of government measures. While aiming for the extension of protective legislation to domestic workplaces and laundries, they also lobbied for fairness in applying factory and workshop regulations to women. Much of the Council's efforts in this work was undertaken by its Legal and Statistical Committee, chaired by MacDonald.

The Council let parliamentary leaders know its views on pending factory legislation. In 1900, when the government introduced a Factory Bill, the Council along with the Industrial Committee of the National Union of Women Workers, the Women's Co-operative Guild and the Manchester Women's Trade Union Council issued a Memorandum 'to call the attention of members of the House of Commons to different ways in which it is felt that the proposed measures would be prejudicial to the interests of workers in general, and of the women workers in particular'. The writers of the Memorandum believed that a proposed double eight hours shift was detrimental to women because it would mitigate against them earning a fair wage, enjoying good conditions of work and also having opportunites for recreation, education and family life. This system would only accentuate the tendency of women workers to view their employment as 'supplementary and casual' because it set a 'distinctly different standard of hours for men and women, and for different groups of women in the same trade'. This was not fair and would lead to a decrease in wages.

This bill was dropped but another introduced the following year. Again, the Council issued a statement, this time in conjunction with the Scottish Council for Women's Trades. Two of the Council's objections were that the bill gave too much responsibility for inspection to the local authorities and that the proposals concerning laundries were insufficient. When the bill became law, the *Women's Industrial News* regretted that the laundry section had been withdrawn. The League also supported extending the Factory Acts to laundry workers.

The Council's support of factory legislation resulted from its investigations into different trades. As early as 1897–8, the Council's Investigation Committee, of which Black and MacDonald were then both members, decided to tackle the question of the economic effects of factory legislation on women's employment. The inquiry was extended to cover the whole issue of the condition of women as workers. The Committee finally concluded in its 1903–4 report that legislation limiting the hours of women's labour did not have a detrimental effect. Their investigations into trades followed by women had shown that men and women did not compete and that women were not dismissed from their jobs because of the legal limit on hours.

This report is of interest because it summarized the practical uses to which investigative results were put. As the report noted, to those who had helped gather the 'information, it has been the basis on which we have formed our views of industrial life and conditions, and it is from that basis that we feel we may suggest some remedies'. The Council's efforts both to bring about better technical training for working-class girls and to help home workers resulted from their understanding of industrial conditions which in turn came about because of investigative efforts.

Both the Women's Trade Union Association and the Women's Industrial Council concluded that 'the inferior position occupied by women in the labour market largely rests upon the inefficient and untrained quality of their work'. Thus the Council saw its mission as promoting 'by all means in its power' the right of girls to technical and trade training and seeing that 'the needs of girls received attention proportionate to that bestowed on boys'. They also campaigned to have working-class girls trained as children's nurses 'with a view to providing an opening for remunerative work and to fitting them for their future lives as wives and mothers'. Thus the dual benefits of industrial training were stressed. The girls would become better workers and be able to support themselves in later life if necessary but they would, in addition, develop skills for proper 'mothering and tending'. Here social feminists were contributing to what Anna Davin has called the 'formation of an ideology of motherhood'.[15]

Margaret MacDonald, according to her husband Ramsay, devoted much time to the subject of industrial training of girls. She believed that girls had to train for their future life. To ensure that some working-class girls at least had the opportunity for training, the Council's Education Committee put pressure on the Technical Education Board in London and eventually industrial classes for women were started. Until that point, Ramsay MacDonald noted, women's interests had been neglected.[16]

The Council continued its efforts in this direction. In October 1908, it sponsored a conference to consider the best way to develop industrial training for girls, a subject which one speaker noted had 'received in the past very little attention'. While the same speaker concluded that increased skill would raise the standard of women's work, a dissenting voice noted that this was not enough. Maud Pember Reeves, a founder of the Fabian Women's Group, another social feminist organization, expressed the view 'that the tendency of turning out large bodies of skilled labour from the Schools into the market would inevitably result, failing legal enactment as a preventive, in the reduction of wages'.

While the view expressed by Pember Reeves had gained increasing support by 1906, not all social feminists were staunch supporters of the Trade Boards legislation. MacDonald and Black, for instance, reached different conlusions over the best path to follow in ameliorating conditions for women workers. This is most apparent when looking at the complex issue of home work and sweated labour. The Council sought to make the problem of home work an issue for public discussion. By 1906, its efforts were somewhat rewarded as both the public and parliamentary leaders became concerned over the larger issue of sweated labour in general, not just in the home industries. The Council was by then not alone in its interest, for social feminists now had other forums such as the League and the National Anti-Sweating League from which to express their views.

In all the discussions, the question of home workers as sweated labourers could not be separated from the issue of women's larger role in the family. Although women were not the only workers who toiled at home, they were in the main those whom social reformers had in mind when discussing the problem. The investigations undertaken by the Council centred on women home workers. Men were considered but primarily because, as Hutchins noted in 1908, 'the two great evils of unemployment and casual labour are closely bound up with the home work of women'. Social feminists did not want to restrict married women's work but they still emphasized that if men were paid enough many women would not work.[17]

The Council's approach to the subject of home work is illustrative of its general method. From 1895, the Investigation Committee's principal task had been an inquiry into the home industries of women in London. Investigators (including MacDonald whose inquiries were mostly in the north-east and east districts) saw 400 women working in 18 different trades. A report, prepared under Black's guidance, was issued in 1897 and was heralded as 'probably the largest collection of facts concerning home-work in London that has yet been gathered'. Two other reports were issued in 1906 and 1908.[18]

After it issued the 1897 report, the Council held a conference on the subject at the London School of Economics in November of that year. About 90 people, representing a number of women's groups, including the Glasgow Council for Women's Trades, the Liverpool Women's Industrial Council, the Women's Co-operative Guild, the National Union of Women Workers, and the Women's Trade Union League, attended. The conference speakers echoed the two themes which the Council's investigations had revealed: the prevalence of child labour and the extremely low wages earned by women home workers.

It is not surprising, after reading the vivid descriptions of the living and working environments of home workers such as fur pullers, that the leaders of the Council looked to more protective legislation to ameliorate the unsanitary conditions of home work. After the conference, the Council's Legal Committee drafted a 'Bill for the Better Regulation of Homework'. It was first introduced in the House of Commons in July 1899 by John Burns and other supporters. The bill was reintroduced many times between then and 1907 when Ramsay MacDonald reintroduced it.

The bill basically sought to extend the protection of the factory acts to home workshops through a system of licensing. Under the Council's plan, an employer could not give work out unless a certificate was presented showing that a factory inspector had ensured the home workshop to be 'a fit place for the carrying on of industry without injury to the health of the persons employed there'. Provision was made for temporary licences to be issued until such time as inspection could take place.

As the title of the bill implied, its object was to regulate or 'organize' home work. The supporters of the bill remained constant in their beliefs about the scheme's benefits. They thought that holding a certificate would make the home worker less casual and therefore in more constant demand. They pointed out that it was not restrictive upon women's labour as it would apply to all home workers, male or female, but it might control child labour. In her 1907 testimony before the Select Committee on Home Work, Margaret MacDonald also stated her hope that indirectly the scheme would increase wages although she was far from sanguine about that happening 'under the present system of industry'.

Because inspection of the worker's home was at the core of its proposal, the Council's Legal Committee hoped its scheme would protect both the consumer and the worker against dirt and disease. It would allow the inspector to see how home workers lived and thus be able, according to Margaret MacDonald, 'to insist on a minimum standard, both of structural and domestic cleanliness'. The inspector could either withdraw or withhold a licence. This power gave 'the necessary support to the moral persuasion and tactful advice which must always be the Inspectors' first weapons in their crusade against dirty rooms and unopened windows'. For Margaret MacDonald, licensing was worth trying because it was a way of protecting children and also a way of making sure the woman of the house would use a little soap and water and make her beds each morning.[20]

While the Council's licensing scheme only dealt with one aspect of the problem of sweating and also smacked of social control, the idea was not a new one and had been proposed earlier by the Women's Trade Union Association. The Council took up where the Association left off. In May of 1899, a memorandum was sent to the Home Secretary, which asked both for the extension of the Factory and Workshop Act of 1878 to domestic workshops and the inclusion of the Council's scheme of licensing in amendments of the Acts of 1891 and 1895. Employers had been obligated to keep lists of outworkers since the 1891 Act (reinforced in the two subsequent Acts of 1895 and 1901) but the Council thought this was insufficient to remedy the problem at hand.[21] In commenting on the Factory Inspectors' Report of 1900, Margaret MacDonald pointed out in the *Women's Industrial News* that the inspectors were really powerless to remedy evils and insanitary conditions such as were found in the homes of fur pullers. She added that 'without more effective legislation such evils must remain unchecked'.

The Council was able to obtain the support of other associations, such as the Trade Union Congress, the Women's Liberal Federation and the Scottish Council for Women's Trades; the latter co-sponsored the Council's bill for a time. The Council's Legal Committee had been able to persuade the Women's Liberal Federation to pass a resolution in favour of its bill. Further, when the Industrial Committee of the National Union of Women Workers, the Women's Co-operative Guild and the Manchester Women's Trade Union Council joined the Council in issuing a statement on the Government's factory bill, it contained the comment that 'it is to be regretted that no serious attempt is made to deal with the sanitary and other evils attaching to Home Work'. The groups thought that unless the homes of workers could be visited by factory Inspectors, the keeping of the names of such workers was useless. In spite of these efforts, the bill was never carried through parliament. In Ramsay MacDonald's opinion 'the problems of homework were gradually absorbed in those of sweating, and were all lost sight of save that of wages'.[22]

MacDonald's view is not completely accurate as home workers

were not overlooked even when wages did become a major issue. The MacDonalds continued to support the licensing scheme and a Select Committee of the House of Commons was instructed to look into the problems of home work in 1907. The major thrust of reformers, social feminists included, from the time of the Sweated Industries Exhibition in 1906 was towards establishing Trade Boards to set a minimum wage in selected trades, whether or not work was done at home.[23] The House Committee recommended the establishment of Boards to help home workers in its 1908 report, but by that time the consensus was that such legislation would be too narrow and that all workers in a particular trade had to be covered.

Social Feminists Debate the Trade Boards

How best to deal with sweated labour was an issue facing both the Council and the League, but the debate was most divisive within the former. Margaret MacDonald wrote to Black that it seemed 'so silly to start from much the same standpoint and go in exactly opposite directions' but that is precisely what happened.[24] MacDonald not only disagreed with Black on the issue of a minimum wage but also with Macarthur.[25] While both Black and MacDonald supported the Exhibition and the Council's home work bill, Black went further and worked actively to secure a legal minimum wage. Her role in the agitation and MacDonald's opposition can be seen in their writings, and at public conferences as well as at Council and League meetings held between 1906 and 1909. They had, as social feminists, created forums from which their views could be heard and on this issue they were considered among those to whom public officials listened.

The division within the Council did not emerge until after *The Daily News* Exhibition of Sweated Industry. In fact, Margaret MacDonald played a role in involving the Council in the Exhibition's organization when she informed the Council's Investigation Committee about the plans for it. MacDonald and Black represented the Women's Industrial Council on the Council of the Sweated Industries Exhibition. Women's Industrial Council members gave lectures at the Exhibition which ran from 2 May to 13 June and the Council was able to supply workers and pieces of work for the Exhibition. Black and MacDonald also contributed to the handbook of the Exhibition.[26]

The Anti-Sweating League was formed after the Exhibition was over. In an article published in *The Daily News* on the last day of the

Exhibition, Black proposed a non-partisan 'Living Wage League', to demand eventual legal enactment 'of a minimum wage for workers in unorganized and ill-paid trades'. To her, this was 'the only real remedy for the evil' of sweating.[27] When the Anti-Sweating League was formed Black became a member of its Executive Committee and played, according to Macarthur, a large role in its work.

The members of the Council and the League both now debated the efficacy of Trade, or Wages, Boards. The Council, divided on this issue, did not take an official position; it did continue as did the League to promote licensing, but here too there was some difference of opinion. While it does not seem to have affected the League's operation, the disagreement within the Council led to Black's temporary resignation from the presidency in January 1909. She was so committed to the establishment of Trade Boards that she could not continue as the Council's leader until the Boards were adopted; she continued, though, to serve as chair of the Investigation Committee.

Within the League, the remedies of Trade Boards and licensing were also often pitted against each other. The debate heated up after the Labour Party's bill was introduced in 1907. During discussion at the League's 1907 annual conference on a resolution to support Ramsay MacDonald's Licensing Bill, Macarthur, speaking in opposition, emphatically stated that 'the remedy for sweating was the raising of wages'. On 20 November 1907, the Central London Branch of the League held an evening educational meeting at which Macarthur and Margaret MacDonald debated the proposed Wages Boards, the latter speaking in opposition.

The division within the League, did not prevent it giving official support to the remedy of Trade Boards. A resolution was passed, after much discussion, at the League's 1908 annual meeting which called for a government bill similar to the Labour Party's Sweated Industries Bill. During the discussion, an opposing amendment was moved which stated that Trade Boards would not improve wages and conditions of work in the sweated trades. Margaret MacDonald spoke for this amendment which called for other remedies, including the right to work for the unemployed, the abolition of child labour, state maintenance of widows with young children and women with sick husbands or other helpless relatives, and old age pensions. MacDonald thought that Trade Boards would not work in sweated trades, especially since much of the work was done at home. She supported the amendment because it pointed out 'other ways of helping those homeworkers . . . who really ought not to be in industrial work at all'. MacDonald was vehemently opposed to Trade Boards and would not accept that they could be, as another speaker said, 'urged side by side – *not instead* of the measures suggested in the amendment'.

MacDonald did try to stop further support for Trade Boards but was unsuccessful in her attempts with the League. At a meeting of the National Executive of the League on 11 December 1908, MacDonald spoke against the League sending a representative on a deputation to Asquith organized by the Anti-Sweating League. She thought that as there was a difference of opinion within the League, a delegate should not be sent. A vote was taken and MacPherson was appointed to represent the league. In June of 1909, MacPherson again took part in a deputation to Asquith; the report of the Executive for the 1910 annual conference noted that on this subject of interest to the League, the answer was satisfactorily embodied in legislation. Earlier, Bondfield had pointed out the League's active involvement in the agitation for Trade Boards. Even the Central London branch of the League had passed a resolution in favour of the government bill.

The Women's Industrial Council, however, an organization that had long worked to help women workers, did not take a stand on Trade Boards. As has been pointed out, support for the boards was widespread and across political lines. The MacDonalds were the main opponents to the legislation. The pages of the *Women's Industrial News* report the debate and highlight the stands taken by Black and Margaret MacDonald. It is clear that Black and MacDonald, especially the latter, were like other social feminists in that they could not always separate reforms in the industrial sphere from women's home life.

One reason why the MacDonalds rejected Trade Boards was that they did not think them workable, particularly in industries with large numbers of home workers. Margaret MacDonald wrote to Black on 3 December 1908 that while they were probably 'most united' on the 'general principle of the desirability of a minimum wage', it was 'on the details of legislation we are at cross purposes. You believe a minimum wage can be successfully worked in homework trades. We believe that to attempt this is "worse than a waste of time", and an obstacle to progress'. Her letter concluded that the Council could not 'possibly make any decision officially, which we can both loyally support'. Because of these differences, MacDonald hoped that the Council would not commit itself to one side or another.[28]

Between April 1908 and January 1909, when Black resigned from the presidency, there were several meetings at which she and MacDonald presented their sides for discussion. While they also spoke at other events and wrote about their views elsewhere, these debates brought the issue to a head. They showed that Black strongly believed in the necessity for Trade Boards and that MacDonald thought them unworkable.

Black's remarks at the Council's meeting on 1 April 1908 indicate her belief in the efficacy of the minimum wage as the 'next step' to check 'unrestricted competition'. She said that their 'method of progress is by slowly advancing steps, and by the avoidance of such suffering as would cause revolutions'. The minimum wage would also 'diminish . . . the amount of employment of married women, because the great cause of married women's work is the underpayment of the husbands'.

According to Black, Margaret MacDonald reproached her for 'being academic' and not sufficiently practical. MacDonald did reiterate her view 'that married women should not be earning money at all', a view that on the surface appeared close to that of her opponent. Black's rebuttal was firm and passionate. She said she thought it time for a legal minimum wage in part because she hoped that 'the bright intelligent' working girls who met in the Council's rooms should 'be kept on the level they occupy, and . . . not become worn dragged-out looking women looking fifty before they are thirty'.

After the House of Commons Select Committee on Home Work recommended that a legal minimum wage be set for some home trades, Black tried to get the Council to pass a resolution not to limit trade boards to home workers. She was afraid that including only some workers in a particular trade would hurt the 'regulated' workers unduly. Elsewhere she had opposed restricting such legislation to women workers only. She hoped here that by modifying her stance it would be more palatable to her critics. She was unsuccessful in her attempt and the Council at its meeting on 20 January 1909 followed MacDonald's lead and passed a resolution indicating it would not take an official position on Trade Boards. Within ten days, Black resigned from the presidency because, in her own words, her 'free time being extremely limited I must devote most of it to what I regard as the most vital of industrial reforms . . .'. In spite of the Executive trying to placate her by suggesting another investigation of Trade Boards, Black was adamant. She did not return to her position as president until after Trade Boards became law.

Because Black believed in the principle of a minimum wage and the practicability of Trade Boards, she worked outside of the Council to effect their enactment. Her acknowledged expertise, gained as a leader of the Council, gave her standing apart from it. *The Daily Chronicle*, for instance, interviewed her after Winston Churchill introduced his Trade Boards Bill. Its correspondent noted that 'among those who have investigated the question of sweating, Miss Clementina Black takes a high place for the thoroughness of her inquiries and the completeness of her knowledge of the subject'. Her interview was soon followed by two articles written by Black, one of which was subtitled, 'Hope for Women Workers in Ill-Paid Industries'.[29]

Unlike Black, MacDonald was troubled by the administrative problems she anticipated and her concern over cleanliness in workers' homes. These two strategists for change who had worked so long together were divided on whether to support Trade Boards because Margaret MacDonald and her husband looked upon the measure 'as illusory and impracticable'.[30] She wrote that by striving to obtain a legal minimum wage, socialists were making a great mistake; that they were 'diverting [their] energies from the direct fight for socialism in order to advocate a palliative which, . . . would be not only effective, but in some cases positively harmful'. She was, however, in favour of licensing, which she saw as another palliative because there was 'a fundamental difference between seeing what money has gone into a worker's pocket and seeing [or smelling] whether his workroom is sanitary'. From their 1897 trip to the United States, the MacDonalds had become 'convinced by the very simple testimony of our eyes, and above all of our noses' that licensing was the answer.[31]

To their credit, the MacDonalds supported other measures which they believed would deal with low wages, for example, those to relieve distress from want of employment and insurance for sickness and old age.[32] They would not, however, change their view, also developed during a visit, this time to Australia and New Zealand, that Trade or Wages Boards would not work because of the difficulty of fixing standard wages.[33] Speaking at the 1907 conference of the National Union of Women Workers, MacDonald made her position quite clear when she said she did not agree with Black in seeing 'Wages Boards' as a remedy for sweating.[34] She added that

> The community . . . must take more responsibility for work. What was wanted were Employment Acts to prevent men from being out of work for long periods and obliging their wives to

support them. The work of married women in looking after their children or sick husbands should be recognised and paid for by the community . . . This idea would not be recognised till more Collectivism was in force; but much could be done even now . . .

While not alone in looking at women workers as wives and mothers first, Margaret MacDonald was in a minority among social feminist leaders on the Trade Boards issue.

Although unable to persuade the Council to act because of the MacDonalds' influence, Black was in the forefront of those who supported Trade Boards. She had long believed that underpayment was the problem and was 'really a more pressing and vital question than that of unemployment . . . Underpayment [was] a direct and quite inevitable result of unrestricted competition in the buying and selling of labour . . .'. Because most women workers were unorganized, they could not compete. The establishment of Trade Boards, however, would encourage unionism among women. Her brand of social feminism was to take steps to remedy the evils of low pay through legislative and other action. She was even willing to accept a minimum wage bill which was obviously limited in scope because it was a new idea which needed to be tried. She thus supported Churchill's bill.[35]

The Establishment of Trade Boards

After Trade Boards were established in four trades, chain making, box making, lace mending and finishing, and ready-made clothing, Macarthur lectured at a meeting of the Women's Industrial Council. She called the Boards a 'legislative revolution'. She was optimistic about their success and again credited Black as having had a large share in the work of the Anti-Sweating League. By 1911, *The Sociological Review* could report that the Boards had given women workers the ability 'to organise and combine together, for mutual protection and self-defence.'[36]

Advocates of Trade Boards did not stop here. At a conference convened by the Fabian Women's Group in December 1912, Black called for 'a basic statutory, national minimum wage, below which no adult, male or female, should be paid.'[37] In 1913, the Council joined with the Anti-Sweating League to promote a demonstration to extend the Boards.[38] When a non-partisan conference was sponsored, in November 1913, by the Conservative and Unionist Women's Franchise Association to discuss extending the Boards,

The Daily Telegraph reported that the women's trade union movement would be presented by 'its three most prominent leaders'. Black was included with Gertrude Tuckwell and Macarthur.[39]

The Trade Board system was extended first by Board of Trade action and then by legislation in 1918; the Boards were eventually renamed Wages Councils.[40] Interestingly, in 1914, the Council, with Black well entrenched as its leader, claimed that its own bill to regulate home work had 'over a long series of years helped to prepare the way for the public interest culminating in the Trade Boards Act'. While the Council itself did not help bring about the 1909 legislation, Black certainly was an important actor in the agitation to secure a legal minimum wage.

Conclusion – The Women's Movement and Social Reform

Social feminist organizations had wide-ranging concerns centred around issues which affected women's lives. They were closely aligned in purpose and method although separately organized. The Council and League are just two representative groups which sought to improve women's economic position in late nineteenth and early twentieth-century England. There was often co-operation and mutual support among the different groups. They united to hold conferences and joined together to form deputations to ministers. They often spoke at each other's meetings.

At times, however, there was disagreement over strategy. This was especially clear in the conflict between Black and MacDonald over Trade Boards. While Black did not completely separate women's role in the family from that in the workforce, she was able to look more broadly at the problem of low wages and support a measure which was applied to men and women as workers.[41] In general, the appraisal of the Trade Boards Act has been positive. Although, as Margaret MacDonald feared, there were administrative difficulties and women were in some cases exempted from the minimum wage, the legislation was 'the first notable blow against the sweating system'.[42]

Social feminists did gain some of their goals. The agitation for Trade Boards is just one case where women were instrumental in achieving social reform. By forming pressure groups which had the express aim of improving women's economic status, they had made a statement to society that women had a voice in politics. They worked to arouse public opinion and influence public officials. They challenged the status quo by claiming that women's responsibilities went beyond the private sphere. They also extended women's sphere by insisting that issues of family welfare were matters for public concern.

While there are numerous examples of feminist agitation to achieve political, economic, and social rights, during the nineteenth century the groups which came into being at the end of the century did so at a time when society was turning away from economic liberalism and towards the idea of a collectivist state. As Barbara Taylor has pointed out, the left-wing revival of the 1880s and 1890s influenced the women's movement.[43] This is most evident when looking at social feminist organizations such as the Women's Industrial Council and the Women's Labour League. Almost any issues which affected women and their families were fit subjects for their efforts. The socialist influence coupled with a feminist approach to social change, made social feminist women a force to be reckoned with in late nineteenth and early twentieth-century England.

Bibliographical Note

In addition to the works on feminists, trade unionism and Trade Boards cited in the footnotes, see Clementina Black, *Sweated Industry and the Minimum Wage* (Duckworth, 1907) and Mrs Carl Meyer and Clementina Black, *Makers of Our Clothes. A Case for Trade Boards* (Duckworth, 1909). For a study of Trade Boards, see Jenny Morris, *The Sweated Trades. Women Workers and the Trade Boards Act of 1909: An Exercise in Social Control* (Unpublished PhD thesis, London School of Economics, 1982). For a survey on women workers by a member of the Women's Industrial Council, see B. L. Hutchins, *Women in Modern Industry* (EP Publishing Limited, East Ardsley, 1978, originally published by G. Bell and Sons, 1915). See also Hutchins and A. Harrison, *A History of Factory Legislation* (Frank Cass, 1966, originally published 1903, 2nd edn rev. 1911). For a study on child and maternal welfare, see Jane Lewis, *The Politics of Motherhood* (Croom Helm, 1980).

Notes

I wish to thank my husband Marc and children Benjamin and Rebecca for their patience and humour while I was writing this essay. I would also like to thank friends and colleagues who over the years have commented on my efforts to define social feminism. Thanks too to Sheila Lockhead for permission to quote from the MacDonald letters, the staff of the London School of Economics and the Public Record Office.

1 I have used the term, social feminism, broadly, in the same way as Olive Banks used the term, feminism. It includes women of diverse political allegiances including socialists and Liberals. Most though not all were from the middle and upper classes. The desire to improve women's economic position in society was their common bond. Many were active in the suffrage movement, but did not forsake other women's rights concerns in their attempts to obtain the vote. Strategies and the degree of commitment to social feminist ideology differed by group and often by individual. For more background see Ellen F. Mappen, new introduction to *Married Women's Work* ed. Clementina Black (1915; Virago, 1983), and Mappen, *Helping Women at Work* (Hutchinson, 1985). See also Olive Banks, *Faces of Feminism* (St Martin's Press, New York, 1981), p.3.

2 Sheila Lewenhak, *Women and Work* (Fontana and St Martin's Press, New York, 1980), p.189.

3 Reported in *The World's Congress of Representative Women*, ed. May Wright Sewell (Rand, McNally, Chicago, 1894), vol. i, pp.426–30; vol. ii, pp.515–21. See esp. pp.517, 518.

4 Ellen Condliffe Lagemann, *A Generation of Women* (Harvard University Press, Cambridge 1979), p.155.

5 Unless otherwise stated, the following sections are based upon official publications of the Women's Trade Union Association, the Women's Industrial Council and the Women's Labour League. These include minutes, annual reports, progress reports, and propaganda materials. Except for the minutes of the Women's Labour League, these are all printed materials.

6 Sheila Lewenhak, *Women and Trade Unions* (Ernest Benn, 1977), p.118.

7 See letters in Labour Party Library, specifically, in LRC 17/311, 18 November 1904, in LRC 17, 313, 8 December 1904, and LP GC 1/340, 1 March 1906. For more background on the formation of the Women's Labour League see Lucy Middleton, 'Women in Labour Politics', in *Women in the Labour Movement*, ed. Lucy Middleton (Croom Helm, 1977), esp. pp.24–6. I would like to thank The Labour Party Library for permission to use these materials.

8 Quoted in Middleton, *Women in the Labour Movement* p.28.

9 The definition of sweating used at the time is based upon that of the House of Lords from its 1888–90 inquiry. In its terms, sweating refers to the conditions of employment and includes unusually low wages, excessive hours of labour, and unsanitary workplaces. See Beatrice Webb, 'How to Do Away with the Sweating System', in Sidney and Beatrice Webb, *The Problems of Modern Industry* (Longmans, Green, 1902), pp.139–40. See essay 3.

10 Lewenhak noted 'the campaign [against sweating] had been building up since 1864' but as Asa Briggs pointed out, it was not until the 1880s that workers in the sweated trades began to attract public notice. See Lewenhak, *Women and Trade Unions*,. p.118, and Briggs, 'Social Background', in *The System of Industrial Relations in Great Britain*, ed. Allan Flanders and H.A. Clegg (Basil Blackwell, Oxford 1954), p.11.

See also John Rickard, 'The Anti-Sweating Movement in Britain and Victoria: The Politics of Empire and Social Reform', *Historical Studies*, 18 (October 1979), p. 583. For a contemporary analysis and some background, see B. L. Hutchins, 'Home Work and Sweating', *Fabian Tract* no. 130, March 1908. See also James A. Schmiechen, *Sweated Industries and Sweated Labor* (Croom Helm and University of Illinois Press, Urbana, 1984). He is correct in pointing out that the Council (p. 162) was one of two groups to seek government regulation of wages and conditions of work in the sweated trades in the 1890s. By only labelling the Council as an 'industrial rights group', however, he denies its feminist bent and looks at its endeavours too narrowly. The Council considered all aspects of women's life even though it purported to assist only 'industrial' women.

11 Clementina Black, 'The Organization of Working Women', *Fortnightly Review*, xlvi (November 1889), pp. 699, 703, 695.

12 Ibid., p. 701.

13 Idem., 'Caveat Emptor', *Longman's Magazine*, 10 (August 1887), pp. 417–20 and 'The Morality of Buying in the Cheapest Market', *The Women's World* (1890), p. 43.

14 Idem., 'The Consumers' League. A proposal that buyers should combine to deal only with employers who pay their workers fairly', (nd), p. 8, and 'Legislative Proposals' in *Women in Industry from Seven Points of View* (Duckworth, 1908), p. 194.

15 Anna Davin, 'Imperialism and Motherhood', *History Workshop*, 5 (Spring 1978), p. 14. See also Mappen, *Helping Women at Work*, pp. 22–4.

16 J. Ramsay MacDonald, *Margaret Ethel MacDonald* (George Allen and Unwin, 1912, 5th edn. 1920), pp. 137–42.

17 Although I have not touched on the issue of the family wage, it should be noted that social feminists like Pember Reeves pointed out that men were not paid enough to support their families and that women were not even considered as needing enough money to support a family. In *Round About a Pound a Week* (1913; Virago, 1979), p. 216, she indicated the difficulties in discussing a minimum wage which at the same time was a family wage.

18 For a short summary of the 1897 report, see *'Women's Home Industries'*, *The Contemporary Review*, lxxii (December 1897), pp. 880–6. For Margaret MacDonald's role, see MacDonald, *Margaret Ethel MacDonald,*. pp. 143–7.

19 *'Select Committee on Home Work,'* PP. 1907, VI, q. 4334–5 and 4392–3.

20 Ibid., q. 4443, 4449, and 4509. The latter response was in answer to a question by Arthur Henderson who was the sponsor of the Labour Party's Sweated Industries Bill.

21 R. W. Cooke-Taylor, *The Factory System and the Factory Acts* (Methuen 2nd edn, rev., 1912), pp. 120–3.

22 MacDonald, *Margaret Ethel MacDonald*, p. 147.

23 The events leading up to the passage of the Trade Boards Act of 1909 have been discussed by numerous writers. Charles W. Pipkin, *Social Politics and Modern Democracies*, vol. i (The Macmillan Co., New York,

1931), pp. 128–35 and Dorothy Sells, *British Wages Boards* (The Brookings Institute, Washington, DC, 1939), pp. 3–22, are two of the classic works which offer good background material. For a contemporary view advocating a minimum wage, see Constance Smith. 'The Minimum Wage', in *Women in Industry*, pp. 27–59. More recently, John Rickard's interesting work notes the role played by women in the agitation (Macarthur, Black, and Hutchins, for example) although he does not, however, give full credit to Black nor does he review in any detail the specific stances taken by MacDonald and Black and the ensuing debates within the Council and the League, for that is outside the province of his article. See 'The Anti-Sweating Movement', pp. 582–97, esp. p. 586, and 588–90. See also Lewenhak, *Women and Trade Unions*, pp. 119–22 and Schmiechen, esp. Ch. 7.

24 MacDonald Collection, Collection J, vol. 1, n. 24, 27 November 1908, British Library of Political and Economic Science (BLPES).

25 Mary Agnes Hamilton, *Mary Macarthur* (Leonard Parsons, 1925), p. 75. Schmeichen notes, as do others (for example, Rickard, 'The Anti-Sweating Movement', pp. 589–90), that the MacDonalds were in a minority in opposing Trade Boards. He points out incorrectly though that this opposition led to the resignation of the MacDonalds from the Council in 1909 (pp. 169–70). The MacDonalds and their supporters did resign in 1910 but not over the Trade Boards issue.

26 Ramsay MacDonald spoke on 'A Bill for the Better Regulation of Home Industries', Black on 'Labour as a Commodity', Margaret MacDonald on 'American Anti-Sweating Laws', and B. L. Hutchins on 'The Position of Women in Industry'. See *Sweated Industries: Being a Handbook of the Daily News Exhibition*, compiled by Richard Mudie-Smith, May 1906 (Reprinted by Garland Publishing, 1980).

27 13 June 1906, p. 6.

28 MacDonald Collection, #25 and #24, 27 November 1908.

29 Tuckwell Collection, TUC, London 200I, 2 April 1909 and 19 and 23 April 1909. Norbert C. Soldon, *Women in British Trade Unions, 1874–1976*, (Gill and Macmillan, Dublin, 1976), notes that Black, along with Lord Dilke, J. Mallon and Mary Macarthur met with William Beveridge, G. R. Askwith, Clara Collet and Winston Churchill when the latter as President of the Board of Trade was responsible for writing the government bill. See p. 66.

30 B. L. Hutchins, 'The Control of Sweating', *The Economic Review*, 17 (October 1907), p. 408.

31 See articles in *The Labour Leader*, 17 May 1907, p. 822 and 5 July 1907, p. 21. See also *Sweated Industries: A Handbook*, p. 27. For their arguments, see J. Ramsay MacDonald, 'Sweating and Wages Boards', *The Nineteenth Century*, lxiv (November 1908), pp. 748–62 and 'The Case for and Against a Legal Minimum Wage for Sweated Workers', published by the Women's Industrial Council, 1909, 'The Case Against' was written by the MacDonalds, pp. 11–24.

32 MacDonald, 'Sweating and Wages Boards', p. 762.

33 The principle of the state setting a minimum wage using Boards as models was not a new one. New Zealand and New South Wales used compulsory arbitration and Victoria, Australia had Wages Boards to set wages. The MacDonalds and others looked at the results, particularly in Victoria in formulating their ideas for or against minimum wage legislation and Trade Boards in England. For a summary of their workings see, for example, B.L. Hutchins, 'Laws regulating conditions of Home Work in Australia and New Zealand', in *Home Industries of Women in London*, Report of an Inquiry by the Investigation Committee of the Women's Industrial Council, 1908, pp.39–41.

34 National Union of Women Workers Conference on Women Workers, 1907, p.24.

35 Black, 'Legislative Proposals', pp.190–1 and Tuckwell Collection 200I; *The Daily Chronicle*, 2 April and 19 April 1909.

36 *The Sociological Review*, iv (1911), pp.50–1.

37 Reported in *The Fabian News*, xxiv (February 1913), p.18.

38 Reported in *The Educational News*, 3 October 1913 in Tuckwell Collection, 340.

39 17 November 1913. Article found in Tuckwell Collection 218.

40 V. L. Allen, *Trade Unions and the Government* (Longmans, Green, 1960), pp.59–60 and Clegg, *The System of Industrial Relations in Great Britain* pp.356–7.

41 While there is a debate over whether the Parliamentary Labour Party and the Trades Union Congress gave little more than 'lukewarm' support to the bill, it is true that it appeared at first to be 'a measure mainly of value to the women trade unionists'. Still, the measure did not exclude one sex or the other. See B.C. Roberts, *The Trades Union Congress 1868–1921* (George Allen and Unwin, 1958), p.217 and Schmiechen, *Sweated Industries*, p.172.

42 Schmiechen, *Sweated Industries*, pp.174–9.

43 Barbara Taylor, *Eve and the New Jerusalem* (Virago and Pantheon Books, London and New York, 1983), p.282.

Left to right: Jessie Stephen, Mary Macarthur, the N.F.W.W. organizer Mrs. Hewson(?), Julia Varley, at the N.F.W.W. Headquarters c. 1908

9

The Bundle of Sticks: Women, Trade Unionists and Collective Organization before 1918

Deborah Thom

> It came to me that the women in the factory were too tired for the revolt urged upon them, too deeply inured to acceptance. I had no doubt as to the utter desirableness of an increase in our wages; I believed that this we could achieve by the organisation advocated by the speech-makers who came to us – if only we could have effected the necessary organisation, unity, and flank attacks.
>
> Forlorn Hope. For the women in the factory continued stonily to eye the preachers of revolt, the liberators who descended on us from unknown worlds of competence and comfort, too palpably unblemished by the experience that was ours. Yet I do not think their insufficiency proved so great an obstacle as the subscription fees to the Trade Union from women to whom even two pennies a week represented a loaf of bread that, for a time at least, would quiet a family of hungry children.
>
> (Kathleen Woodward, *Jipping Street*, Virago, 1983, pp. 120–1)

Kathleen Woodward's account of women workers in Bermondsey reflects the basic facts of women's lives at work in early twentieth-century England. Trade union organizers who tried to improve those lives were often too distant from such women, who were too poor to pay their dues and too bowed down with family cares. The question should thus be, not why did so few organize but why did so many, against such considerable odds? Working women's organizations of the late nineteenth century were shaped more by the interests of social reformers than by the demands of working women themselves. Trade unions would, it was hoped, prevent both exploitation and degradation and thus improve the condition of the nation as a whole. The process of organisation did not follow in any simple way from this founding impulse. The national leaders of women in trade unions were either middle-class women or men – but that did not mean that when women first planned to join a union or keep one going they were passive recipients of the ideas and principles of others.[1]

It has often been argued that the first 'take-off' for women's organization in trade unions was the result of an unusually strong organizing impulse led by one outstanding woman – Mary Macarthur.[2] In the years between the foundation of the National Federation of Women Workers (NFWW) in 1906, and the end of the First World War in 1918, women's organization did increase both absolutely and relatively.[3] However, this increase arose from a muliplicity of factors against which the individual contribution of leaders needs to be measured.

I am going to look at the organizing practices, and principles, of two trade union leaders in order to assess the contribution made by individuals to this union growth. In doing so I shall argue that in some respects their ideology of organizing women put a brake on the women who applied to join unions, ran strikes and entered the labour market, as well as being a shaping force for women's trade unionism. The two individuals are Mary Macarthur and Julia Varley. Macarthur is well known. She was the heroine of books by Mary Agnes Hamilton, Kathleen Woodward and Barbara Drake written in the 1920s. She was middle-class by origin and only ever worked as union organizer for the Women's Trade Union League (WTUL) and the NFWW. Varley, on the other hand, was active as a suffragette, mill worker and Poor Law Guardian – as well as a trade union organizer for the Birmingham Trades Council, the NFWW and the Workers' Union.

We have to allow for heroism and the force of character but we must also examine the specific details of the growth in women's trade unionism during this period. The balance between the interests of a union's members and that of trade unionism as a whole was not a dilemma peculiar to women but it was often discussed as though it were.

In looking at the nature and theories of women's collective organization the historians of women's trade unionism have adopted two stances. The most recent of the feminist accounts of unionism, that by Heidi Hartman, has argued that women were both oppressed and excluded from the benefits of trade unionism by male workers, particularly male workers organized in trade unions. The First World War has been seen as the period when this was most true, since women were welcomed into war-work when needed and then later excluded when the government honoured its commitment to male craft unions to 'restore pre-war practices'. This view is valid in the case of a few small specialist trade unions in war time, particularly the Society of Women Welders, but it is not a true description of the fate of the majority of women in general unions, whether those unions were women only, such as the National Federation of Women Workers, or mixed, such as the Workers' Union.

Gail Braybon has shown how the wartime admission of women to men's jobs was constricted, or constructed, by the needs and attitudes of male workers. I want to argue that a part of that construction was made by women, as trade union organizers, and that its roots are to be found in the late nineteenth-century experience of women workers. Nor does the alternative conventional explanation for the changes in women's unionism quite work. In this socialist or labourist explanation, as in the books by Sheila Lewenhak and Sarah Boston, women represent a part of the 'forward march of labour'. They are organized late and in specific forms because of the force with which the tradition of the past weighed on the attitudes of the present. These historians attribute success to success in leadership.[4] I look at the careers of two outstanding leaders to show the processes and ideology of the organization of women. Growth was as much to do with social change as heroic individual action. The argument is that the organization of women was highly structured by ideological notions of the weakness of women at work and in society at large and that in looking at such a formation notions of patriarchy are inadequate and ignore the activities and ideas of women themselves. Women of whatever class did differ in their strategy and tactics of organization and this difference mattered and cannot be explained in class terms.

In 1918 the historian of the Ministry of Munitions described women workers as they were seen in 1914 when their use in wartime factories was being discussed in government circles.

> Women were badly organised, prone to manipulation by employers ignorant of workshop practices, in particular defensive, restrictive practices, and content to work in lowly positions for low pay. Women did not enjoy the protection of custom, they were not organised in strong Trade Unions, nor could such organisations be built up in an emergency.[5]

This viewpoint could have been stated at any time in the preceding 30 years – indeed was still being stated in variant forms until the Second World War. It strikingly reveals the vicious circle that women unionists tried to break. The history of women workers was used to argue a case based on notions of what was natural, and inherent in all women. Notions of trade union organization reflected this bifurcated vision. Discussion about trade union organization among women reflects, in the same way as did all general discussions about women at that time, the belief that women are more strongly affected than men by their gender – and that this is a problem.

The sources for the history of women's trade union organization add to the historian's problem. Biographies and autobiographies emphasize the individual contributions. Mary Macarthur was very much loved and her biography by Mary Agnes Hamilton reflects this love; as does the shorter account by Margaret Cole. Both accounts obscure the sharper, astringent even autocratic woman portrayed by the oral evidence of Dorothy Elliott and Grace Robson.[6] Margaret Bondfield's biography reflects a long career in public service, in which trade unionism was an unproblematic part. On the other hand official or government sources have the immediacy of being recorded during or near the events they describe so they are less able to use hindsight to construct a palatable narrative. If they record trade union views at all they tend to be those of the leaders. They emphasize trade unions as a problem. We know far more about women's life in factories in war time than we do in peacetime because they were so closely scrutinized by government agents. In the 1900s women were widely discussed because of concern for 'the race', feminist agitation and welfare politics, and a great deal is known about their public activities. The fact that the government was not then concerned does not mean that women were not as active in the privacy of their workplaces as the war-workers of 1917.

The records of women's organizations themselves provide a valuable counter to official records and memoirs. Unfortunately the most important organization – the NFWW – lost its records on amalgamation into the General and Municipal Workers' Union (GMWU) in 1922.[6] The Trades Union Congress houses such records of the Women's Trade Union League (WTUL), together with the large collection of press-cuttings, leaflets, handbills and pamphlets that are known as the Tuckwell Collection which Gertrude Tuckwell, secretary of the League, built up in the course of her life's work for women's trade unionism. This source has been used for a large number of secondary works on women's trade unionism, but it should be used with caution. It represents the interests of one woman, or one organization, and therefore includes a large amount about the NFWW (which the WTUL set up) and a great deal about activities in London and nearby. Its coverage of the biggest single group of women workers, and women trade unionists – workers in wool and cotton – is limited and unrepresentative.

The writings of the Fabian Women's Group, particularly those of Barbara Drake, tend to suffer from the same geographical and political limitations. Drake's book, *Women in Trade Unions*, first published in 1924, remains the best account of women's unionism. It is thorough, detailed, lucid and makes its viewpoint explicit. It is, however, very much a work of its time. It is partly based on Drake's war time work on *Women in the Engineering Trades* and the historical memorandum for the War Cabinet Committee on Women in Industry which reported in 1919.[7] Women had been engaged to do war-work. They had demonstrated what feminists had always argued, namely that most women could do what most men could do. War-work was, however, seen primarily as temporary war-service based on patriotic impulse rather than any more enduring intention to compete on equal terms with men. She therefore emphasizes the overwhelming force of history and the state as the main agency of change in the face of history. It was, after all, the state, she argued, that had convinced employers of women's capacity by using travelling shows depicting women at work, displaying excellent photographs (now in the Imperial War Museum), pamphlets and all the evidence gathered by dilution officers. The other main component in Drake's analysis was the assumption common to many in the Fabian tradition of familial feminism; women were inhibited by biology and the social order from certain activities – potential or actual motherhood was their main function. As Drake said in her evidence to the Atkins committee, as a representative of the Fabian Women's Group, 'The residue of women would provide a margin of labour for periods of good trade. If either sex is to be short of employment it had better be the women'.[8]

There was an alternative to the tradition which placed a woman firmly in the family as her primary sphere of operations. In such an analysis, women were united by their sex and oppressed by men who excluded them from political power by withholding the vote. Both suffragettes and suffragists organized independently from men, although both included men as supporters. Feminist historians have recently begun to rediscover the vitality and variety of suffrage organization at the local level. The same vigour and difference is noticeable in looking at trade unionism in any women's trade. The two were not integrally related. Women were divided by class, region and occupation more than they were united by gender except in a very few areas of suffrage movements. Julia Varley's early life campaigning for women's suffrage with her sister in Bradford was distinctly separate from her life as a union organizer in the Black Country. In an individual career the one might well lead to the other, but far fewer women went from suffrage to trade unionism than the other way around. The lessons of such an experience, whether direct and personal or not, were learned and expressed. Julia Varley's feminism was explicitly directed at working-class women, working women: 'We work shoulder to shoulder with the men in the mills and in the councils of the workers; why should they deny us the right to help to choose the men who make the laws that govern the workers . . . Our motto is "Rise up, Women" and the battle-cry, "Now"!'[9] The first half of this statement is characteristic, while the second is conventional, echoing the Pankhursts, since Varley worked closely with Sylvia Pankhurst at this time.[10] She argued that working-class women particularly *needed* the rights of a citizen from which they were excluded by their lack of the vote, because they were especially in need of legal protection. Mary Macarthur, who supported the Adult Suffrage Association (as did Margaret Bondfield), thereby expressed her view that the vote was a class matter, since the demand for the vote for all adults was to demand it for excluded men as well as women.[11]

The other strand in the theory and motive force of trade union organization among women was the Anti-Sweating Campaign. Macarthur was particularly closely associated with the London campaign and was given freqent access to the Liberal *Daily News* at periods when she was not editing the *Women Worker* for the Federation. In 1906 the *Daily News* had organized an exhibition of Sweated Industries in which women had worked at their sweated trades to educate the public in what it meant to sew shirts, make nails or paper-boxes and so on. It also produced some vividly expressive photographs which were reproduced in the handbook to the exhibition which sold widely. The Anti-Sweating League which resulted was a powerful force for change; Macarthur sat on its executive after 1906.[12] Julia Varley's return to trade unionism came through association with an anti-sweating organization. She was invited to Birmingham by Edward Cadbury in 1909 after she had successfully organized the chain-makers of Cradley Heath into the NFWW in 1907. She was employed by the Birmingham Committee

for the Organization of Women as secretary, sat on the Trades
Council and was a member of its Executive Committee. She
successfully organized card-box makers, bakery workers and chain-
makers, as a member and organizer for the NFWW. Cadbury wrote
the book on sweating that exposed the working and living conditions
of sweated workers and argued that the concept involved no moral
description of the workers themselves but was a material condition
caused by income inadequate for basic expenditure.[13]

Cadbury's argument about the need for organization among
women to compensate for the disadvantages of being a woman
worker in Edwardian Britain smuggled back the notion of the
inherent incapacity of women to defend themselves properly for
social reasons: 'The competition between the inefficient, unmarried
girls, the wife whose husband is out of work or drunken or dissolute,
and whose children must have food, and the widow who also has
many mouths to feed, plays into the hands of the unscrupulous
employer'.[14] Varley was the most explicit exponent of a theory of
organization based on the defencelessness implicit in the description
sweated, when she described democracy in the inspirational words of
her Chartist great grandfather, 'When you grow up you'll know what
the word means and then you will work for the people, think for the
people and live for the people – for they don't know how to do it for
themselves'.[15]

Varley and Macarthur were both pragmatists. Macarthur's
biographer pointed out that she was not an intellectual and did not
claim to be one. Like Varley she had a facile pen and a powerful
speaking presence. Mary Macarthur's use of the homely metaphor of
the bundle of sticks illustrates the style which she adopted in *The
Woman Worker* and in her leaflets. Macarthur's picture is explicitly
defensive. One stick can be broken, a bundle cannot, 'A Trade
Union is like a bundle of sticks. The workers are bound together and
have the strength of unity. No employer can do as he likes with
them. They have the power of resistance. They can ask for an
advance without fear'.[16] Later she wrote of girls who do not join.
'They are not only selfish they are short-sighted'. It is a personal,
direct approach arguing that women have a duty to society to
organize in unions. She described her power over meetings to Arthur
Salter when she gave an account of an angry speech she made to the
girls of a North London factory after their employer had refused
their wages rise. 'I suddenly realised', she told me, 'that if I didn't at
once stop them they would tear him limb from limb'.[17]

Julia Varley did not have that power, or, it would seem, reading the accounts, the charm of Macarthur, but she had force and wit as well as a quick tongue. She often told an anecdote about marriage in which she explained that she had not seen many advertisements for the married state in the course of her career and instanced the woman in the casual ward when she was 'on the tramp' who told her how to deal with a husband, 'Always go for his nose with something sharp, my dear'.[18] Neither woman wrote any systematic statement of beliefs and principles but both expressed a consistent set of attitudes which can be used to understand the different trajectories they took.

Julia Varley moved trade unions after 1912. She left the NFWW and her work for the Birmingham Committee and became women's organizer in Birmingham for the Workers' Union, the Union's first women's organizer. She described her decision in the union's journal, 'Believing that where women work with men they should be organised in the same Union, she finds the Workers' Union more fully in accord with those ideas, and when her work under the voluntary committee came to a close she had little difficulty in accepting the position our Union had to offer'.[19] In some respects there was no major change in Varley's activities. She had been organizing men and women together as a member of the Trades Council Executive and as a supporter of the anti-sweating movement. The NFWW had been founded because women had got in touch with the WTUL in order to join a union but had found that either the union in their trade did not admit women or that there was in fact no union in that trade. It had not been founded on any feminist principle. When Macarthur negotiated the transfer of the Federation into the General and Municipal Workers' Union (GMWU) (a mixed general union) she said that she had always intended such a merger.[20] She did argue, however, together with her organizers that it was both more successful, and *right*, to organize women as women in women's branches using women organizers. There had already been the occasional conflict of interest between the two unions since they were attempting to organize in the same occupational and geographical areas at a time of labour unrest. There is no record of any quarrel but the Workers' Union account of the transfer strongly implies that there was one, as does the hint of bitterness in relations between Varley and the Federation thereafter. It is certain that the Workers' Union did begin to have a sizeable women's membership and that much of the growth in membership among women was in Varley's area.[21]

The Federation did suffer from a lack of internal democracy as Dorothy Elliott agreed when looking back in 1975. In 1913 a Miss

Hedges attempted to challenge the leadership on these grounds but failed. (By 1918 the membership carried a motion giving greater powers to shop stewards on the same grounds.) But in this case Varley remained sufficiently friendly with the Federation to take Miss Hedges's place at the TUC in 1913.[22]

There was no simple division between the two organizers or their organizations based on a different conception of men and women. They shared the same view. The difference lay in their understanding of the processes of organization. It did not even appear significant until 1913, but a year later, at the onset of war, the differences in organizational theory were to prove crucial to war-workers. Since the experience of Macarthur and Varley and the other trade union organizers of the war years had been gained from the principles and practice of the ten years preceding the war, it was this, added to the theory of nineteenth-century unionism, that was then most influential, rather than the war experience.

In July 1914, a month before war was declared, Mary Macarthur wrote (in a series of articles titled 'Women's Discontent'), 'I am most concerned with the industrial unrest among women, and I don't think it is any sense a sex unrest; it is merely that the general industrial unrest is now being shared by women'.[23] The industrial unrest of the years 1907–14 has been described by historians as the 'great unrest'. In parts of the country it was in fact unrest among women, for example in London and the Black Country.[24] Women did join unions in greater numbers than before, they went on strike more frequently, they were more often to be seen on the public platforms of the labour movement. But it is not true to say that this was women catching up with men. There were specifically female characteristics to the unrest. Women were more likely to take strike action, they used suffrage tactics of propaganda and demonstration and produced many leaflets, songs, postcards, ribbons and badges to publicize their struggles. Women were much more likely to attempt a public display of their conditions of work and their grievances, possibly because of the legitimation given to their demands by both feminism and the advocates of improvements for the nation's mothers. Contemporaries saw and wrote of a sex war, some women felt that that was what they were urging. Macarthur did not, but she was mistaken in denying its existence.

The 'sex war' in industry resulted in, as well as accompanying, a general expansion in union membership. Women's trade union membership expanded greatly in the years before the war. The problem of describing this growth is demonstrated by the table of

TABLE 9.1   TRADE UNION MEMBERSHIP

Year	Men Actual membership (000s)	Men Potential membership (000s)	Men Density of membership (%)	Women Actual membership (000s)	Women Potential membership (000s)	Women Density of membership (%)	Total Actual membership (000s)	Total Potential membership (000s)	Total Density of membership (%)
1900	1869	11,194	16.7	154	4,763	3.2	2022	15,957	12.7
1901	1873	11,325	16.5	152	4,775	3.2	2025	16,101	12.6
1902	1857	11,433	16.2	156	4,833	3.2	2013	16,267	12.4
1903	1838	11,541	15.9	156	4,890	3.2	1994	16,433	12.1
1904	1802	11,649	15.5	165	4,948	3.3	1967	16,599	11.9
1905	1818	11,757	15.5	180	5,005	3.6	1997	16,765	11.9
1906	1999	11,865	16.8	211	5,063	4.2	2210	16,932	13.1
1907	2263	11,973	18.9	250	5,120	4.9	2513	17,098	14.7
1908	2230	12,080	18.5	255	5,178	4.9	2485	17,264	14.4
1909	2214	12,188	18.2	263	5,235	5.0	2477	17,430	14.2
1910	2287	12,296	18.6	278	5,292	5.3	2565	17,596	14.6
1911	2804	12,404	22.6	335	5,350	6.3	3139	17,762	17.7
1912	3027	12,453	24.3	390	5,380	7.2	3416	17,841	19.1
1913	3702	12,502	29.6	433	5,410	8.0	4135	17,920	23.1

Year									
1914	3708	12,551	29.5	437	5,440	8.0	4145	17,998	23.0
1915	3867	12,600	30.7	491	5,470	9.0	4359	18,077	24.1
1916	4018	12,649	31.8	626	5,500	11.4	4644	18,155	25.6
1917	4621	12,698	36.4	878	5,530	15.9	5499	18,234	30.2
1918	5324	12,747	41.8	1209	5,560	21.7	6533	18,312	35.7
1919	6601	12,796	51.6	1326	5,591	23.7	7926	18,391	43.1
1920	7006	12,845	54.5	1342	5,621	23.9	8348	18,469	45.2
1921	5627	12,894	43.6	1005	5,651	17.8	6633	18,548	35.8
1922	4753	12,334	38.5	872	5,470	15.9	5625	17,804	31.6
1923	4607	12,436	37.0	822	5,528	14.9	5429	17,965	30.2
1924	4730	12,539	37.7	814	5,587	14.7	5544	18,125	30.6
1925	4671	12,641	37.0	835	5,645	14.8	5506	18,286	30.1
1926	4407	12,743	34.6	812	5,703	14.2	5219	18,446	28.3
1927	4125	12,847	32.1	794	5,762	13.8	4919	18,609	26.4
1928	4011	12,950	31.0	795	5,821	13.7	4806	18,771	25.6
1929	4056	13,054	31.1	802	5,880	13.6	4858	18,934	25.7
1930	4049	13,158	30.8	793	5,938	13.4	4842	19,096	25.4
1931	3859	13,261	29.1	765	5,997	12.8	4624	19,259	24.0
1932	3698	13,302	27.8	746	6,038	12.4	4444	19,340	23.0

Source: Based on A. H. Halsey (ed.), *Trends in British Society since 1900* (Macmillan, 1972), p. 123. [The figures include the whole of Ireland.]

'Trade Union membership' (see table 9.1). Women were under-recorded in two ways. The first is that women's employment was generally under-recorded in employment statistics. Their work did not count as 'occupied'; they did not choose to let officials know (as Ellen Smith noted in her survey for the Fabian Women's Group of 1915); their employers did not wish officials to know (in the case of women returning early after having children for example); it was seasonal – tennis-ball making, for example.[25] Their union affiliations, for some of the same reasons, may have been limited by time and place. While of perhaps even greater importance, women's work fell into some categories in which union organization, despite all attempts, was almost impossible, pre-eminently domestic service, in which one-third of all occupied women were employed. If one excludes from the potential membership all domestic servants, the figures for union density might be a more accurate representation of the expectations of union organizers. There were also of course reasons for general labour unrest which, added to women's campaigns, gave powerful impetus to unionization.

The context for a general growth in trade unionism was an economy in which real wages fell; high unemployment in some trades; increased production in consumer trades. There was also widespread discussion of the rights and duties of the individual and of the state as both Labour and Liberals demanded old age pensions, unemployment insurance and provision for infants and children in the interests of the state. Working women, particularly mothers, found or placed themselves in the middle of the political discussions of a highly political period.[26]

One of the specific causes of the growth in women's unionism was the development of the Trade Boards system. The Trade Boards had been set up to prevent sweating as both a moral and an economic evil. The main effect of the imposition of a Trade Board was the development of a list of minimum wages organized by task but also by the age and sex of the worker. The trades of the first Boards were mainly women's trades but they also included occupations which were effectively organized on the family lines of early capitalist enterprise. They were nearly all to be found in major conurbations as many of these trades had developed around the finishing processes so that the small employers who predominated could be near their outlets in both retail and wholesale trade. The shirt-making processes were in London while the chain makers who supplied the engineering trade were to be found in the Midlands. These trades also depended on the existence of surplus labour. Margins of profit were slight and trade fluctuated. As a result they tended not to be found in areas of steady, respectable, artisan employment for men where a part of male respectability was based on a non-working wife. An example of the contrast in local trade union organization is that between Plumstead and Charlton in South-East London. In the latter the work for men was seasonal casual labour, housing was poor and overcrowded and large numbers of women were engaged in a variety of 'sweated' occupations – making tennis-balls for Slazenger, working in the Wood Street shirt factory or gut-scraping in Deptford, or doing other smelly, unpleasant, arduous work on 'food processing' elsewhere in South or East London. In Plumstead, with owner-occupation and artisan work amongst the highest in London, few women worked, very few at sweated occupations.[27] Any trade union organization had to recognize the specificity of the female labour market and the domestic surroundings of work described as sweated if it were to succeed in the difficult task of organizing in any new trade. In women's trades there was the added problem of the social aspiration of any women's movement at a time of such intense activity.

In 1909 the first Boards were set up for Tailoring (Ready-Made and Bespoke), Paper-Box Making, Lace Making, and Chain Making. In 1913 those for Embroidery, Hollow-ware, Shirt and Tin-Box Making, Sugar Confectionery and Food Processing were added. The definition which made a trade liable to the imposition of a Board was that the wages were 'exceptionally low compared with those in other employments'.[28] The effect does appear to have been to raise women's wages from an extremely low average to a low one.[29] Were the Trade Boards, as Gertrude Tuckwell argued, the basis for the growth in women's trade unionism, or were they a product of it? They were of course both, but it was as a component in the ideology of organization that I wish to argue that they were important, representing as they did the culmination of a set of demands current in women's unionism since the 1890s, when Sir Charles and Lady Dilke first attempted to improve both the wages and conditions of work to stop the rearing of 'our industrial structure above an abyss of inefficiency and misery'.[30]

The campaign for the Trade Boards increased the emphasis in women's unionism on the need to make demands on the state. Although women did tend to a syndicalist style in agitation and organization they did not follow a syndicalist politics, i.e. organize to achieve socialism at the point of production rather than through political parties. The absence of women from the literature of British syndicalism is not the omission of partriarchal attitudes, it is the representation of their absence in fact. There was a real disjunction between the needs and demands of women from the working class at that time and those of syndicalist men. Syndicalism was most successful in heavy industry, single occupation areas which were also areas of heavy domestic work for women and little paid work outside the home. Organization at the point of production excluded women who did not work at the face in the mines or in the docks where syndicalism was strongest. Women's agitation was directed at a state which they felt could provide the reforms they desired – infant welfare centres, family allowances, the reform of the poor law. Women in paid employment tended to want more intervention, not less, in the form of factory inspection, wages legislation and limited hours of work. There was a similar lack of contact with the systematic rejection of legality by some suffragette groups. Trade unionists shared the demand for representation but did not thereby reject the state as an agent of change. They were reformists, however much Macarthur chose to shock polite society by describing herself as a 'Tolstoyan'. As Julia Varley said at the end of her long life, 'God has enabled me to live to see the fruits of my labours – a joy denied to most reformists'.[31] The Trade Board route to improvement in the condition of women in industry was emphatically not one that challenged the social and political order; it was one which asked for women's participation in it.

A second effect was to emphasize the mediating role of trade union officials. Trade Boards had an equal number of representatives of employers and employees. Worker representatives often sat on several Trade Boards as representatives of the workers in the trade in the same general union. There had to be a woman representative on a Board for a trade in which the majority of the workers were women so the small number of women officials sat on several Boards at once. Mary Macarthur, Susan Lawrence, Margaret Bondfield and Gertrude Tuckwell all sat on Boards. They met in London fairly frequently and this excluded many other activists. Their role was to negotiate wages *minima* in the light of the state of the trade and general conditions of wages. The *minima* thereby established quickly became *maxima*. The women who sat on the Trade Boards, and in wartime on the arbitration tribunals and other negotiating bodies set up for war-work for women, were those who had education and negotiating experience. They were the women who were least likely to have direct personal experience of work in the trades they represented. The class difference between men and women trade union officials was noticeable in the case of Macarthur, Lawrence and Tuckwell – it did not exist in the case of Varley or Bondfield. It remained true that the most public representatives of working women were not and had not been working women themselves and that representation on the Boards accentuated this phenomenon.

The final contribution of the Trade Boards to the nineteenth-century image of working women was the persistent belief that low wages were a permanent feature of women's work. The wage-scales established in protected trades were much higher than their previously shameful levels since that was the justification for the existence of a Board in the first place. But they remained relatively low within the trade and in general when compared with men's wages. They remained at about one-half the male average – and the Board perpetuated this relationship. Beatrice Webb tartly remarked in her minority report on Women in Industry (1919) that there was nothing logical or rational about this ratio but that the only way to abandon it would be to pay for the job done rather than to pay the worker who did it. As contemporary commentators pointed out women's low wages were based on the assumption that the wage was secondary to a main breadwinner's contribution. They argued against this assumption that it was the least well paid women who were most likely to have no other support, because they were able only to take work that could fit in with family commitments. The solution advocated by Clementina Black in *Married Women's Work*, Mrs B. L. Hutchins in *Women in Modern Industry* and Edward Cadbury in *Women's Work and Wages* was double-pronged.[32] First it was for union organization among working women to prevent employers paying low wages; secondly it was for state support for motherhood and wages to remove the weakest competitors from the industrial struggle. There was no challenge to this notion of motherhood as primary even if these authors did argue that the 'good mother' could be the one who worked out of the home.

The implications of this set of attitudes for trade union organization were direct. Women tended to be perceived by their familial role before any other description of them was made. Oral evidence shows how much family relationships did in fact influence union affiliation.[33] However, with so few women belonging to unions for any length of time, family tradition tended to go from fathers to daughters rather than mothers. Union members are often described as girls as though they were young and speeches of trade union organizers to their members tend to be as from older women. Julia Varley was quoted (a long time after she made the speech), as convincing factory workers thus:

I can't understand you women. You used to walk around the fields of Bournville with the lads and they'd whisper sweet nothings in your ears and tell you if you'd only marry them they would make heaven for you. And what sort of heaven have you got? A seventeen-and-tenpenny one – eighteen bob a week and twopence off for the hospital.[34]

There were many other examples of such speeches, but rarely did they get made to male workers. Women were seen as particularly concerned with and related to their households and their industrial demands were perceived in that context; industrial organization was often argued in general almost sociological terms as if women should take on the wider social burdens as well as their own immediate material needs. Trade union organization was also their way of meeting male objections to their being in the workforce at all. Lady Dilke argued this in a pamphlet for the WTUL in 1891 in a neat summation of the argument, 'once women are brought within the rates of the callings that they seek to pursue, the just objection to and fear of their labour felt by men will disappear, and not only so but the whole social position of women themselves will be advanced'.[35] Women were also expected to improve the moral tone of industry. This could lead to exclusionary policies being argued in the name of the greater good of society. A delegate from the Postmen's union argued for the 'wholesale prohibition of married women's labour' at the 1909 Labour Party conference on the grounds that 'the woman is the greatest humanising factor we possess'.[36] In arguing that women's work contributed to civilization, trade union organizers had to be careful not to allow their role as improvers of society to conflict with their role as representatives of existing women workers.

More immediately practical problems added to the ideological loading of the concept of womanhood. Women were particularly difficult to organize, suffering from such major deficiencies as workers as to be secondary in organizational terms as well as in employment. To argue, as did the union organizers, that there was more urgency in dealing with the weakest was not to undercut the argument – merely to restate it. Women did have a dual burden of domestic work in the home and paid work outside it. Evening meetings were difficult to organize and often unsuccessful – any account of a working woman's day shows how the evening was often used for sewing, baking, pressing and cleaning – with little time for rest or reading, let alone two hours sitting listening to speakers. The best procedure was to organize on the job or at the factory gates, but although this was also true of men (except in the craft unions), it was generally attributed to women's lack of motivation rather than to lack of time.

Many women participated in the 'great unrest' of 1910 and 1911. At its peak in London, in the summer of 1911 Mary Macarthur organized some two thousand women in the course of 20 concurrent strikes. The process was generally that the women struck and the union then intervened to negotiate for them and so won negotiation rights. Macarthur argued that this was a demonstration of the power of unions to control their members, a clear instance of unions as mediators rather than agents of struggle:

> A strike of unorganised workers should always be utilised to form a trade union amongst them. In such cases one is frequently able to point out that had an organization existed, the strike in all probability would not have occurred, because the employer would not so confidently have ventured to assail the rights of Trade Union workers. It is quite a mistaken idea that strikes are caused by Trade Unions.[37]

Macarthur did, however, accept the reverse although her officers denied it, not liking to associate with striking even as an agent of organization. Mrs Hewson wrote, 'She did not believe in strikes which were very bad things, but when she talked to some of the girls the only thing they knew of trade unionism was strikes.'[38] Gertrude Tuckwell also argued that trade unions prevented strikes. She approved the result in a Christian Socialist pamphlet on the organization of women 'Again and again strikes have been averted by the power of bargaining that combination gives'.[39] Organization was advocated to remove women's weakness and dependence but some argued that women needed to take on their own affairs on a permanent basis if that power was to be maintained.

Margaret Bondfield saw this lack of persistence, or of experience, as the central difficulty among these new women members, 'The problem was a lack of continuity of membership and it is a notable fact that a large part of the membership [of the NFWW] was built up as its organisers came to the help of unorganized groups of strikers'.[40] Barbara Drake wrote of this period ten years later as if it was characteristic of women as a sex to depend on outsiders, or figures of authority to do their bargaining for them. She did argue that the experience of striking should be seen as educational, so that the use of the strike weapon should not be regarded as evidence of inherent instability among women workers.

> Women learn very slowly the fact that their union is inside and does not consist of an organizer outside. They undertake no

> duties of shopstewards and seldom interview the firm or
> manager but call in the organizer in every difficulty. To get
> women to take up these duties with any enthusiasm they must
> go through a strike and lose their fear.[41]

She was here quoting an unnamed organizer who was probably
reporting on war-workers who were mostly new to the type of
workplace and associated organization in which they found
themselves. As was often the case, what was as much to do with
inexperience was attributed to gender. It is almost impossible to
detach the expectations of the organizers from the practices of the
organization they undertook. What we can do is see how far what
people thought they were doing determined what they did do.

Paradoxically the greatest successes of the women's trade unions –
the campaigns against sweating – were later to confine them most. In
particular, the organization of the chain makers added such weight
to a general picture of the waged work that women did that in
wartime, when their labour was in demand, they were organized as if
it was still subject to the same constraints as the sweated labour of
peacetime. The chain maker's strike is a distillation of women's
trade unionism at the period. It displays its magnificence and its
deformation by the way it posited women's need for protection as the
dominant force in the agitation. Women chain makers at Cradley
Heath struck work in 1911 over the employers' attempt to evade the
provision of the Trade Board. The strike was organized by Julia
Varley with Charles Sitch. She appealed to them as women, and
helped to orchestrate the public campaign that emphasized
womanhood in chains.

> We went in and out of the forges, talking to the women as they
> hammered away, awakening their consciousness to their
> responsibilities; appealing to their pride and their
> motherhood[42]

and

> At the end of the agitation I had about twenty women between
> the ages of 60 and 90 parading the streets with necklaces of the
> chains they had made, and the words, 'Britain's disgrace, 1d an
> hour'![43]

Women in chains appeared at demonstrations, on public platforms,
in dramatic woodcuts on song-sheets and in some very effective,
though less emotional, photographs which are still at the TUC. It
was a powerful visual image of the servitude of the industrial woman

– a servitude from which she was released by the benign intervention of the state mediated by trade unions. Women were exhorted to organize, to act for the general good, for their own good only in their role as mothers.

The ideology of woman as the sweated worker, defenceless, in need of protection was reinforced by the organizational practices of women's unions. They tended to rely more on organizers – paid or voluntary helpers from outside – than on elected officials. This was a circular argument often used against the organization of women. It was seen as making them more expensive to organize but less 'worthwhile' because they contributed less from their low wages in union dues. Will Thorne told Mrs Hutchins that he did not think women should be organized because he said 'they do not make good trade unionists'.[44] Despite the slightly contradictory association of women and insurrectionary behaviour in strikes, women were thought to be less capable of self-activity. Women did stay less time in jobs than men in some trades; they did remain in unions for a shorter period. Contemporaries described women as 'meantime workers', in work until marriage and therefore interested only in the short-term benefits of work. The unions themselves often encouraged this view. The NFWW, for example, paid a marriage benefit to members on leaving their employment; its organizers regularly left their jobs on marriage. But not all did and Mary Macarthur made little change in her domestic life when she married since she continued to live above the office of the WTUL and NFWW. Marriage and the career of a union organizer were rarely combined and the personal cost was enormous – but such a counter example was impressive and was seen as such.

Low wages tended to lead to a similar difference in organization among women unionists. Dues collection was important to all unions but it was the single most regular contact most members had with the union at all. Oral evidence indicates that women, far more than men, continued to contribute their wages to a family pool, leaving less money under personal control. Many women also had regular commitments to clothing and shoe clubs whereby a group of friends or workmates could pool slender resources for large purchases. Many branches reported difficulty with dues collection in the *Woman Worker*, the paper that Macarthur founded and edited for the Federation from 1907 to 1908 and revived in 1916. The solution was to develop organization by using someone on the job, the shop steward. Women's unions were using shop stewards in the decade before the war without the anti-leadership implications of the office often described in the case of the skilled men's unions.[45] There were implications involving the power and experience women could develop by performing this role. Oral evidence indicates that shop stewards were often the older, married women who had the authority to collect money and the experience to speak formally with management. The few local disputes recorded in the press that took place in organized shops (i.e. not to obtain recognition) were over shop stewards. There were distinct maternalistic overtones to workshop organization among women. Margaret Bondfield exhorted a meeting of the Women's Co-operative Guild, 'Every mother should get her girl a union card'.[47]

The principle of organization was one of protection, of help for the weak rather than of self-activity, but because many of the leaders and their philanthropic supporters felt this way about their organizations did not mean that their members saw themselves in the same way. There was certainly disagreement within organizations about both tactics and organization as well as pay. One union for example split over the question of organization – the National Union of Boot and Shoe Operatives. The woman who remained in the NUBSO, Mary Bell, continued to believe in women officials for women members but also believed in industrial unionism. She addressed a meeting thus,

> Men might think they could organize women but they could not do it as well as women. (Laughter) Girls would be more frank about conditions in the factory than they would be with men. Women and men ought to be summoned to joint branch meetings so that the women could be educated in unionism.[48]

Women were excluded from some unions as they had always been. In 1914 one union excluded them for the first time. When the National Union of Railwaymen was formed from several unions it included the Amalgamated Society of Railway Servants (which had organized women); it then excluded these members on the grounds that 'although a woman might be a railway "servant" . . . she was not a railwayman and therefore ruled out by the title of the new body'.[49] Reorganization could as easily mean the removal of women from a union in this way as it could the extension of their organization. It was against this sort of disregard, or Will Thorne's view that women were not good trade unionists, that the women's trade union leaders set their face. The aim to demonstrate that women were as good trade unionists as any man increasingly tended to dominate the direction of the NFWW and the WTUL. Hence their policies were tailored to the dominant voice in trade unionism, the craft unions, particularly the Amalgamated Society of Engineers and the Boilermakers. Those who saw the future for women as lying with general unions took a different line on pay and on organization.

The division was clearest in the war but it was already evident before then. Julia Varley's activities in the Black Country had led to a surge of activity in the engineering shops of the Black Country and a great growth of union membership in 1912 and 1913. The Workers' Union negotiated a general wages agreement with the employers' federation which raised the basic rate for all workers but, relative to previous wages, it was almost doubled for women. It was not, however, the rate for certain jobs that the ASE wanted and it was scorned by both the ASE and the NFWW who regarded it as selling the pass to the employer for the sake of negotiating rights. The ASE was particularly angry because recent bitter battles within the union over local autonomy had meant their control over engineering processes had been slackened. In the context of a general growth in union membership for women, the question of which interest within trade unionism they should ally with became crucial. That women would act in unity with others was not questioned. Women were participating in a move towards unionization in all types of occupations and union settings – co-operative workers, women working on poisons in chemist shops, printing workers. The separate women's unions merely articulated the position more clearly and tended to stand in as representative of all women workers. The change in the working woman's perception of herself and her capacity to organize in defence of her own interests was not fully recognized until the war but in fact that change was revealed, and diverted and delayed, by war rather than created by it. Mrs Fawcett still saw women in industry with nineteenth-century spectacles when she wrote in 1918, 'The war revolutionised the industrial position of women. It found them serfs and left them free'.[50]

War did not find women serfs. They were already emancipating themselves by organization and agitation. Nor did it leave them free. In the context of trade unionism the war severely restricted the field of operations of women's unions and helped to institutionalize a position for women in trade unions that presumed their inadequacies in the labour market and in self-organization. Women's initial reaction to war ensured that this was built in from the start. War caused unemployment for women as people reduced consumption by sacking servants, cutting back on clothing, hats and shoes and other luxury trades. The textile trades had already been 'half-recumbent' and war cut off both supplies and markets.[51] Women's position as the disposable part of the workforce had never seemed more apparent; their defencelessness never more evident. There was also a moral panic associated with troop embarkation which added force to the speeches of people who argued that unemployed women should be provided for.[52] Mary Macarthur was particularly prominent in the campaign to provide for unemployed women. She was secretary for the Queen's Work for Women Fund which ran workrooms for the unemployed. Sylvia Pankhurst protested to Macarthur about the wages in the workrooms and the fact that they would neither train women nor compete with private manufacture – she argued that they were effectively sweating women to keep them off the streets and out of trouble. The workrooms did attempt to retrain women in domestic skills and they were given second-hand clothes to remake for their children, or orange crates to make into cradles if their hands were 'too rough to hold the needle'.[53] Pankhurst appeared to think in her account of the meeting that Macarthur had been corrupted by mixing with royalty – but there was an easy evasion of the problem in her account.[54] Macarthur did have an industrial motive. She was anxious to prevent women becoming what some male trade unionists had always said they were, desperate competitors in the industrial struggle who had neither the experience nor the organizations behind them to prevent them accepting low wages and thereby reducing everyone's wages and conditions of work.

By 1915 the need for more armaments had changed the labour market utterly. Women had begun to demand the right to participate in the war effort. Mrs Pankhurst used all her skills as a publicist and spent twice the funds Lloyd George had promised her to produce a pageant which started as a Right to Work march and become a Right to Serve march.[55] The women's War Register was set up in which women who wished to do war-work were encouraged to record their desire to serve. Women were thereby reduced to units of labour power and all differences of experience, training or skill submerged in their gender. The fact that women who replaced men as dilutees (doing the work of a skilled man) would get equal pay was not discussed with the representatives of women at all, 'this was not in itself unreasonable as the women at the time had no *locus standi* in the matter'.[56] The agreement made was one for the men in the interests of the men but it was accepted, even policed, by the

NFWW, which came to an agreement with the ASE that, if the ASE would help them organize, they would be the union for women war-workers and would withdraw their members from such work so that the men would have their jobs back. The Workers' Union on the other hand made no such commitment on the grounds that they would not be the same jobs, that the women were as good as the men and deserved to be judged on the work not their gender.

The difference between the two principles of organization showed in the way unions carried out their work. All took on organizers but the NFWW had nearly 200 women, mostly unpaid volunteers, to the Workers' Union's 20 women. For example, the two unions competed hotly in the Woolwich Arsenal for the 27,000 munitions workers there. The NFWW employed Dorothy Elliott to work for the union as a part of her social work diploma at the LSE. She hardly went into the Arsenal, never sat on the shop stewards' committee, and did not hold branch meetings. She was very dependent on her shop stewards and they organized the two big demonstrations involving women in 1917 and 1918. Mary Macarthur, Margaret Bondfield and Susan Lawrence came down to speak but did so at meetings organized jointly with the ASE. The Workers' Union organizer, Florence Pilbrow, relied less on big name speakers and certainly did not ring up her union General Secretary at home as Dorothy Elliott was encouraged to do. She said she was left pretty much to do what she liked.[57] The implications of this organizational inertia are ambigious. The Workers' Union did have meetings, many of which were socially directed and the advertising for members emphasized the social side, 'All the handsome boys and all the beautiful girls are joining the Workers' Union'.[58] On the other hand such activity could be said to reflect a belief that these members were temporary ones, only there for wartime and therefore not to be taken, nor encouraged to take themselves, very seriously. Within the factory it does not appear to have made very much difference to which union, (if any) women belonged. They demonstrated a formidable strength in the face of poor conditions, unequal pay and exacting supervision. Protest often borrowed the language of trade unionism but was as likely to be settled by union officers as by management.

Two other factors accentuated the social work aspects of trade unionism for women. The first was the increase in the amount of welfare provision for munitions workers in particular. 'No word is more hated by the women worker than welfare', said Mary Macarthur, 'They object to being done good to'.[59] Yet many women did not object to welfare provision at all, they found it more salient to their working lives than their trade union. The competition for the workers' allegiance could result in the union becoming more like a welfare organization, concerned with every aspect of its members' lives. The second factor was the growth in arbitration. Wartime bans on striking meant that other means of dealing with disputes had to be found and the experience of the Trade Boards provided a valuable basis for the Special Arbitration Tribunal (for women) which dealt with increasing protests from women who realized that they were not getting equal earnings at all, and certainly not getting the equal rates for the job that the government had promised. Mary Macarthur sat on most of the important committees of the Ministry of Munitions, the Labour Party and the TUC. She was increasingly seen as the voice of all women workers. As G. D. H. Cole commented, her views were not shared by all women workers or all trade unionists but she did represent the dominant trend in British women's trade unionism.[60] Arbitration procedure, union recognition and membership all melted away at the end of the war, however. The NFWW did talk bravely of 'old faces in new places' but they lost members even more dramatically than other general unions as their war-members were forced out of industry altogether. Macarthur said, 'The new world looks uncommonly like the old one rolling along as stupidly and blindly as ever, and all it has got from the war is an extra bitterness or two'.[61]

War was the culmination of a long process by which women's union organization was to compensate both for women's weakness at the workplace and society's inadequacies in dealing with motherhood. Women were seen as especially vulnerable not only because of their inexperience but also because of their short life in the workforce, their lack of commitment to work and their docility. Those who organized women in trade unions did so in order to prevent wider social evils, to provide British society with a model of female co-operation. Class differences between organizers and organized were most crucial in this respect – that they tended to lead to too much direction from on high or too little democracy below. Women never gained the experience they needed to rise through their union organization to the top from an occupational base within their trade. The social aims of unionism dominated over the occupational ones.

The relationship to male unionists varied widely but the two main strategies, independent organization as in the NFWW or general, mixed unions as in the Workers' Union, both recognized the need to overcome male reluctance to allow women any place in trade unionism at all. To win that recognition Mary Mcarthur was prepared to accept the exclusion of her members from their war-work and even to enforce it. Julia Varley was not. The difference in principle was not that great, the difference in leadership style was, but ultimately it made little difference to the large numbers of women who joined trade unions in the period, developed shop stewards' organizations, struck for more pay and campaigned for mothers' pensions and maternity allowances within the trade union movement. They were not the victims of employers or male trade unionists at all; they did not generally accept the description of themselves that their leaders were attempting to undercut. The chain makers, the munitions workers, the Cornish clay workers' wives demonstrated that the help of a Julia Varley was invaluable in presenting their case to the rest of the world but that the case itself was one that they organized and stated. Their leaders were far more inhibited by the history of previous campaigns and by their experience of the difficulties of organization than they were.

The history of women's collective organization has been dominated by the history of its leaders and thence by their ideology of the weakness of working women. More work needs to be done on the way in which that organization worked at a local level for us to make any sense of what it meant to be member of a trade union, and that must mean more use of the recollections of participants. For too long women have been the stage army of history, particularly labour history. We need less of seeing them as others saw them, more of seeing them as they saw themselves.

Bibliographical Note

The best single source for women's trade unionism is Barbara Drake, *Women in Trade Unions*, (published in 1920 by the Labour Research Department and George Allen and Unwin, republished by Virago in 1984). Sarah Boston, *Women Workers and the Trade Union Movement* (Davis Poynter, 1980), is the most lively of its successors; Sheila Lewenhak, *Women and Trade Unions* (Ernest Benn, 1977), tends to follow the TUC line too closely and is of more use the nearer it gets to the present day. The best biographies of leading figures in the movement are to be found in the *Dictionary of Labour Biography*, eds John Saville and Joyce Bellamy (vol. 2, 1974; vol. 5, Macmillan, 1979) (DLB), which contain Bondfield and Macarthur, and Varley respectively. Contemporary biographies of Mary Macarthur are to be found in Mary Agnes Hamilton, *Mary Macarthur, a biographical sketch* (Leonard Parsons, 1925), and Margaret Cole, *Women of Today* (Thomas Nelson, 1922); both are fairly adulatory. Margaret Bondfield wrote an autobiography, *A Life's Work* (Hutchinson, 1951), and Mary Agnes Hamilton also wrote about her in *Margaret Bondfield* (Leonard Parsons, 1924).

Primary sources are mainly to be found at the TUC which holds the Tuckwell Collection (GT), annual reports of many trade unions including the NFWW and the WTUL. The *Women's Trade Union Review* and the *Woman Worker* provide extremely valuable material as does the *Workers' Union Record*. Julia Varley has not, surprisingly perhaps, inspired a full-length biography but her surviving papers have been deposited in the University of Hull, Brynmor Jones Library (classified as DJV). There is a large amount of relevant material on women in trade unions in the Imperial War Museum's Women's Work Collection, particularly the files on Employment (IWM Emp.) but these records were selected to show what women had achieved in the war and tend to overstress the novelty of much that is described or attribute behaviour to war conditions that may represent a consistent pre-war trend.

There are few expositions of trade union theory or organization by women at this period. Mary Macarthur contributed to several collections of essays on the trade union point of view including *Women In Industry from Seven Points of View* (Duckworth, 1908), (as did Gertrude Tuckwell), and *Women in the Labour Party*, ed. Marion Phillips (Headley Bros, 1918). Oral history provides an excellent source for the sort of information needed for the rediscovery of the hidden history of women in trade unions. See for example J. Liddington, *The Life and Times of a Respectable Rebel* (Virago, 1984).

Notes

My interest in this topic was aroused by discussion with, and the work of, Marion Kozak. For editorial advice and help I am grateful to Angela John and Ian Patterson.

1 Gladys Boone, *The Women's Trade Union Leagues in Great Britain and the United States of America* (Colombia University Press, New York, 1942); Robin Miller Jacoby, 'Feminism and Class Consciousness in the British and American Women's Trade Union Leagues, 1890–1925', in *Liberating Women's History*, ed. Berenice A. Carroll (University of Illinois Press, Urbana, 1976).
2 Hamilton, *Mary Macarthur*, for example; Lewenhak, *Women in Trade Unions* following Drake, *Women in Trade Unions* also.
3 Table 1 in Drake, *Women in Trade Unions* (folded in at the back).
4 Heidi Hartmann, 'Capitalism, Patriarchy and the case for job segregation by sex' in *Capitalist Patriarchy and the Case for Socialist Feminism*, ed. Zillah R. Eisenstein (Monthly Review, Monthly Review Press, 1980); G. Braybon, *Women Workers in the First World War* (Croom Helm, 1981).

5 *History of the Ministry of Munitions*, vol. iv, part L, p. 57.
6 Interview with Dorothy Jones, who as Dorothy Elliott was an organizer for the NFWW and then an official in the GMWU when the Federation merged with it, D. Thom, Summer 1975; interview Grace Robson, D. Thom, Summer 1980.
7 Barbara Drake, *Women in Engineering Trades* (Fabian Research Department, 1917, PP 1919, XXXI, Cmd. 135, Report of the War Cabinet Committee on Women in Industry.)
8 PP 1919, Cmd. 167, minutes of evidence to the War Cabinet Committee. Evidence of the Fabian Women's Group.
9 DJV 6, *Bradford Daily Argus*, 15 February, 1907.
10 Obituary by George Horwill (though S. Pankhurst does not mention her in her history of the suffragette movement).
11 Biographies by M. A. Hamilton.
12 R. Mudie-Smith (ed.), *Sweated Industries: Being a Handbook of the 'Daily News' Exhibition* (1906); vol. 2, p. 256.
13 E. Cadbury and G. Shann, *Sweating* (Headley Bros, 1907).
14 E. Cadbury, H. Cecile Matheson and G. Shann, *Women's Work and Wages* (T. Fisher, Unwin, 1906), p. 283.
15 DJV 6, *Daily Herald*, 23 May 1915.
16 Leaflet in Tuckwell Collection, also Hamilton, *Mary Macarthur* p. 40.
17 A. Salter, *Slave of the Lamp* (Weidenfeld and Nicholson, 1957), also cited in *DLB*, vol. 2, p. 246.
18 See note 15, also cited in *DLB*, vol. 5, p. 217.
19 *Workers' Union Record*, July 1914, p. 7.
20 Interview Dorothy Elliott.
21 Richard Hyman, *The Workers' Union* (Oxford University Press, Oxford, 1971).
22 GT 357 (i), no date but seems to be 1913.
23 GT 604, *Daily Graphic*, 2 July 1914.
24 Teresa Olcott, 'Dead Centre: The Women's Trade Union Movement in London, 1874–1914', *The London Journal*, vol. 2, 1 (May 1976).
25 Mrs B. L. Hutchins, *Women in Modern Industry* (G. Bell and Sons, 1915); Ellen Smith, *Wage-earning women and their dependents*, Fabian Women's Group (1915).
26 Cadbury et al., *Sweating;* Hutchins, *Women in Modern Industry*.
27 D. Thom, '"Nice girls and rude girls", Women Munition Workers in the Woolwich Arsenal in the First World War,' in *Patriotism and the making of the national identity*, ed. R. Samuel (Routledge and Kegan Paul, 1985).
28 D. Sells, *The British Trade Boards System* (P. S. King and Sons, 1923), p. 2.
29 Ibid., p. 79.
30 Gertrude Tuckwell, *A short life of Sir Charles Dilke* (Students' Bookshops, 1925), p. 13.
31 Kathleen Woodward, *Queen Mary* (Hutchinson, 1927), p. 190; DJV 6, *T & GWU Record*, December 1951.
32 Clementina Black, *Married Women's Work* (G. Bell and Sons, 1915;

Virago, 1983). See essay 8; also Jane Lewis's essay in Lewis, *Women's Experience.*

33 J. Bornat, 'Home and Work: A New Context for Trade Union History', *Oral History*, vol. 5, 2 (Autumn 1977).

34 DJV 7, *Bournville Works Magazine*, June 1951, p. 180.

35 GT 506, Lady Dilke, 'Trade unionism among women', pamphlet (1891).

36 GT *Reynolds' News*, 25 April 1909.

37 Drake, *Women in Trade Unions*, p. 46.

38 GT, *Morning News*, 27 March 1914.

39 IWM Emp. viii, 471.

40 Bondfield, *Life's Work*, p. 58.

41 Drake, *Engineering Trades*, p. 129.

42 DJV 6, *Railway Service Journal*, November 1921, p. 145.

43 DJV 6, *T & GWU Record*, December 1951.

44 BLEPS, Webb TU collection, Thorne to Hutchins, 30 March 1910.

45 James Hinton, *The First Shop Stewards' Movement* (George Allen and Unwin, 1973). G. D. H. Cole, *Workshop Organisation* (Oxford University Press, Oxford, 1923).

46 *Woolwich Pioneer*, 5 May 1916.

47 Drake, *Women in Trade Unions*, p. 50.

48 Ibid., pp. 62–3; A. Fox, *A History of the NUBSO* (Oxford University Press, Oxford, 1958), pp. 312–3; GT, *Daily Citizen*, 5 June 1914.

49 GT, *Evening News*, 8 June 1914.1 This goes completely unremarked in the history of the NUR when the amalgamation is described, P. Bagwell, *The Railwaymen*, vol. 1 (George Allen and Unwin, 1963), p. 330, though it is mentioned later, p. 357.

50 Millicent G. Fawcett, *The Women's Victory and after* (Sidgwick and Jackson, 1920), p. 106.

51 S. D. Chapman, 'War and the Cotton Trade', Oxford pamphlet (1915), pp. 8–9.

52 Fabian Women's Group, 'The War, Women and Unemployment', FRD (1915).

53 *Interim Report of the Women's Employment Commission*, PP 1914–16, XXXVIII, Cmd. 7848, pp. 4–11; Hamilton, *Mary Macarthur* (1925), p. 138.

54 Pankhurst Collection, International Institute for the Study of Social History, Amsterdam, doc. 27, minute books of the ELFS, 1915; E.S. Pankhurst, *The Home Front* (1932).

55 Records of the Ministry of Munitions at the Public Record Office, MUN 5.70.26, 11 August 1915, 28 August 1915.

56 Mary Macarthur in her memorandum to Drake, *Engineering Trades*, pp. 111–12.

57 I am very grateful to Richard Hyman for the chance to see his notes on the interview with Mrs Pilbrow and other information from his thesis on the Workers' Union.

58 Advertisement, 1917, *Woolwich Pioneer*, several issues.

59 IWM, Transcripts of evidence to the War Cabinet Committee on Women in Industry, 4 October, 1918, evidence of Mary Macarthur,

pp. 10–11; D. Thom 'The Ideology of Women's Work, 1914–1924, with special reference to the NFWW and other trade unions', PhD thesis, for the CNAA at Thames Polytechnic 1982, ch. 6, has more details on this.

60 Drake, *Engineering Trades*, p. 109.

61 GT 324A, *West Sussex Gazette*, 11 December 1919.

Index